Jeanette Winterson

Susana Onega

Manchester University Press
Manchester and New York

distributed exclusively in the USA by Palgrave

Copyright © Susana Onega 2006

The right of Susana Onega to be identified as the author of this work has been asserted by her in accordance with the Copyright, Designs and Patents Act 1988.

Published by Manchester University Press
Oxford Road, Manchester M13 9NR, UK
and Room 400, 175 Fifth Avenue, New York, NY 10010, USA
www.manchesteruniversitypress.co.uk

Distributed exclusively in the USA by
Palgrave, 175 Fifth Avenue, New York,
NY 10010, USA

Distributed exclusively in Canada by
UBC Press, University of British Columbia, 2029 West Mall,
Vancouver, BC, Canada V6T 1Z2

British Library Cataloguing-in-Publication Data
A catalogue record for this book is available from the British Library

Library of Congress Cataloging-in-Publication Data applied for

ISBN   0 7190 6838 X   *hardback*
EAN   9780 7190 6838 6

ISBN   0 7190 6839 8   *paperback*
EAN   9780 7190 6839 3

First published 2006

15 14 13 12 11 10 09 08   07 06   10 9 8 7 6 5 4 3 2 1

Typeset
by Northern Phototypesetting Co Ltd, Bolton
Printed in Great Britain
by Bell & Bain Ltd, Glasgow

Who then devised the torment? Love
Love is the unfamiliar Name
Behind the hands that wove
The intolerable shirt of flame
Which human power cannot remove
We only live, only suspire
Consumed by either fire or fire.

(T. S. Eliot, 'Little Gidding' IV, ll. 8–14)

For Paco, Jorge and Alberto, with love

Contents

Series editor's foreword

Contemporary British Novelists offers readers critical introductions to some of the most exciting and challenging writing of recent years. Through detailed analysis of their work, volumes in the series present lucid interpretations of authors who have sought to capture the sensibilities of the late twentieth and twenty-first centuries. Informed, but not dominated, by critical theory, *Contemporary British Novelists* explores the influence of diverse traditions, histories and cultures on prose fiction, and situates key figures within their relevant social, political, artistic and historical contexts.

The title of the series is deliberately provocative, recognising each of the three defining elements as contentious identifications of a cultural framework that must be continuously remade and renamed. The contemporary British novel defies easy categorisation and rather than offering bland guarantees as to the current trajectories of literary production, volumes in this series contest the very terms that are employed to unify them. How does one conceptualise, isolate and define the mutability of the contemporary? What legitimacy can be claimed for a singular Britishness given the multivocality implicit in the redefinition of national identities? Can the novel form adequately represent reading communities increasingly dependent upon digitalised communication? These polemical considerations are the theoretical backbone of the series, and attest to the difficulties of formulating a coherent analytical approach to the discontinuities and incoherencies of the present.

Contemporary British Novelists does not seek to appropriate its subjects for prescriptive formal or generic categories; rather it aims to explore the ways in which aesthetics are reproduced, refined and repositioned through recent prose writing. If the overarching architecture of the contemporary always eludes description, then the grandest ambition of this series must be to plot at least some of its dimensions.

Daniel Lea

Acknowledgements

The research carried out for the writing of this book forms part of a research project financed by the Spanish Ministry of Science and Technology and the European Regional Development Fund (no. HUM2004–00344/FIL). Originating in a longstanding interest in the work of Jeanette Winterson, this book is partly indebted to a number of journal articles and book chapters published by the author between 1993 and 2005, which are referenced in the bibliography

The author wishes to acknowledge Jeanette Winterson's permission to reprint extracts from her fictional, dramatic and critical work; Alfred Douglas for permission to quote from *The Tarot: The Origins, Meaning and Uses of the Cards*; and David Sheridan for permission to reproduce his design of a Tarot spread in the frontispiece of Douglas's book. She is most thankful to Tim Bozman for reading the manuscript and to Ricardo Sáez for his help in the most practical aspects of this project. Her thanks are also due to Daniel Lea, the series editor, for his very detailed and useful editorial comments, to Alison Kelly, the copy-editor, for a most efficient job, and to Matthew Frost, the Head of Editorial at Manchester University Press, for his unfailing support.

Abbreviations

AL   *Art & Lies: A Piece for Three Voices and a Bawd.* London: Jonathan
        Cape, 1995 (1994).
AO   *Art Objects: Essays on Ecstasy and Effrontery.* London: Jonathan Cape,
        1995.
B   *Boating for Beginners.* London: Methuen, 1990 (1985).
GMA   *Great Moments in Aviation.* London: Vintage, 1994.
GS   *Gut Symmetries.* London: Granta Books, 1997.
KC   *The King of Capri.* London: Bloomsbury, 2003.
L   *Lighthousekeeping.* London and New York: Fourth Estate, 2004.
O   *Oranges Are Not the Only Fruit.* London, Sydney, Wellington: Pandora
        Press, 1990 (1985).
OS   *Oranges Are Not the Only Fruit. The Script.* London: Pandora, 1990.
P   *The Passion.* Harmondsworth: Penguin, 1988 (1987).
PB   *The.PowerBook.* London: Jonathan Cape, 2000.
SC   *Sexing the Cherry.* London: Vintage, 1990 (1989).
WB   *Written on the Body.* London: Jonathan Cape, 1992.
WOP   *The World and Other Places.* London: Jonathan Cape, 1998.

Introduction

In an article entitled 'Fiction at the Centre and at the Fringe' (1989), Peter Lewis briefly analysed the general panorama of contemporary European literature and concluded that: 'At the end of the 1970s the two younger British writers being most hyped in the direction of immortality were Martin Amis and Ian McEwan, claimed by some to be the authentic voices of their generation. At the end of the 1980s Julian Barnes and Peter Ackroyd seem to occupy a similar position.'[1] With a few notable exceptions, Lewis's short list of representatives of British writing in the 1970s and 1980s would have been endorsed at that time by most analysts of contemporary British fiction, as well as by virtually every British bookseller, well aware as they are of the best-selling capacity of these four male writers.[2] However, together with Ian McEwan, Martin Amis, Julian Barnes and Peter Ackroyd there were also other significant writers in the late 1970s and 1980s, including Angela Carter, Iain Sinclair, Marina Warner, Graham Swift, Salman Rushdie, Charles Palliser, Maggie Gee, Sara Maitland, Alan Hollinghurst and Jeanette Winterson.

All these writers received a university education in literature and at some stage combined their creative activity with literary criticism and/or the teaching of literature, so that they have a wide knowledge of literary theory as well as of canonical literature. All of them share a keen interest in history and in the problematic relationship of self and world, and, in various degrees, a relish for metafiction; that is, they share a self-conscious and playful tendency to foreground the artificiality and linguistic nature of their own literary texts, revealing the constructedness of the realism-enhancing mechanisms employed in them. In the case of Winterson, Carter, Rushdie, Warner, Gee and Maitland, irony and parody are often allied to fantasy, a literature

whose subversiveness lies in its tendency to dissolve structures,
moving both towards an ideal of entropic *undifferentiation*, 'of transgression of the limits separating self from other, man from woman,
human from animal, organic from inorganic objects',[3] and towards
constant metamorphosis, with its stress upon instability of natural
forms, expressive of its rejection of the notion of the self as a coherent, indivisible and continuous whole, a basic tenet of realist
fiction. Helena Grice and Tim Woods have suggested that there is 'a
specific tradition of British women writers who employ fantasy and
the fabulous in their fiction'.[4] However, fantasy has never been the
exclusive realm of women and there are many contemporary writers,
both male and female, who use fantasy and the fabulous in their
work, such as Kathy Acker, Margaret Atwood, Julio Cortázar, Gabriel
García Márquez, Isabel Allende, Italo Calvino, Neil Gaiman or
Michael Moorcock. It is within this international experimentalist
trend, which she considers to be a direct descendant from Modernism, that Jeanette Winterson has often aligned herself:

> working off Calvino [in *The Passion*] was a way of aligning myself with
> the European tradition where I feel much more comfortable. That's a
> tradition which uses fantasy and invention and leaps of time, of space,
> rather than in the Anglo-American tradition which is much more
> realistic in its narrative drive and much more a legacy of the nineteenth
> century. Modernism here really moved sideways and has been picked
> up much more by European writers. We lost it completely [. . .], whereas
> writers like Borges and Calvino and Perec wanted to go on with those
> experiments and didn't see modernism as a cul-de-sac, but as a way
> forwards into other possibilities.[5]

In general, the work of these experimentalist British writers of the
1970s and 1980s may be called 'postmodernist', since it combines
the self-referentiality characteristic of metafiction and the pleasure
in the equivocal truths and epistemological hesitation characteristic
of the fantastic with an apparently contradictory realism-enhancing
interest in history and in the traditional storytelling aspect of fiction.
In the case of Carter, Maitland, Warner and Winterson, a further distinctive element may be added: the pervasive influence of feminism
and, in the case of Winterson, of lesbian theory as well. As Lynn
Pykett has pointed out, this fact has led academic criticism to place
Winterson's work in one or other of 'the boxes labelled "lesbian fiction" or "postmodernist fiction"'.[6] However, the writer rejects both
qualifications, particularly that of 'lesbian writer', and insists that she

expects to be called simply 'a writer', as male authors usually are. As she puts it with reference to Virginia Woolf:

> I see no reason to read into Woolf's work the physical difficulties of her life. If I said to you that a reading of John Keats must entertain his tuberculosis and the fact that he was common and short, you would ignore me. You should ignore me; a writer's work is not a chart of their sex, sexuality, sanity and physical health. (*AO* 97)

Winterson's refusal to be called 'a lesbian writer', like Bharati Mukherjee's claim that she is not an 'Indian-American', but 'an American without hyphens', evinces the vital need of all minorities 'to alert ourselves to the limitations and the dangers of those discourses that reinforce an "us versus them" mentality'.[7] Winterson is, then, right to ask her readers, with Lawrence, to '[j]udge the work not the writer' (*AO* 192). At the same time, however, the writer draws attention to herself in various ways; she cultivates her public image to the point of keeping a website for her fans.[8] And she likes showing off and playing 'the bad girl'. Thus, when she was asked by the *Sunday Times* to select 'her favourite author writing in English', she chose herself.[9] And she told a Sunday newspaper that her choice 'Book of the Year' was *Written on the Body*.[10] She also loves teasing the media with shocking stories about herself that she then dismisses as fictional, like the famous one about having serviced married women with casual sex and having being paid with Le Creuset cookware.[11] She is always ready to answer questions about her private life, but equally explicit about showing her disagreement when the criticism is adverse.[12] What is more, some knowledge of her life and background is indispensable for an understanding of her work, since one of the games she recurrently plays in her fictions is the confusion of her identity with that of her protagonists.

Jeanette Winterson was born in Manchester on 27 August 1959 and brought up in the nearby mill-town of Accrington, Lancashire, by her adoptive parents, Constance (*née* Brownrigg) and John William Winterson, in a strict Pentecostal Evangelist faith. In *Art Objects* she points out how her adoptive great-grandparents had 'worked a twelve-hour day in a Lancashire cotton-mill' (*AO* 159); her father was a worker in a television factory and her mother a housewife. As a Northern, low-church working-class girl she was expected to do militant religious work, to accept compulsory heterosexuality and to avoid developing her intellectual and artistic capacities. Winterson admits to being a keen collector of rare books, mostly signed first editions of her favourite Modernists (*AO* 119–32), an activity surely meant to compensate for the enforced deprivation she endured during her childhood. As she has often explained, her parents 'owned six books between them. Two of those were Bibles and the third was a concordance to the Old and New Testament. The fourth was *The House at Pooh Corner*. The fifth, *The Chatterbox Annual 1923* and the sixth, Malory's *Morte d'Arthur*' (*AO* 153), a book that she read 'over and over again'.[13] This is the book, then, that provided the young writer with two central *topoi* in her fiction: the archetypal quest and the love triangle. With her inborn deadpan comicity, Winterson explains how she spent her childhood and youth devising cunning ways to circumvent her mother's ban on reading: using the outdoor toilet as a bathetic version of Virginia Woolf's 'room of one's own' (*AO* 153); hiding books under her mattress until her mother found and burnt them (*AO* 154); and, eventually, convincing her to let her work at the Public Library, on the mistaken assumption that 'I would be unable to read and work at the same time' (*AO* 154).

One positive side to her otherwise extremely demanding and unusual education was that she was encouraged to memorise long texts. She admits, for example, to having learnt all of Eliot's *Four Quartets*: 'I know it by heart (Pelmanism is a low-church virtue)' (*AO* 129). This habit helped improve her excellent natural ear for the rhythms of English and encouraged a reverential attitude to language: 'I grew up not knowing that language was for everyday purposes. I grew up with the Word and the Word was God. Now, many years after a secular Reformation, I still think of language as something holy' (*AO* 153). In *Oranges Are Not the Only Fruit*, the protagonist, Jeanette, is told by her foster mother that 'This world is full of sin', and that she 'can change the world' (*O* 10). This key Evangelical message has ruled Winterson's own life, as it surely provided her with the stimulus for her experimental attitude to writing.

Winterson attended Accrington Girls' Grammar School and Accrington College of Further Education, an experience reflected in some of the most comic passages of *Oranges*. But she was destined to undertake missionary work, and she became a preacher at the age of twelve. As Nicci Gerrard has pointed out, her mother's prospects for her only daughter came to an abrupt end when 'at 16 [she] was found in bed with another woman and thrown out of her home and the Pentecostal Church'.[14] After this, she tried several jobs – in an undertaker's parlour, selling ice cream and working in a mental hospital – before she could pay her way to university. Her determination to acquire an education was so firm that, 'Having failed to impress an interview panel at St Catherine's College, Oxford, she camped outside till they reconsidered. She went up to read English in 1978'.[15] As the writer herself has noted, at Oxford she felt as if she 'had been dropped into the middle of a special practical joke. Not only did everybody read books, they were expected to read books, and given money to read books. Did I really not have to prepare my essay in the toilet?' (AO 158). After obtaining a BA in English in 1981, Winterson attempted a job in advertising, but with little success. In 1982 she went to London and was employed at Roundhouse Theatre to do odd jobs. In 1983 she worked as editor at Brilliance Books and, between 1983 and 1984, at Pandora Press.[16] By then she was already writing Oranges Are Not The Only Fruit, having begun it at the age of 23. The novel was published in 1985 by her boss at Pandora, Philippa Brewster, earning the Whitbread First Novel Award. In 1990, Oranges was made into a TV drama, winning two BAFTA awards (for Best TV Drama Series and for Best Actress) and the Prix d'argent for Best Script in 1991.

On the strength of this success, Winterson was commissioned to write a book for the Methuen Humour List and she wrote Boating for Beginners (1985) in a few weeks. This novel has often been omitted from Winterson's list of publications or set apart from her main works as 'a comic book' or 'a comic book with pictures'. Next came The Passion (1987), which won the John Llewelyn Rhys Prize; and Sexing the Cherry (1989), which won the E. M. Forster Award. The growing success and popularity that characterised the decade of the 1980s suffered a first check in 1992 with the publication of Written on the Body, a novel which met with the divided opinion of the critics. In Britain, reviewers like Julie Burchill branded it as 'the Great Bad Novel of the 90s',[17] while, in the United States, it became the bestseller that made Winterson's name as a lesbian writer. The irate reaction of the author, who, according to Maya Jaggi, 'felt herself judged in Britain not for literature but lifestyle', initiated a battle with the media that did Winterson's public image a lot of damage, and which she now fully regrets: 'About 1992 I should have had an operation to sew up my mouth, and kept it closed until 1997 [. . . .] You can't make more of a mess of it that I did. I was mad and behaved like an idiot. But I was very hurt, I didn't have the resources or sophistication to deal with it, and no one to say, "calm down and let it pass"'.[18]

The publication of her next novel, *Art & Lies*, in 1994, marks the lowest point in what Winterson has described as 'a dark decade for me, in personal terms and in terms of the work I wanted to do'.[19] As Jaggi notes, Winterson speaks of 'mental collapse' and a growing fear that she was suffering from writer's block. The publication of *Gut Symmetries* (1997) marks the end of this dark period. Still, its reception was not as positive as expected and, according to Winterson, it was not until she moved from her house in Highgate to the countryside that she fully recovered her peace of mind and her confidence in her writing capacity. After a period of seclusion in the Cotswolds, she wrote *The.PowerBook* (2000), which again met with a mixed reception.

At present, Jeanette Winterson shares her time between her main home, a riverside cottage 15 miles from Oxford, and the 1780s house in Spitalfields that appears in *The.PowerBook*. During the winter of 2003–4 she spent a lot of time in Paris, supervising a theatre version of *The.PowerBook*, and she likes its intellectual atmosphere so much that she is thinking of moving there permanently. Her latest novel, *Lighthousekeeping*, published in March 2004, has been unanimously welcomed as a return to the type of writing that launched her to fame in the 1980s. During the early months of 2005 Jeanette Winterson has been working on *Tanglewreck*, a children's book scheduled to be published by Bloomsbury on 1 January 2006, whose protagonist, like that of *Lighhousekeeping*, is an orphaned child called Silver; and *Weight*, a novella on the myth of Atlas that Winterson was commissioned to write for a series called *Myths* launched by Canongate, for publication on 1 September 2005.

In an interview with her former partner, the Australian critic Margaret Reynolds, Jeanette Winterson described the seven (since she excludes *Boating for Beginners*) fictions that she wrote between 1985 and 2000 as forming part of a cycle:

MR: Why do you quote yourself in your books?
JW: Because all books speak to each other. They are only separate books because that's how they had to be written. I see them really as one long continuous piece of work. I've said that the seven books make a cycle or a series, and I believe that they do, from *Oranges* to *The PowerBook*.[20]

These words bring to mind Winterson's description of Robert Graves's lifelong endeavour to arrange his poems sequentially rather than chronologically, with a view to creating 'an organic continuity, so that the individual poems flow together, a river of writing unstopped by dates and collections and themes' (AO 174). According to Winterson, 'This organic continuity brings Graves, as a poet, close to George Herbert (1593–1633) whose meditative religious lyrics form a pattern outside of their pattern, so that when read together, they seem to the reader to be some great arc made of many colours and perfectly broken into one another' (AO 174). To Herbert and Graves could be added other poets like Yeats, Eliot or Pound, who also tried to arrange their poems according to the ancient Greek principle of 'organic unity'. Thus, in *Ezra Pound and his World*, Peter Ackroyd points out how, although *A Draft of XXX Cantos* was left unfinished and is made up of fragmented extracts needing to be completed with the reader's collaboration, Pound was convinced that he had achieved organic unity by means of two main mechanisms: the juxtaposition of the general with the particular, of all kinds of voices, genres and modes, of history, autobiography and literature; and by having the *Cantos* crisscrossed by the figure of the poet as a wandering Odysseus, a mythical quester travelling across time zones and ontological boundaries in order to 'shock the readers [. . .] into an awareness of the disturbed and complex world around them'.[21] Interestingly, these seem to be the same mechanisms used by Winterson to grant overall unity to her fictions, as she herself suggested when she told Margaret Reynolds that, in her work, the same themes 'do occur and return, disappear, come back amplified or modified, changed in some way, because it's been my journey, it's the journey of my imagination, it's the journey of my soul in those books'.[22] Strikingly echoing Pound's poet as wandering Odysseus, then, Winterson presents herself as a mythical quester cutting across the boundaries of her own books and knitting them together by means of slightly differing repetitions of recurrent themes or *leitmotifs*, in an attempt to unify the individual works into a single art object that may be said to have the shape of Winterson's own process of artistic or spiritual maturation.

Winterson further characterises her writing by aligning herself with 'those writers who were obsessed by a single all-consuming idea; in Herbert's case, God, and for Graves, the goddess as lover and Muse' (AO 174). Her words bring to mind Isaac Berlin's famous contention that there are two basic types of writers, the 'foxes' and the 'hedgehogs'. The foxes 'pursue many ends, often unrelated and even contradictory, connected, if at all, only in some *de facto* way', while the hedgehogs 'relate everything to a single central vision, one system

[. . .] in terms of which they understand, think and feel'.[23] Berlin's prototypical representative of the 'fox' type is Shakespeare; of the 'hedgehog' type, Dante. Like Dante, Herbert, Blake, Graves, Yeats, Eliot or Pound, then, Jeanette Winterson is a 'hedgehog' type of writer, with love as the single central vision around which all her fictions develop.

Winterson discusses this issue at length in *Art Objects: Essays on Ecstasy and Effrontery*, a book that may be considered her poetic manifesto. As its subtitle suggests, the book contains a collection of essays on art and literature written in the first person and with constant references to her personal development as a writer. She wrote this book in the middle of her personal and creative crisis, in what may be interpreted as an attempt to systematise her ideas about art and literature in a way comparable to Virginia Woolf's *A Room of One's Own* (1928), Peter Ackroyd's *Notes for a New Culture* (1976), John Fowles's *The Aristos: A Self Portrait in Ideas* (1964) or D. H. Lawrence's *Pansies* (1929), whose title, as Winterson herself notes, 'puns with pensées' (*AO* 125). The writer begins her reflections by analysing her response to pictorial art. She observes that, if she had previously failed to respond adequately to its aesthetic demands, it was because she did not master pictorial language as she did the language of literature. This observation leads her to contend that 'the language of art, of all art, is not our mother-tongue' and that 'human beings can be taught to love what they do not love already' (*AO* 4, 6). In consonance with the reverential attitude to language she had developed as a child, Winterson defines art in strictly linguistic terms: every art object offers its own imaginative version of reality in a foreign language that must be mastered if we are to apprehend its beauty. Quoting Harold Bloom, she describes aesthetic experience in romantic and transcendentalist terms as 'the ecstasy of the privileged moment', a heightened and cathartic experience that brings about 'insight', 'rapture' and 'transformation' (*AO* 5–6); and she defends the independence and autonomy of art, its inalienable right to offer its own imaginative version of reality, even if its interpretation demands a great effort of concentration since, as she explains, the intensity demanded by the art object is always rewarded by the intensity of feeling that comes together with the epiphanic apprehension of a higher truth that only art can aspire to express (*AO* 10–11). Echoing John Fowles's definition of art as 'a human shorthand of knowledge, [. . . .] the expression of truths too complex for science to express',[24] Winterson concludes that

'It is the poet who goes further than any human scientist' in the pursuit of knowledge (AO 115).

Winterson further defines art as 'the realization of complex emotion' (AO 111, 112), and the artist as someone who combines 'an exceptional sensibility with an exceptional control over her material' (AO 112). As she notes, the need to express complex emotion determines the *forbidden* nature of art's subject matter: 'Complex emotion often follows some major event in our lives; sex, falling in love, birth, death, are the commonest and in each of these potencies are strong taboos' (AO 113). Thus, in her search for a higher truth, capable of providing 'the shape we need when our own world seems most shapeless', the artist creates 'emotion around the forbidden' (AO 114). However, the world the artist's imagination creates 'is not a private nightmare, not even a private dream, it is a shared human connection that traces the possibilities of past and future in the whorl of now. It is a construct, like science, like religion, like the world itself. It is as artificial as you and me and as natural too' (AO 117). Winterson's specification that artistic constructions are not private dreams but collective (i.e. archetypal) visions, points to the artist's function as 'mediator' between the lower and the upper worlds. That is, it points to a visionary conception of the artist as Hermetic quester or shaman with the task of shaping and giving overall significance to the anarchy and futility of particular phenomena and of unifying them into a common vision by means of the imagination.[25] This is the mythopoeic and transcendentalist vision of art which Jeanette Winterson endorses as her own. Originating in Plato and Dante, it was transmitted by Thomas Aquinas and the metaphysical poets, coming to a climax with William Blake and the Romantic poets (and, in the US, with Emerson and Agassiz), who handed it down to Yeats, Graves, Pound, Eliot and Joyce. This visionary or 'hedgehog' conception of art was continued by transition-to-postmodernism writers like Lawrence Durrell, Malcolm Lowry, John Fowles, Doris Lessing and Maureen Duffy, who in their turn have handed it down to postmodernist writers like Peter Ackroyd, Iain Sinclair, Marina Warner and Jeanette Winterson.[26]

It is in the light of this transcendentalist tradition that we should interpret Winterson's contention that 'Realism is not a Movement or a Revolution, in its original incarnation it was a response to a movement, and as a response it was essentially anti-art' (AO 30–1), as well as her claim that she does not write 'novels' and that 'the novel form is finished' (*AO* 191). Clearly, by 'novel' Winterson understands a wholly realistic genre, born alongside the development of patriarchal humanism in the seventeenth and eighteenth centuries, reaching plenitude in the Victorian period and its point of exhaustion with the advent of Modernism, though still lingering on in the writing practice of 'The Movement', the trend initiated by Kingsley Amis, Philip Larkin and John Wain in the late 1940s and the 1950s. Avowedly, Winterson's fictions are not novels in this sense. Still, her definition is rather restrictive, since, as Mikhail Bakhtin demonstrated once and for all, the novel can be the most polyphonic of all literary genres. When Cervantes wrote the first modern novel, he did not make the resilient realist Sancho Panza the protagonist, but rather Don Quixote, Sancho's chivalrous and visionary master. We laugh at Sancho's pedestrian commonsensicalities and truisms, but it is Don Quixote we love, precisely because he mistakes windmills for giants, treats tavern maids as damsels and falls in love with a Dulcinea that only exists in his imagination. Indeed, it is out of the dialogic inter-play of the two characters' competing and complementary worldviews that the novel is born, rather than out of Cervantes' realistic accuracy of depiction.

Winterson's refusal to call her fictions 'novels' is the more puzzling since she does not seem to have any theoretical grudge against the genre as such, as becomes evident, for example, when she criticises the Victorian writers for their 'denial of art as art'. Significantly, she does not put the blame on the novel as a genre, or on the novelists themselves, but rather on 'the spirit of the age', which, she concedes, 'no writer can escape' even if at the cost of 'neurosis'. Thus, she admits that Dickens is 'the most interesting example of a great Victorian writer, who by sleight of hand convinced his audience that he is what he is not: a realist' (*AO* 31). What Winterson seems to dis-like, then, is the banality of the Victorian attitude to art, what she describes as the absurd attempt of Victorian writers to transform art into 'a version of everyday reality' (*AO* 31). Her suspicion of realism is such that she even disparages one of her own most valuable and distinctive features: storytelling. Thus, she self-consciously justifies the inclusion of 'stories within stories' in her fiction as 'a trap for the reader's attention', insisting that she is 'not particularly interested in folk tales or fairy tales' and that she is 'a writer who does not use plot as an engine or foundation' (*AO* 189). Her words provide evidence for Linda Hutcheon's contention that one of the defining traits of postmodernist fiction is its problematic and ambivalent relationship to storytelling.[27]

At the same time, implicit in Winterson's rejection of plotting and storytelling is a reluctance to associate her works with other less realistic genres, such as the romance, so that the writer is constantly forced to use periphrastic expressions to refer to her books, such as 'piece of work' (for example, in the interview with Reynolds quoted above).[28] The ultimate reason for the writer's refusal to employ the words 'novel' or 'romance' to define her prose fictions seems to stem from her conviction that 'the calling of the artist, in any medium, is to make it new' (AO 12). Popularised by Ezra Pound as a battle-cry for Modernist poets, the phrase 'to make it new' points to Jeanette Winterson's concern with presenting herself as the inheritor of Modernism and her desire to bring about what John Barth announced as a 'literature of replenishment' capable of renewing the 'exhausted' literary forms of the 1950s and 1960s.[29]

In 'Tradition and the Individual Talent', T. S. Eliot famously contended that no 'individual talent' can flourish that is not firmly rooted in the literary tradition.[30] In A Room of One's Own, Virginia Woolf likewise claimed that 'masterpieces are not single and solitary births; they are the outcome of many years of thinking in common'.[31] Similarly, in Art Objects, Winterson carefully qualifies her defence of innovation by stressing the importance of the past: 'I do not mean that in new work the past is repudiated; quite the opposite, the past is reclaimed. It is not lost to authority, it is not absorbed at a level of familiarity. It is re-stated and re-instated in its original vigour' (AO 12). The past tradition Winterson signals as her own excludes realism and 'concentrates itself [on the period] 1900–1945 on those Modernists whose work I think vital. That includes major and minor writers of poetry and prose; H D, Marianne Moore, Gertrude Stein, Virginia Woolf, Sitwell, Mansfield, Barney, Radclyffe Hall, Eliot, Graves, Pound and Yeats' (AO 126). However, with the important exception of Virginia Woolf – and, to some extent, of Joyce and Gertrude Stein, to whom she devotes a chapter in Art Objects (45–60) – the writers Winterson constantly feeds on are (male) poets, Eliot primarily, but also others like Donne, Blake, Keats, Shelley, Marvell, Yeats, Graves and Pound. This apparent incongruity, given the fact that Winterson has explicitly said that she does not think of herself as a poet,[32] is solved by the writer herself when she explains in Art Objects that Modernism is the movement that questioned the boundaries between poetry and prose:

> For the ordinary reader, the Modernist writer looked desperately diffi-
> cult (Eliot) desperately dirty (Joyce) desperately dull (Woolf). Novels
> were meant to be novels (stories), and poems were meant to be poetic
> (pastorals, ballads, and during the war, protests). Amongst its other
> crimes, Modernism was questioning the boundaries between the two.
> (*AO* 38)

Thus, Winterson describes the Modernists as 'that group of people
working towards returning literature to its roots in speech (which is
not the same thing as forcing literature down to speech)' (*AO* 38). Her
emphasis on the linguistic nature of literature echoes Peter Ackroyd's
distinction, in *Notes for a New Culture*, between what he calls the
'humanist' (Winterson's 'realist') and the 'modernist' attitudes to language.[33] As Ackroyd explains, while for the humanists language is
transparent, a mere aesthetic vehicle for the communication of the
experience of the moral self, for the Modernists language is an
autonomous entity, a self-begetting universe of discourse without referent or content.[34] Once language is defined as a self-sufficient and
autonomous sign-system without meaning or referent, the traditional
boundaries between the literary genres and between the literary and
non-literary genres collapse, as Winterson accurately notes when she
defines Stein's *Autobiography of Alice B. Toklas* as 'an act of terrorism
against worn-out assumptions of what literature is and what form its
forms can take' (*AO* 50). Thus, the notion of genre is substituted by
more general notions: Derrida's 'writing', Barthes's 'text' or Kristeva's
'intertext'.

These are, in a nutshell the motivations that seem to have led
Jeanette Winterson to reject labels such as 'novel' or 'romance' for her
work. However, calling her works 'texts' or 'pieces of writing' seems
unnecessary, much more so since all her fictions may be said to
belong to a specific kind of novel: that claimed by Virginia Woolf for
the woman writer of the future with enough 'money and a room of
her own [to ensure her] freedom to think of things in themselves'.[35]
Reflecting on the contribution of eighteenth- and nineteenth-century
women to the literary canon, Woolf explains in *A Room of One's Own*
that women probably wrote novels because '[t]he novel alone was
young enough to be soft in her hands'. However, as she further
reflects:

> who shall say that even this most pliable of all forms is rightly shaped
> for her use? No doubt we shall find her knocking that into shape for her-
> self when she has the free use of her limbs, and providing some new

vehicle, not necessarily verse, for the poetry in her. For it is the poetry that is still denied outlet.[36]

In a prophetic paragraph that foreshadows the focal point of feminist theory, Woolf closes her reflections on the future of literature by drawing the reader's attention

> to the great part which must be played in that future so far as women are concerned by physical conditions. The book has somehow to be adapted to the body, and at a venture one would say that women's books should be shorter, more concentrated, than those of men, and framed so that they do not need long hours of steady and uninterrupted work.[37]

Shorter, more concentrated than those of men, crucially concerned with physicality and the human body, and written in a poetic prose capable of expressing 'the poetry in her', Winterson's experimental fictions in poetic prose, with their generic and formal ambiguities – reminiscent of Virginia Woolf's *The Waves* (1931) – may be said to materialise Woolf's prophetic dream of a new novelistic form created by women with the intellectual and material freedom to express their own sensibility and worldview. This is what Woolf herself tried to do, and other Modernist women writers as well, like Gertrude Stein or Dorothy M. Richardson, each knocking the realist novel into her own shape, just as each Modernist male writer, Lawrence, Joyce, Proust, Kafka or Thomas Mann, had tried to adapt the inherited form to his own ends.

Although Ezra Pound was convinced that Joyce had taken the novel form to a dead end with *Finnegans Wake*, the fact remains that the novel did not die with Modernism but, as Winterson herself suggests in the interview with Reynolds, it once again showed its astounding capacity for metamorphosis and renewal at the hands of late Modernists like William Faulkner, Samuel Beckett, Flann O'Brien, Malcolm Lowry, Lawrence Durrell, William Golding and, a genera- tion later, John Fowles, Doris Lessing, Maureen Duffy, Muriel Spark and Alasdair Gray. Indeed, the best proof of the novel's capacity for survival and renewal is Jeanette Winterson's own work, since no matter how different from the realist novel they are, or precisely because they are so different from it, her nine short novels (or novel- las) still have the basic ingredients of Cervantes' masterpiece, includ- ing the psychological realism, the love interest and (in various degrees) the glittering 'lure of a good story' (*AO* 189), and may indeed be regarded as apt examples of the further turn of the screw given to

the novel form by a woman writer who happens to be lesbian, writing
at the end of the twentieth century and the beginning of the twenty-
first.

Notes

1 Peter Lewis, 'Fiction at the Centre and at the Fringe', *Stand Magazine* 30.3
   (1989): 66–73; 71.
2 A case in point would be James Wood, who, in his survey of the contemporary English novel, praises the fiction of the 1960s and dismisses the
   writers of the 1970s and 1980s *en bloc*, on the grounds that their writing
   is characterised by 'the breaking up of the apparent coherence of English
   literary culture' and a 'turning outwards both to European models and to
   America'. James Wood, 'England', in John Sturrock (ed.), *The Oxford
   Guide to Contemporary Writing*. Oxford: Oxford University Press (1996):
   113–41; 134. See Susana Onega, 'The Visionary Element in the London
   Novel: The Case of Iain Sinclair and Peter Ackroyd', *Symbolism – An
   International Journal of Critical Aesthetics* 2 (2002): 151–82.
3 Rosemary Jackson, *Fantasy: The Literature of Subversion*. London and New
   York: Methuen (1981): 73.
4 Helena Grice and Tim Woods, 'Reading Jeanette Winterson Writing', in
   Grice and Woods (eds), *'I'm telling you stories': Jeanette Winterson and the
   Politics of Reading* (Postmodern Studies 25). Amsterdam and Atlanta, GA:
   Rodopi (1998): 11–16; 6.
5 In Margaret Reynolds, 'Interview with Jeanette Winterson', in Margaret
   Reynolds and Jonathan Noakes (eds), *Jeanette Winterson: The Essential
   Guide*. London: Vintage (2003): 11–29; 19.
6 Lynn Pykett, 'A New Way With Words? Jeanette Winterson's Post-
   Modernism', in Grice and Woods (eds), *'I'm telling you stories'*: 53–60; 53.
7 Bharati Mukherjee, 'Beyond Multiculturalism: Surviving the Nineties',
   Journal of Modern Literature 20.1 (Summer 1996): 29–34; 33.
8 The Official Jeanette Winterson Website, www.jeanettewinterson.com.
9 In Tania Unsworth, '*Art & Lies*: Contempt and Condescension' (1999).
   www.geocities.com/WestHollywood/Heights/3202/ARTANDLIES.HT
   ML. Consulted on 14 January 2002.
10 In Nicci Gerrard, 'The Ultimate Self-Produced Woman', *Observer* (5 June
   1994): 7.
11 Libby Brooks, 'Power Surge'. *The Guardian Weekend* (2 September
   2000): 10–6; B. Ruby Rich, 'In Profile: Jeanette Winterson', *Advocate* (24
   June 1997): 105.
12 Nicci Gerrard, 'Cold Blast at the Door', *Observer* (3 July 1994): 11; Claire
   Longrigg, 'Get Out of My Life – Get One of Your Own', *Guardian* (8 July
   1994): 24.

13 In Helen Barr, 'Face to Face – A Conversation between Jeanette Winter-son and Helen Barr', *English Review* 2.1 (September 1991): 30–3; 31.

14 Nicci Gerrard, 'The Prophet: Nicci Gerrrard Talks with Jeanette Winter-son, The Novelist Who Says If It Doesn't Shock It Isn't Art', *New States-man and Society* 2.65 (1 September 1989): 12–13; 13.

15 Maya Jaggi, 'Redemption Songs', Saturday Review: Profile: Jeanette Winterson, *Guardian* (29 May 2004). http://books.guardian.co.uk/departments/generalfiction/story/0,6000,1226858,00.html. Consulted on 5 August 2004.

16 Gerrard, 'The Prophet', 13.

17 In Jaggi, 'Redemption Songs'.

18 *Ibid.*

19 *Ibid.*

20 In Reynolds, 'Interview with Jeanette Winterson', 25.

21 Peter Ackroyd, *Ezra Pound and his World*. London: Thames and Hudson (1980): 75.

22 In Reynolds, 'Interview with Jeanette Winterson', 25.

23 Isaac Berlin, *The Hedgehog and the Fox: An Essay on Tolstoy's View of History*. New York: Simon and Schuster (1970): 1–2.

24 John Fowles, *The Aristos* (1964). Revised edition. London: Jonathan Cape (1980): 151.

25 See Evans Lansing Smith, *Rape and Revelation: The Descent to the Under-world in Modernism*. Lanham, NY and London: University Presses of America (1990). See also Susana Onega, 'The Descent to the Underworld and the Transition from *Ego* to *Eidos* in the Novels of Peter Ackroyd', in Ramón Plo Alastrué and María Jesús Martínez Alfaro (eds), *Generic and Ontological Boundaries in Literature and Film*. Heidelberg: Univer-sitätsverlag Carl Winter (2002): 157–74; and 'Jeanette Winterson's Visionary Fictions: An Art of Cultural Translation and Effrontery', in Jürgen Schlaeger (ed.), *Structures of Cultural Transformation: Yearbook of Research in English and American Literature* (REAL) 20. Tübingen: Gunter Narr Verlag (2005): 229–41.

26 See Susana Onega, 'The Mythical Impulse in British Historiographic Metafiction', *European Journal of English Studies* 1.2 (1997): 184–204; and 'The Visionary Element in the London Novel'.

27 Linda Hutcheon, *A Poetics of Postmodernism: History, Theory, Fiction*. New York and London: Routledge, 1988, 124–25.

28 For an interesting analysis of the ethical element in Jeanette Winterson's ambivalent relation to the romance, see Jean-Michel Ganteau, 'Hearts Object: Jeanette Winterson and the Ethics of Absolutist Romance', in Susana Onega and Christian Gutleben (eds), *Refracting the Canon in Contemporary Fiction and Film*. Amsterdam and Atlanta: Rodopi (2004): 165–85. See also Christine Reynier's 'Jeanette Winterson's Cogito –

"Amo Ergo Sum" – or Impersonality and Emotion Redefined', in Christine Reynier and Jean-Michel Ganteau (eds), *Impersonality and Emotion in Twentieth-Century British Fiction*. Present Perfect 1. Montpellier: Publications de L'Université Paul Valéry Montpellier 3 (2005): 299–308 on the related subject of impersonality and emotion in Winterson's fiction.

29 John Barth, 'The Literature of Exhaustion', *Atlantic Monthly* (August 1967): 29–34; 'The Literature of Replenishment: Postmodernist Literature', *Atlantic Monthly* (January 1980): 65–71.

30 T. S. Eliot, 'Tradition and the Individual Talent', in *The Norton Anthology of English Literature* II, M. H. Abrams (general ed.), New York, London and Canada: W. W. Norton & Co. (1979) [1919]: 2293–300.

31 Virginia Woolf, *A Room of One's Own*, in *A Room of One's Own and Three Guineas*. London: Vintage (2001) [1929]: 1–98.

32 In Reynolds, 'Interview with Jeanette Winterson, 22.

33 Peter Ackroyd, *Notes for a New Culture*. London: Alkin Books (1993) [1976]: 115.

34 See Susana Onega, *Metafiction and Myth in the Novels of Peter Ackroyd*. Columbia: Camden House (1999): 6–8.

35 Woolf, *A Room of One's Own*, 2, 32.

36 *Ibid.*, 66.

37 *Ibid.*, 66.

1

Of priests and prophets

Oranges Are Not the Only Fruit was published as a paperback by Pandora Press in 1985. As Jeanette Winterson notes in the Introduction to the Vintage edition of the novel, she wrote it 'on a £25 office Goliath with an industrial quantity of Tipex', 'during the winter of 1983 and the spring of 1984', at a time when 'I was unhappy in London, didn't want to be in advertising or banking like most of my Oxford contemporaries, couldn't bring myself to hold down any job that hinted of routine hours'.[1] Patricia Duncker has pointed out how the mid-eighties was a significant moment for the women's movement, 'after the defeat of the miners' strike, during the consolidation of Thatcher's right-wing rule over Britain', and how *Oranges* 'would not have been published at all without the 1970's revolution in feminist writing and the demand for women's books'.[2] The book was accepted for publication on the recommendation of Philippa Brewster, the Pandora Press publisher to whom the Vintage edition of the novel is dedicated. As Duncker recalls, Pandora Press was 'an imprint of a mainstream publisher, Routledge and Kegan Paul [which] had been set up in competition with the other feminist houses, Virago, Onlywomen, Sheba Feminist Publishers and The Women's Press'.[3] Launched by this important publishing house, *Oranges* soon became a bestseller, winning the 1985 Whitbread Award for First Novel. Its unexpected success brought the twenty-four-year-old writer to general notice, including that of large book chains like W. H. Smith, whose monopolistic policy largely determines the failure or success of new writers, books and publishers.[4]

The back cover of the 1990 Pandora Press edition described *Oranges* as the 'touching and humorous account of an unusual childhood with an extraordinary mother'. The unusual child is a little girl

teasingly called Jeanette who, like Jeanette Winterson, lives in a working-class town in Lancashire with her adoptive parents, Jack and
Louie. Like Winterson's own mother, the fictional Jeanette's foster
mother is a militant member of the Pentecostal Evangelical Church
and has taken great pains to educate her daughter in her faith.[5] The
novel relates Jeanette's process of maturation from admiring and
obedient child, to rebellious adolescent and ideologically self-assured
and free adult, as the progressive revelation of her lesbianism clashes
with her mother's religious and moral ideas. Given its subject matter
and the imprint under which it appeared, *Oranges* was unanimously
classified by its early reviewers as a realistic and heavily autobiographical comedy of 'coming out', in line with the feminist novels
that had begun to appear in small marginal presses in the English-
speaking world from the 1960s onwards. In general, these early
feminist novels followed the traditional hero's quest pattern of the
Bildungsroman, adapted to express the process of self-assertion of a
heroine invariably at odds with the social roles of housekeeper, wife
and mother allotted to her by patriarchal ideology.

Like the reviewers, Winterson's publishers were eager to stress
the autobiographical element in *Oranges*, in their case because they
thought it essential for the young writer's career. Thus, in the note on
the author that appears in the Penguin edition of *The Passion*, the
publisher selected from the writer's real life the same episodes that
make up the stages in the quest for maturation of the fictional
Jeanette, purposely confusing Jeanette Winterson's life with that of
her literary namesake. However, as Roz Kaveney acutely pointed out
in a review of *Oranges*, there is no way of knowing '[w]hether or not
what seems unequivocally presented as fiction is literally autobiographical – the shamelessness could be that of photographic veracity
or that of audacious invention – '.[6] Kaveney's rational doubt was
enhanced by the author herself in the Introduction to the Vintage
edition of the novel when, to her self-posed question 'Is Oranges an
autobiographical novel?' she responded: 'No not at all and yes of
course'.[7] Winterson has said several times that *Oranges* is not a realistic novel of 'coming out', but rather 'experimental' and 'anti-linear' (*O*
vii) so that 'you can read it in spirals'.[8] Further, in *Art Objects*, she compares it to Virginia Woolf's *Orlando* and Gertrude Stein's *Autobiography of Alice B. Toklas*, and contends that the three books belong to a
hybrid new type she describes as 'a fiction masquerading as a
memoir' (*AO* 53).

The incompatibility of the critics' and the author's descriptions of the novel points to the fact that *Oranges* is *both* linear and realistic *and* anti-linear and experimental. Its main storyline follows the traditional narrative pattern of the *Bildungsroman*: it is narrated retrospectively by the adult protagonist, beginning with her childhood recollections at the age of seven and ending in the adult narrator's present at the age of twenty. This type of apparently realistic and simple 'autobiographical' narration is a well-worn literary technique that has been used from *Lazarillo de Tormes* and Defoe's *Moll Flanders* to Dickens's *Great Expectations*, a novel which, like *Oliver Twist* and *David Copperfield*, tells the story of a child trying to survive in the most extraordinary circumstances of family and social milieu.[9] In this type of retrospective narration the adult narrator-character focalises the past events from the perspective of his or her childish self, thus producing an ironic distance between the all-knowing adult narrator and the purblind character which increases the suspense, since the reader can only grasp the facts narrated as they are being lived by the child, understanding them imperfectly or completely misunderstanding them, and has to wait until the end of the novel to discover the truth about them. This is an important narrative limitation that not only subjects the reader's understanding of the events narrated to the childish perception of the protagonist, but also colours the narration with the child's fanciful interpretation of events. Focused from the childish perspective of the protagonists, the adult characters in Dickens's novels often become oddly bizarre and grotesque, either huge and threatening monsters or ludicrously absurd speaking parrots caught up in some foible or peculiarity of their own.

A similarly grotesque and comic effect is perceptible in *Oranges*. From little Jeanette's perspective, some adult characters are ludicrous and bizarre, like old, stone-deaf Mrs Rothwell, who is always having spiritual trances, or Mrs Arkwright, the owner of the vermin shop, who likes giving the 'nipper' empty tins of various pesticides, to 'keep its marbles and stuff in' (*O* 14–5). Or also Mrs Butler, the former owner of the Morecambe guest house, and her friend, the once 'official exorcist to the Bishop of Bermuda', who was allowed by Mrs Butler to 'practise voodoo on some of the more senile patients' at the local old folk's home where she now worked (*O* 176). Also in Dickensian fashion, minor characters in *Oranges* are often associated with a ruling passion or a distinctive personal trait, so that, as Rebecca O'Rourke has noted, the reader has the impression that 'everyone in the novel but Jeanette is one-dimensional'.[10] A pointed example of this is Betty, the ill-tempered waitress at Trickett's snack bar, who is always scolding her customers and has been wearing the same pair of glasses 'stuck together with band aid' for many years (O 81, 169). By contrast, other characters, usually men, are depicted as monstrous, terrifying or disgusting – for example, Pastor Finch, the expert in demons, who terrified Jeanette in the presence of her mother and other members of the religious community the first time they met (O 11–12).

Although apparently realistic, some episodes in Jeanette's life story in fact have a distinctive fairytale flavour. Jeanette feels for her mother the type of unquestioning love associated with fairytale heroines, and she is treated by her with the harshness and cruelty of a fairytale stepmother. Like Cinderella's stepmother, Jeanette's foster mother expects perfect obedience from her, never thanks her for doing all types of odd jobs and errands, and is totally blind to the child's sense of shame or self-respect. Thus, she hires her to do the washing up at Trickett's while she is having a cup of Horlicks with her friends (O 82), and when Jeanette falls ill with an inflammation of the adenoids she leaves her unattended for days on end. When, eventually, a member of their religious community takes her to the big and frightening Victoria Hospital, Jeanette is left there alone with the only comfort of a bag of oranges, while her mother busies herself 'with the Lord' or waits at home for the plumber (O 26–9). Like a fairytale heroine, the only weapon Jeanette has to console herself is the power of her imagination. Thus, she attempts to overcome her fear and misery by transforming a boring and sticky orange peel into an empty igloo, the site of a fully engaging and dramatic story about 'How Eskimo Got Eaten' (O 27).

Like the story and characters, the setting is clogged with intertextual echoes of various canonical literary texts. Although the industrial Lancashire town where Jeanette lived with her adoptive parents might resemble Accrington (Winterson's real home town), in fact, its description produces a baffling effect of *déjà lu*, insistently bringing to mind D. H. Lawrence's description of the Bottoms, the 'great quadrangles of dwellings on the hillside of Bestwood' where the Morels went to live with other miners' families at the beginning of *Sons and Lovers*.[11] The Morels' house was 'an end house in one of the top blocks, and thus had only one neighbour'.[12] Jeanette's family house is also 'almost at the top of a long, stretchy street' (O 6), and their only neighbours are a family Jeanette's mother hates because they are not religious and because they used to live at the 'Factory Bottoms', a place frequented by gypsies and the very poor, where Jeanette is forbidden to walk on her own (*O* 14). A great amount of Mrs Morel's frustration with her married life stemmed from the fact that she had lost contact with her Puritan middle-class family when she married Mr Morel. Likewise, Jeanette's mother, Louie, went down in the social ladder when she married Jack, a factory worker and a gambler she had 'reformed', just as Mrs Morel hoped to make her husband give up drink. By marrying Jack, Louie incurred the wrath of her middle-class father, who 'promptly ended all communication. So she never had enough money and after a while she managed to forget that she'd ever had any at all' (*O* 37).

At the beginning of *Sons and Lovers*, Mrs Morel reluctantly allows her seven-year-old son William to go to the wakes.[13] The boy's struggle between staying longer on his own or yielding to his mother's entreaties to return home with her and Annie inaugurates a recurrent pattern in the relationship between Mrs Morel and her two favourite sons, William and Paul, pointing to the crucial factor in the boys' quest for maturation. This episode is echoed by Jeanette's remark at the beginning of *Oranges* that from the top of her hill one could see 'Ellison's tenement, where we had the fair once a year' (*O* 6). The narrator then goes on to explain how, on one occasion when she was there alone, an old gypsy had taken her hand and told her her future: '"You'll never marry," she said, "not you, and you'll never be still"' (*O* 7). This episode has a similarly proleptic function, foreshadowing the crux in Jeanette's maturation process, while the fact that the episode has to do with a fortune teller further enhances the literariness of the chapter, expanding its intertextual indebtedness to Lawrence's novella *The Virgin and the Gipsy* (1930) and to numberless romances and fairytales that have the fortune teller as a *topos*.[14]

The realism of Jeanette's autobiographical narration is further undermined by the novel's division into eight chapters called after the 'Octateuchus', that is, the first eight books of the Old Testament: 'Genesis', 'Exodus', 'Leviticus', 'Numbers', 'Deuteronomy', 'Joshua', 'Judges' and 'Ruth'. This establishes a parodic equivalent, between, on the one hand, the stages in Jeanette's quest for maturation and, on the other, the biblical narration covering God's creation of the world, his designation of the Israelites as his chosen people, their search and struggle for the Promised Land, coming finally to 'Ruth' – that is, to

the story of redemption of a woman enduring threefold marginalisation, as a woman, as a poor widow and as a stranger with a different
religion.

What is more, the linearity of Jeanette's retrospective account is
constantly interrupted by the interpolation of fairytales and fragments
of myth which recur with a difference and/or elaborate on key motifs
in Jeanette's narration, like musical variations in a symphony, adding
to the realistic and the biblical, a fictional and a mythical layer. In the
first chapter, Jeanette's adoption is described as the materialisation of
one of her mother's dreams (O 10). In it, Jeanette's adoption is narrated like the story of Christ's birth in the Bible, thus equating
Jeanette's prescribed role as an Evangelical preacher with Jesus's mission to save the world. The fundamental idea in this chapter, namely,
that Louie had 'chosen' Jeanette, like God the Father did with his Son,
to share with her her wisdom and prepare her to save the world, is
repeated allegorically in the tale of 'a brilliant and beautiful princess'
who was taught 'the secrets of magic [. . .] by an old hunchback' so
that, when she died, she could take over her duties as advisor and
friend of a small village community (O 9). The same *topos* is repeated
again, but with a 'contrary' ending,[15] in the tale of 'Winnet Stonejar
and the Wizard', – itself a version of the fairytale 'Rapunzel' (O 161) –
in the last chapter of the novel, after Jeanette has accomplished her
maturation process and found at last a Woolfian 'room of [her] own'
(O 158). In this final version of the tale, Winnet learns the secret
wisdom imparted to her by the old wizard who had adopted her, but,
unlike Jeanette in Louie's dream, and unlike the princess in the earlier tale, she refuses to abide by his rules and to accept his prohibition
to marry the young man she loves, choosing instead exile and independence on 'the other side' of the sea, even though she knows that
'she can't go back' (O 160).[16]

In the second chapter, 'Exodus', Jeanette, like the Israelites leaving
Egypt, leaves the security of home in order to attend school. This is
her first encounter with an alternative worldview, and Jeanette has
great trouble with her teachers, who are as incapable of accepting her
outlook on things as her mother is of accepting theirs. Thus, her
teacher of English is so shocked with her essay on 'What I Did in my
Summer Holiday' that she does not let her finish reading it out for
fear that she might scare the other children (O 37–8). Jeanette also
thoroughly disturbs her needlework teacher, fittingly called Mrs
Virtue, by making a sampler, predominantly black, with the biblical

text 'THE SUMMER IS ENDED AND WE ARE NOT YET SAVED' (O 39). The narration of this episode brings about the first major frame break in the autobiographical narration when, disrupting the convention of focalising the events from the perspective of her younger self, the adult narrator interrupts the narration in order to give her own interpretation of the events:

> my needlework teacher suffered from a problem of vision. She recog- nised things according to expectation and environment. If you were in a particular place, you expected to see particular things. Sheep and hills, sea and fish; if there was an elephant in the supermarket, she'd either not see it at all, or call it Mrs Jones and talk about fishcakes. But most likely, she'd do what most people do when confronted with something they don't understand:
> Panic. (O 45)

Thus, Mrs Virtue's problem of vision becomes an emblem of the narrow and totalising mentality Jeanette must oppose if she is to open up a space for the definition of her own (lesbian) self. The third chap- ter, 'Leviticus', develops this *topos* further. After listening to Pastor Spratt's definition of 'perfection' as 'flawlessness', Jeanette 'began to develop her first theological disagreement' (O 60). This disagreement is allegorically 'varied' in the tale of the prince who wrote a book about how to 'build a perfect person' (O 67) and then set out in search of the perfect and flawless wife, only to discover many years later that what he wanted 'does not exist' (O 66).

In the fourth chapter, 'Numbers', Jeanette's general disagreement with received ideas progressively narrows down to a growing revul- sion for heterosexual relations as she becomes a teenager. This is expressed in a recurrent dream with psychoanalytical and fictional components. She dreams that she is about to marry and, after approaching the altar with increasing difficulty, she finds that her groom is sometimes 'blind, sometimes a pig, sometimes my mother, sometimes the man from the post office, and once, just a suit of clothes with nothing inside' (O 71). This dream is triggered off by Jeanette's discovery that married women like her aunt do not like their husbands at all, and call them 'pigs', thus confirming her own feelings about men in general and her uncle Bill in particular. After reading 'Beauty and the Beast' and 'Little Red Riding Hood', the teenager concludes that there are three types of people in the world: women, men and beasts (O 72). In order to confirm her theory,

Jeanette then spies on two married neighbours, Doreen and Betty, 'hid[ing] in the dustbin to hear what the women said [. . . . w]hen it was washday' (O 75). This ludicrous scene is intertextually indebted to the one in Salman Rushdie's *Midnight's Children* in which puzzled Saleem Sinai hides in 'the washing chest' and sees his sexually starved mother's hands 'caress[ing] her bare midriff' and 'stray[ing] below decks'.[7] The chapter ends with Jeanette and Melanie's first love-making, just before the Harvest Festival Banquet, and their fear that their exciting and wonderful new feeling might be the product of an 'Unnatural Passion' (O 89). The impending clash between Jeanette's sexual orientation and the views on homosexuality of her mother and their religious congregation is the *topos* of a short tale describing a scene in which 'a table [is] set at feast, and the guests are arguing about the best recipe for goose' (O 89). The mention of the goose links this tale with the tale of the prince in search of the perfect woman, since the prince's advisor is a goose he beheads for daring to contradict him (O 62). In the new tale, the 'elect', who 'have always been this way' – like the members of the Pentecostal Evangelist con-gregation – try to enjoy the banquet even though the hall is derelict and very cold, with the bare-shouldered women suffering most, while outside 'the rebels' get ready to 'storm the Winter Palace' (O 89).

When Melanie and Jeanette fall in love, they naturally take for granted the purity of their relationship, so they 'read the Bible as usual, and then told each other how glad we were that the Lord had brought us together' (O 88). However, what they think to be holy, Jeanette's mother and Pastor Finch consider to be a particularly dreadful example of 'Unnatural Passions' (O 85, 105, *passim*) caused by demonic possession (O 104), the result of Jeanette's training in the 'male' role of preacher (O 133). The struggle with her mother and the religious community con-stitutes the core of Chapter 6, 'Joshua'. In the Bible, Joshua won the Battle of Jericho following God's instructions to walk around the walls of the city and to blow a trumpet. Likewise, Jeanette must fight the reli-gious community alone, armed only with her trust in God's words: 'To the pure all things are pure' (O 303). The climax of this unequal battle is the exorcism she is submitted to by Pastor Finch. In the *Gospel accord-ing to Mark* we learn that Jesus Christ 'was there in the wilderness forty days, tempted of Satan; and was with the wild beasts; and the angels ministered unto him (Mark, 1: 13). Parodying this, Jeanette sees an 'orange demon' in a hallucination – which makes her think 'about William Blake' (O 108) – after thirty-six hours of seclusion and fasting.

The demon asks her to choose between repenting and having a prede-termined and easy life, or keeping it as her counsellor and having 'a dif-ficult, different time' (O 109).[18] Unlike Jesus, who resisted Satan's temptations, Jeanette decides to keep this (bisexual) orange demon, which she acknowledges as her own. As it tells Jeanette, all human beings have their demons: 'We're here to keep you in one piece, if you ignore us, you're quite likely to end up in two pieces, or lots of pieces, it is all part of the paradox' (O 109). As the demon suggests, then, if she is to mature, Jeanette has to overcome the fragmentation of her self into 'Jeanette' (her conscious, or ego) and 'the orange demon' (her unconscious, or id), brought about by the exorcism. Accompanied by glandular fever and a deathlike slumber, Jeanette's climactic struggle to preserve her self-identity is comparable to the mythical hero's ritual death and rebirth. The danger she is facing at this stage is allegorised in a dream in which she sees everyone 'who can't make the ultimate deci-sion' in 'the city of Lost Chances' and is shown 'the Room of the Final Disappointment', which, no matter how high you climb, is where you end up 'if you've already made the Fundamental Mistake' (O 111).

After this, Jeanette's mother ransacks Jeanette's room, burning all her private correspondence, a violent *auto da fé* that transforms Louie from the 'White Queen' (O 112) into the 'Queen of Spades' in *Alice in Wonderland* (O 127). The shattering effect of this experience is reflected in the fragmentation and incoherence of the interpolated 'literary' version of the same, which, instead of a tale, consists of a series of short, inchoate and mixed-up 'variations' on the sentence 'She had a heart of stone', taken from a range of biblical, historical and fictional texts: (1) 'The Forbidden City' of Amiens ransacked by the Black Prince; (2) Christ's injunction to the Pharisees, who had asked him to condemn an adulterous woman: 'He that is without sin among you, let him cast the first stone at her' (St John, 8:7); (3) a stone lion, where the world ends; (4) a gryphon made of stone, in the West; (5) the Northern corner of a stone turret; (6) a gritty beach in the South;[19] (7) Humpty Dumpty's fall from the wall, from *Alice in Wonderland*; and (8) the City of Lost Chances 'full of those who chose the wall' of her earlier dream (O 112–13). In this interpolated text, the 'stone wall' and 'turret' built by Louie's 'stone heart' echo 'Rapunzel', the fairytale of a little girl who was taken from her parents by a witch and was kept in utter isolation and misery in a stone tower until she was saved by a prince. Opposed to this stone turret that imprisons the body is 'the chalk circle' that protects 'the soul' (O 113).

The beginning of the following chapter, 'Judges', opens with two lines from *Alice in Wonderland* in which the Queen of Spades warns Alice: '*Either you or your head must be off*' (*O* 127). This quotation summarises the main motif in this chapter, namely, Jeanette's expulsion from home and congregation and her mother's treacherous behaviour. The motifs of exile and betrayal are then repeated in an interpolated fragment from Thomas Malory's *Morte d'Arthur*, which tells how Sir Perceval, 'the youngest of Arthur's knights, at last set forth from Camelot' (*O* 128). Echoing the stone wall and turret, Camelot is described as a 'high-walled castle' (*O* 128), where Arthur lingers, betrayed and old, while Perceval wanders across the waste land in search of the Holy Grail (*O* 129). In the Arthurian myth, the stone is also a central symbol, since Arthur proves his right to assume kingship by removing the king's sword, Excalibur, from the stone: 'There was a stone that held a bright sword and no one could pull the sword because their minds were fixed on the stone' (*O* 129). Refracting this idea, Jeanette manages to endure her trials by holding 'on tight to [a] little rough brown pebble' (*O* 135), the symbol of her self-integrity.

The interpolation of the Perceval story adds a mythical and archetypal dimension to Jeanette's autobiographical life story, providing the unitary quest pattern into which the other subsidiary texts can be integrated, in a way that brings to mind the unity-within-fragmentation effect produced by the figure of the poet as mythical quester crossing time zones and ontological boundaries in Ezra Pound's *A Draft of XXX Cantos*.

Set against the Arthurian myth, the tale of the princess and the hunchback and its 'contrary', the tale of Winnet Stonejar and the Wizard, become alternative and complementary fairytale variations on Sir Perceval's archetypal quest for the Holy Grail. At the same time, the fact that the Holy Grail is the Christian symbol of perfection points to the tale of the prince in search of the perfect and flawless woman as the fairytale 'contrary' to Perceval's own quest, since, where his finding of the Grail brings about Perceval's spiritual wholeness and the renewal of the waste land, the prince's search ends with the woman telling him that what he is looking for does not exist (*O* 66). The prince is so furious that he has the woman's head chopped off and all his advisors and most of the court are instantly drowned in the lake formed by her spilt blood (*O* 67). Parodying Jeanette's mother's habit of comforting her daughter with an orange whenever she is unhappy, the despondent prince comforts himself at this stage by buying a dozen oranges from a vendor who 'only does oranges' (*O* 67), and who offers him a book that 'tells you how to build a perfect person, it's all about this man who does it, but it's no good if your ain't got the equipment. [. . .] this geezer gets a bolt through the neck' (*O* 67), thus ironically suggesting that the road he has taken will not lead him to spiritual renewal and wholeness, but to the crude sewing together of the split facets of a monstrous human being, as in the case of Mary Shelley's *Frankenstein*.

In the fifth Book of the 'Octateuchus', God commands Moses to restate the Ten Commandments. Parodying God's commanding voice, the fifth chapter of *Oranges* is narrated by the godlike voice of an external author-narrator who interrupts Jeanette's narration in order to reflect on time and history. Unlike that of Jehovah, the ring of this authorial voice is strikingly literary and derivative as well as parodic, turning T. S. Eliot's categorisation of time in *Four Quartets* upside down:

> Time is a great deadener. People forget, get bored, grow old, go away. There was a time in England when everyone was much concerned with building wooden boats and sailing off against the Turk. When that stopped being interesting, what peasants there were left limped back to the land, and what nobles there were left plotted against each other.
>
> Of course that is not the whole story, but that is the way with stories, we make them what we will. It's a way of explaining the universe while leaving the universe unexplained. (*O* 93)

Where for Jehovah, all human beings can be ruled by the application of ten commandments, and where for Eliot 'history is a pattern / of timeless moments',[20] developing cyclically, with 'a time for building / And a time for living and for generations / And a time for the wind to break the loosened pane / And to shake the wainscot where the field-mouse trots / And to shake the tattered arras woven with a silent motto',[21] for the godlike author of 'Deuteronomy' history is rather depressingly mixed up and confused, 'a ball of strings full of knots' made up of often contradictory and always partial individual stories and perspectives, without the possibility of univocal interpretation: 'The only thing for certain is how complicated it all is, like string full of knots. It's all there but hard to find the beginning and impossible to fathom the end. The best you can do is admire the cat's cradle, and maybe knot it up a bit more' (*O* 93).[22] Rejecting the Aristotelian separation of 'storytelling which is not fact from history

which is fact', the authorial voice concludes that those who defend the
objectivity and truthfulness of history 'do this so that they know what
to believe and what not to believe' (O 93). Her refusal to distinguish
between storytelling and history and her insistence on the provision-
ality and partiality of historical versions of reality echo both the
postulates of the New Historicism and the general denunciation in
the postmodernist period of the 'myths of totality' endorsed by the
patriarchal system in favour of competing 'ideologies of fracture' –
that is, the ideologies of social minorities, whether sexual, political,
ethnical or religious.[23] Therefore, this short metaleptic chapter, which
is thematically linked to the adult narrator's reflection on Mrs Virtue's
'problem of vision' in Chapter 2, may be said to encapsulate in a nutshell the ideology informing the novel as a whole, namely, a postmodernist rejection of the overall 'truths' of dominant discourses that
condemn individual 'difference' to invisibility and erasure,[24] a position which, according to Patricia Waugh, has its roots in Nietzsche's
reading of Romantic individualism.[25] In the authorial voice's own
words:

> And when I look at a history book and think of the imaginative effort it
> has taken to squeeze this oozing world between two boards and typeset,
> I am astonished. Perhaps the event has an unassailable truth. God saw
> it. God knows. But I am not God. And so when someone tells me what
> they heard or saw, I believe them, and I believe their friend who also
> saw, but not in the same way, and I can put these accounts together and
> I will not have a seamless wonder but a sandwich laced with mustard of
> my own. [. . .] Here is some advice. If you want to keep your own teeth,
> make your own sandwiches. (O 95)

For all its flippant tone, the authorial voice's advice to make our
'own sandwiches' if we are to preserve our individual outlook on life
is strongly reminiscent of the poet/prophet Los's climactic declaration of individual creativity to his weeping Spectre in Blake's visionary poem *Jerusalem: The Emanation of the Giant Albion* (1804–18?): 'I
must Create a System or be enslav'd by another Man's / I will not
Reason & Compare; my business is to Create'.[26]

At the very beginning of the novel Jeanette says that her mother is
'very like William Blake; she has visions and dreams and she cannot
always distinguish a flea's head from a king' (O 8–9). Like the visionary writer and engraver, Louie had an inborn talent for drawing and
storytelling. When teaching little Jeanette, she used to draw for her

'all the creatures mentioned [in the Book of Deuteronomy]' (O 42);
she loved reading out to her daughter a version of *Jane Eyre* with an
'improved' ending she had herself invented (O 74); and she was
always telling her stories of conversion, such as the one 'about a brave
person who had despised the fruits of the flesh and worked for the
Lord instead' (O 7); the story of the 'converted sweep' (O 7); and the
story of the 'Hallelujah Giant' (O 8). Louie's own conversion story was
so romantic that Jeanette compares it to a Mills and Boon novelette:
Pastor Spratt had succeeded in converting her because 'he looked like
Errol Flynn, but holy' (O 8). Yet another story invented by Louie was
the story of Jeanette's adoption (O 10). In it, as we saw above,
Jeanette's birth was equated to that of Jesus Christ. Louise's 'biblical'
version is then 'varied' by Jeanette-as-narrator, who compares her
own birth to that of Athena springing from Zeus's head.[27] Thus, a
further equation is established between the Greek virgin goddess who
played 'a central role in the institution of war, reserved for the male',[28]
and the role of preacher prescribed for Jeanette by her mother in
the equally patriarchal institution of the Church. Further still, the
fact that Jeanette's mother is compared to Zeus – the male god who
established patriarchal hegemony in Olympus – may be read as a proleptic warning both of Louie's militant – and according to Jeanette,
treacherous – subservience to the patriarchal values upheld by the
Pentecostal Evangelical Church and of her own forcefully repressed
lesbianism.[29] More significantly, it may also be read as evidence of
Louie's godlike creativity, her visionary capacity to create life, like
Blake's poets/prophets, not by means of 'the jolt beneath the hip, but
[by means of] water and the word' (O 10).

Potentially, Louie has all the qualities of Blake's poet/prophet. In
'The Marriage of Heaven and Hell' (1792), Blake describes him as
'The just man' inhabited by 'Poetic Genius', like Isaiah or Ezekiel. He
is the creator of the metaphors that give birth to gods existing within
the field of language (plates 11 and 12), someone whose 'senses discovered the infinite in everything' ('Preludium'). Opposed to this
figure is that of the 'priest', 'the villain' who conceptualises the
metaphors of desire, giving birth to transcendental gods (that is, to
gods that have become supernatural referents) and dogmas that he
uses as instruments of power:

> The ancient Poets animated all sensible objects with Gods or Geniuses,
> calling them by the names and adorning them with the properties of

woods, rivers, mountains, lakes, cities, nations, and whatever their
enlarged and numerous senses could perceive.
    And particularly they studied the Genius of each city and country,
placing it under its Mental Deity;
    Till a System was formed, which some took advantage of, and
enslav'd the vulgar by attempting to realise or abstract the Mental
Deities from their objects – thus began Priesthood;
    Choosing forms of worship from poetic tales.
    And at length they pronounc'd that the Gods had order'd such things.
    Thus men forgot that All Deities reside in the Human heart.[30]

Neatly following Blake's distinction, Jeanette sees the success or failure of her own individuation process as a choice between these two
conflicting roles:

I could have been a priest instead of a prophet. The priest has a book
with the words set out. Old words, known words, words of power. Words
that are always on the surface. Words for every occasion. The words
work. They do what they're supposed to do; comfort and discipline.
(O 161)

Since her adoption, Jeanette had been trained to undertake the role
of 'priest' (or 'preacher'). It involved learning the biblical 'words of
power' and administering them to the flock for their 'comfort and discipline', without ever, however, questioning their truthfulness. Her
maturation, therefore, involves the rejection of this prescribed role,
and her assumption of the role of 'prophet': 'The prophet has no book.
The prophet is a voice that cries in the wilderness, full of sounds that
do not always set into meaning. The prophets cry out because they are
troubled by demons' (O 161).
    Discussing the influence of Romanticism on postmodernism,
Patricia Waugh has pointed out how 'Nietzsche includes Romantic
"vision" as an idealism implicated in the decadence of the principle of
individuation'. However, 'he too is caught up in the belief that not to
invent one's own system is to be enslaved to someone else's'. Consequently, Nietzsche 'advocates the need for a positive decadence; a self-
conscious awareness of our fictionalising powers which will prevent
us accepting another fictionalised will to power as the collectively val-
idated truth of myth'.[31] Thus, Nietzsche opposes the salutary self-conscious awareness of the individual's fictionalising powers to 'the
mode of the liar who deceives by imitating truth. It is the mode of conventional morality, a sickness masquerading as health and producing

that attitude of "ressentiment" or revengefulness against life which is anchored in self-deception and characteristic of the herd mentality'.[32] As the authorial voice curtly puts it in 'Deuteronomy': 'Knowing what to believe had its advantages. It built an empire and kept people where they belonged' (O 93).

It is this self-deceptive 'herd mentality', then, that has transformed Jeanette's mother – as well as Pastor Finch, Pastor Spratt and the other members of her religious community – from potential vision-ary poets/prophets into 'priestly' religious bigots of monolithic con-victions.[33] The key exception is Jeanette's old friend, Elsie Norris, who was always reading romantic and metaphysical poetry, loved Wagner's operas (O 46–7), and told Jeanette 'all about Swinburne and [. . .] William Blake. [. . .] read [her] Goblin Market by a woman called Christina Rossetti' and admired W. B. Yeats most, because he 'knew the importance of numbers, and the great effect of the imagination on the world' (O 30). Although 'Testifying Elsie' seems to be slightly crazed and ludicrously absentminded, in fact, like the old hunchback in the tale, who taught 'the secrets of magic' to a beautiful and bril-liant princess before she died (O 9–10), it is Elsie the old magician, rather than Louie, who (also on the point of death) taught Jeanette the visionary wisdom that would transform her from priest, or power-seeking recipient and transmitter of ancient wisdom, to poet/prophet, someone with the godlike capacity to interpret the signs and to create the shape of her own life.

As we have seen, Jeanette's retrospective narration is intertwined with a series of subsidiary fairytales and fragments from myth, narrated by an external author-narrator. Though fragmentary and scattered within Jeanette's narrative, these subsidiary texts are thematically knitted to each other and to specific episodes in the main narrative by means of repetitions-with-a-difference of recurrent motifs, thus creating what Mónica Calvo has described as a pattern of 'recursive symmetry' along the different narrative strands. Develop-ing Winterson's contention that Oranges can be read in spirals, Calvo compares the novel's structure to the spiralling structure postulated by Chaos theory for the behaviour of thermodynamic molecular sys-tems in non-equilibrium conditions.[34] As an incomplete circular structure aiming towards the infinite, the spiral constitutes 'an appo-site structural correlate of the lesbian view of human identity as dif-fused and disintegrating'.[35] As such, it has become 'a recurrent motif in lesbian film iconography'.[36] Her interesting conclusion is that the

spiralling structure of *Oranges* evinces Jeanette Winterson's attempt
to create a new type of *lesbian writing* as distinct from the usually
circular writing propounded by feminist theorists.[37] A key antecedent
in this respect would be Maureen Duffy's *The Microcosm* (1966), a
novel that displays a convoluted, cyclical structure and grows on the
accumulation of elements from myth, saga, romance and fairytale.[38]

Calvo's interpretation shows *Oranges* as a sophisticated example of
a specifically lesbian type of *Bildungsroman*, which it surely is. But
Oranges is not just an experimental novel about the maturation
process of a lesbian heroine. It is a novel about the making of a lesbian *artist*, as is suggested by its central 'poet/prophet' motif, by the
deliberate confusion of protagonist with writer and by the allusions to
Sons and Lovers, which, besides a novel about mother–son relationships, is also a key modernist *Künstlerroman*. Lynn Pykett suggested
as much when, comparing *Oranges* to another canonical modernist
Künstlerroman, James Joyce's *A Portrait of the Artist as a Young Man*,
she defined Winterson's novel as 'a portrait of the artist as a young
working class lesbian who flees the nets of religion and community
[in order to become] an artist/prophet'.[39]

Analysing James Joyce's *Ulysses*, Northrop Frye famously contended that if this encyclopaedic and most ambitious modernist
Künstlerroman gives an impression of shapelessness it is simply
because it is not organised according to familiar principles. Frye's
path-breaking contention was that *Ulysses* is built on a systematic
combination of elements taken from the four basic literary forms –
the novel, the romance, the confession and the anatomy – with the
aim of creating 'a complete prose epic' whose 'unity is built up from
an intricate scheme of parallel contrasts'.[40] According to the archetypal critic, Joyce went a step further in *Finnegans Wake*, as he moved
from the combination of these four basic literary forms to the creation
of 'a fifth and quintessential form. This form is the one traditionally
associated with scriptures and sacred books, and treats life in terms of
the fall and awakening of the human soul and the creation and apocalypse of nature. The Bible is the definitive example of it.'[41]

With Northrop Frye's words in mind, it is easy to see a similar
attempt in *Oranges* to combine elements from the four basic literary
forms – the novel (the realistic elements in Jeanette's life), the
romance (the fairytale and mythical elements), the confession (the
Bildungsroman elements) and the anatomy (the satiric and ironic elements) – and to unify them under the quintessential 'fifth' biblical

form, by framing them in eight chapters named after the eight books
in the 'Octateuchus'.

In the Introduction to the script of *Oranges*, Jeanette Winterson
explained that 'the fairy tales and allegorical passages that weave
themselves within the main story [are] a kind of Greek Chorus commenting on the main events' (*OS* viii). The comparison to a Greek
Chorus is misleading in that it takes for granted the secondary function of these passages, obscuring the fact that these apparently
subsidiary narratives – and also the whole of Chapter 5 – are narrated
by a godlike external narrative instance comparable to God's voice
speaking to Moses in 'Deuteronomy', thus suggesting that they stand
at a *higher* narrative level than Jeanette's narration. Although the
reader is prone to assume an identity between the voices of the internal (or intradiegetic) narrator (the adult Jeanette) and the external (or
extradiegetic) authorial voice (a 'paper' Jeanette Winterson), in fact
these authorial interruptions of Jeanette's narration are metalepses,[42]
that is, unlawful trespassings on ontological levels conveying the dis-
quieting possibility that the extradiegetic might be the same as the
diegetic, so that not only Jeanette Winterson but also her addressee
(that is, ourselves as readers) are included within the text. Taken
together, these parodic literary and mythical texts may be said to constitute a paradoxical and dislocated *mise en abyme* of the type
described by Lucien Dällenbach for the *nouveau roman*,[43] that is, a unitary though fragmented mirror-text of Jeanette's 'realistic' account,
that can only have been written by a godlike, visionary writer enjoying
the 'fourfold vision' of a truly creative poet/prophet.[44]

This interpretation is enhanced by the spiralling structure of
Oranges, since, before becoming an icon in lesbian film iconography,
the spiral was recurrently used by visionary poets/prophets – from
Dante, Milton, Blake and Goethe to Yeats, Graves and Eliot – to symbolise the cycle of human life. As Northrop Frye has pointed out, in
Blake's poem 'The Mental Traveller' the cycle of human life from
birth to death to rebirth is symbolised by 'a male and a female figure,
moving in opposite directions, one growing old as the other grows
young and vice versa' in a fourfold or 'lunar' cyclical relation. While
the male figure represents humanity, the female figure represents the
natural environment. Consequently, in this, as in other visionary
poems, the cycle of human life is associated with 'an ambivalent
female archetype [. . .] sometimes benevolent, sometimes sinister,
but usually presided over and confirming the cyclical movement'.[45]

Winterson creates her own version of this archetype in her short story 'Turn of the World' (*WOP* 149–60), where we find at 'the heart of the island [of Fyr], at the point of zero coordinates, [standing in] a ring of serpentine fire, [. . .] a man and a woman, back to back, holding hands'. This 'twinned royal pair [. . .] youthful but older than the fire in which they wait [are m]ale and female, like for like, separate and identical. A man's face in the woman's. A woman's face in the man's, and both faces the face of the traveller' who manages to find them (*WOP* 152–3).

As Frye further notes, the spiral is also found in the *Divine Comedy*, where 'Beatrice presides over not a cycle but a sacramental spiral leading up to deity, as does, in a far less concrete way, the *Ewig-Weiblische* of *Faust* [. . .]. Eve in Milton, who spirals man downward into the Fall, is the contrasting figure to Beatrice'.[46] Yeats's *A Vision*, which the poet himself associated with 'The Mental Traveller', is also based on this symbolism, as is, according to Frye, Robert Graves's *The White Goddess* and T. S. Eliot's *The Waste Land*.[47] To these may be added 'The Library of Babel', Jorge Luis Borges' 'total' textual universe, made up of hexagonal galleries and bottomless wells arranged around a spiralling stair without beginning or end, reduplicated by mirrors ad infinitum and containing every possible combination of the twenty-odd orthographic symbols, that is, everything that is thinkable.[48]

From a visionary perspective, the 'fourfold' mirror-text in *Oranges* becomes the perfect symbolic expression of Jeanette/Winterson's individuation process, since to the question of whether the visionary writer who has created this complex though unitary spiralling world/book is the mature fictional Jeanette, or the flesh-and-blood Jeanette Winterson, the only possible answer is that it is *both*. In this 'fourfold' visionary world there is no difference between inside and outside, between the fictional and the real, as there is no difference between subject and object, since the imaginative act that creates the world/book is the same act that transforms the artist-to-be into a fully creative poet/prophet. Thus, in the last reading, *Oranges Are Not The Only Fruit* reveals itself as an astonishing *tour de force*, a truly innovative and self-conscious experiment in *écriture lesbienne* giving shape *both* to the fictional Jeanette's maturation process and to Jeanette Winterson's own development as a poet/prophet with the power to create selves and worlds by means of her visionary imagination.

Later in the year that saw the publication of *Oranges*, the young writer published *Boating for Beginners*. Because it appeared in a collection of comic books, the Methuen Humour list, this novel was generally ignored by the reviewers, rarely mentioned by the critics, and even systematically omitted by Winterson herself from her list of publications until the 1990s.[49] In the foreword to the 1990 Pandora edition of *Oranges*, it is mentioned as a novel in its own right.[50] However, in later publications by Winterson *Boating* is carefully differentiated from her 'serious' fictional and non-fictional works as 'a comic book' or, as is the case on the Official Jeanette Winterson Website, as 'a comic book with pictures'. In the course of an exchange of e-mails between myself and Jeanette Winterson's secretary, Jayne, regarding the question of royalties, I was told that I would not be able to quote at length from *Boating for Beginners* because 'JW finds it v boring when the book is included in her main oeuvre, because that was never intended by her' (23 December 2004). As she explained in a later e-mail, *Boating for Beginners*

> was commissioned for the Methuen Humour List, and was never viewed by JW as her second novel – it was a way of funding herself while she was working on The Passion. She also wrote a fitness book at this time for much the same reasons. Only after she won the Whitbread with Oranges did her publishers try and re-package the book differently. So she gets a bit fed-up with all the rumours of not liking it etc. It is what it is – a bit of flotsam written in a few weeks. (26 December 2004)

Although *Boating* is admittedly less complex than *Oranges*, Jayne's description of it as a mere 'bit of flotsam' written for money, like *Fit for the Future* (1986), does *Boating* little justice. In a review of *The Passion*, the critic and bestselling author of comic novels, David Lodge, said that he preferred *Boating* to *Oranges* and *The Passion*: 'Although it won no prizes and has not been published in America it gave me more simple pleasure than the other two, which did, and have.'[51] And, as Eileen Williams-Wanquet demonstrates in a pathbreaking essay, *Boating* is as ideologically charged as Winterson's other novels, making 'constant use of a baroque aesthetics and themes to raise ethical questions about how we ought to live, about individual responsibility and the future of humanity'.[52] What is more, *Boating* displays the same bent for artistic experimentation, the same preoccupation with linguistic exactness and stylistic neatness and the same concern with totalitarian ideology and the excesses of religious fundamentalism that informs *Oranges*.

The novel begins with an epigraph taken from an item of news published in the *Guardian* on 28 August 1984 about the discovery on mount Ararat of what were thought to be the archaeological remains of Noah's Ark, and the announcement of their transportation to the United States for laboratory analysis. Thus, the epigraph synthesises the book's central motif, namely, the need to prove the truthfulness or falsehood of the biblical account by the analysis of historical records. Until the turn of the nineteenth century, the very idea of such research was shocking for most Christians, who believed that every word in the Bible was divinely inspired and its truth guaranteed. The secular humanist movement initiated in Tübingen that became known in England through George Eliot's translations of David Friedrich Strauss's *Life of Jesus* (1846) and Ludwig Feuerbach's *Essence of Christianity* (1854), with its focus on the historical, rather than the divine Jesus, marks the beginning of a new trend among biblical scholars which stands in diametrical opposition to Evangelicalism, with its emphasis on faith, rather than good works or the sacraments, and its insistence on the importance of the individual's personal relationship with God our Saviour.

Medieval scholasticism regarded God as the Author of the only two original books, the Book of Nature and the Book of Scriptures. Therefore, once the need for historical confirmation is admitted, the biblical account loses its unique originality and becomes just one version, among others, of a potent human myth. As the external narrator puts it in a key authorial comment:

> People have believed for centuries, on the authority of the book of Genesis, that there was once a deluge over the whole world. Maybe Genesis is less important than it was, but we still like flood stories – whether they're Plato's Atlantis or yarns about the Loch Ness monster. Freud says we are preoccupied with deluges as a safeguard against bed-wetting. This may or may not be true; what remains true is the potency of the myth. (*BB* 65–6)

Boating fictionalises this sceptical attitude to the Bible, offering the reader a puzzlingly anachronistic and bizarre 'alternative' account of Noah's relationship to God, of the making of the Ark, and of the Flood that brought about the extinction of Noah's pre-Babelian civilisation, which might be compared in comicity and subversiveness to 'The Stowaway', the first chapter in Julian Barnes's *A History of the World in 10½ Chapters*.[53] This self-conscious and parodic version of the Book

of Genesis is narrated by an external narrative instance with the oracular quality of the narrative voice in the Bible, or rather, of the omniscient and ubiquitous narrator of multiplot Victorian novels since,
whereas the divine narrator of the Book of Genesis never enters the
minds of the biblical characters, the godlike author-narrator of *Boating* has the capacity to get in and out of the minds of every character,
particularly of Gloria, the protagonist, and to move freely in space and
time. As in the highly organised plots of Victorian fiction, the narration in *Boating* is structured by means of juxtapositions of several
plotlines and perspectives. Thus, the narration of what Gloria is doing
at a particular moment in the story's present is interrupted by the narrator in order to record what Gloria's mother, Mrs Munde, is doing at
the same time; this account is in its turn interrupted in order to relate
what Noah or some other character is doing, and so on and on, providing a panoramic view of the actions and thoughts of Gloria and her
mother and friends, on the one hand, and of Noah and his sons, on
the other, as they are taking place at the same time in various parts of
Nineveh. However, where in Victorian multiplot novels like, for
example, George Eliot's *Middlemarch*, the events are clearly situated
in a specific past time and space, and where in the Book of Genesis
the events are placed in a remote past and situated in the southern
area of Canaan (now Palestine) or the northern area of Harran and Ur
of Kasdim (or of the Chaldeans) (now Syria), in *Boating*, the city of
Nineveh is incongruously described as both ancestral and modern,
both the biblical city situated in 'Ur of the Chaldees' (*BB* 15, *passim*)
and a contemporary metropolis, with all the advantages and shortcomings of a late twentieth-century capitalist society in the Western
world. In contrast to the chronological linearity of the Bible, from
Genesis to Apocalypse, this 'incongruous juxtaposition of the modern
and the biblical', in Emma Fisher's words,[54] suggests a circularity of
events that precludes the need for myths of origins and advocates
instead the cyclical recurrence of myth.

This is the lesson taught by Mrs Munde to her daughter Gloria
through the tale of the traveller in search of the secret of the world:
'The secret of the world is this: the world is entirely circular and you
will go round and round endlessly, never finding what you want,
unless you have found what you really want inside you' (*BB* 65). These
words and those that follow ('The end of all your exploring will be to
cease from exploration and know the place for the first time') foreground the intertextuality of *Boating*, since they are a pastiche of the

well-known lines at the end of 'Little Gidding': 'We shall not cease
from exploration / And the end of all our exploring / Will be to arrive
where we started / And know the place for the first time.'[55] A similar
effect is produced by the text(ile) metaphor used by Mrs Munde when
she concludes her speech with the observation that the world is like a
jumper and that 'if you've dropped a stitch somewhere in the jumper
of life, you have to pick it up again or your pattern will come out lop-
sided' (*BB* 65). This observation, which recalls both the 'ball of strings
full of knots' in *Oranges* and Henry James's contention that reading a
story to uncover its meaning is like discovering the repeated figure in
a carpet, may be said to function as a *mise en abyme* of the whole novel,
warning the reader about the intertextual nature of *Boating* and the
fictionality of characters inhabiting a wholly textual world. In keeping
with this, on the very first page, the external narrator sets the absur-
dist tone of the novel by presenting Gloria as a diminished version of
Eugène Ionesco's *Bald Primadonna*. The purblind, eighteen-year-old
heroine, whose 'recent experiment with ash-blond tint had left her
threadbare' and who is trying to make up her mind whether to
become a secretary or a prostitute, sadly rejects the latter option, on
the reflection that 'There's no such thing as a bald prostitute' (*BB* 9).
A few pages later, Gloria's friend Doris is similarly associated with the
theatre of the absurd, in this case, with Beckett's *Waiting for Godot*,
since, with the tramps Vladimir and Estragon, she believes that
'[D]ecay is the key' and, with Pozzo and Lucky, characters existing in
a master/slave relationship, that 'some of us are lucky and some of us
aren't' (*BB* 24).

Besides Eliot, Ionesco and Beckett, *Boating* is also intertextually
indebted to Swift and Mary Shelley. Just as the satiric effect in, for
example, Gulliver's description of the 'leaping and creeping game'
played by the Lilliputian courtesans hoping for preferment wholly
depends on the reader's ability to grasp the similarity between this
strange physical activity and the equally humiliating intellectual
games played in George I's court,[56] so the satiric effect in *Boating* is
built on the incongruous mixture of modern with ancestral and of
realistic with fantastic elements. Thus, in a quotation from *Time Out*
cited in an advertisement for the Vintage edition of *Boating*, Noah is
described as 'Howard Hughes crossed with Frankenstein – an eccentric overseer of thriving capitalism who makes "God" by accident out
of a piece of gateau and a giant electric toaster'.[57] The association of
Noah with Frankenstein signals him as the Promethean creator of a

nameless monster. As Ham's wife, Desi, discovers in a manuscript written by Noah in what turns out to be a ludicrous pastiche of Mary Shelley's *Frankenstein* (*BB* 82–3), Noah had created a creature who calls himself 'YAHWEH THE UNPRONOUNCEABLE', by a combination of scientific *hybris*, chance and electricity (*BB* 13, 83–4). Needless to say, once created, the Unpronounceable, like Frankenstein's creature, soon turned out to be uncontrollable and much more powerful than his creator.

The fact that, in this 'alternative' version of Genesis, it is Noah who creates God, and not the other way round, is in keeping with Feuerbach's radical view that the idea of God was created by man to express the divine within himself, and that the beginning, middle and end of Religion is MAN. But the Unpronounceable is not only a human creation, he is also a transcendental god, as is suggested by the fact that he lives with the angels in a cloud (*BB* 85) hovering above Nineveh, and descending to the ground at will, in clear parody of Laputa, the floating island in *Gulliver's Travels.*[58] The Unpronounceable's transcendence makes Noah a 'priest' in Blake's sense of the word – that is, a villainous and evil creator of transcendental gods and religious dogmas to be used as instruments of power over other human beings.

Noah's physical aspect enhances this interpretation. Gloria despises him because he looks like 'a transvestite [wearing] frocks and stacked heels and make-up' (*BB* 18) and, while his three sons call him 'Dad' (*BB* 109), the Unpronounceable calls him 'mother' (*BB* 89, 111, 122). This suggested androgyny is in keeping with the description of the creation of humans as male and female in the first chapter of Genesis.[59] In the biblical account, these androgynes 'were giants in those days' (Genesis, 6: 4). By contrast, Noah is painfully short – 'around four feet tall' (*BB* 50) – and looks like 'a spherical man with a bright bald head' (*BB* 50), that is, he has the spherical (or orangelike) shape of the original androgynes as described by Aristophanes in Plato's *Symposium* (189a–193d). In Aristophanes' account, the androgynes were split into two by Zeus as a punishment for their ungodliness. Similarly, the God of Genesis decided to punish humankind with the Flood when he 'saw that the wickedness of man was great in the earth, and that every imagination of the thoughts of his heart was only evil continually' (Genesis, 6: 5).

At the same time, the association of Noah with Howard Hughes (1905–1976), the aviator, movie producer, billionaire and hypochon-

driac considered to be the father of cybernetics, points to Noah as the
contemporary capitalist and mass-media tycoon, who has risen from
affluent owner of 'a thriving little pleasure boat company called Boating for Beginners' (BB 12), to power-seeking, 'priestly' writer of religious bestsellers and producer of large-scale documentary films and
worldwide touring stage epics on the creation of the world. Thus, displaying an astute command of the mechanisms of mass-media
manipulation, Noah summons a press conference to spread the news
that the Lord, who had originally been reluctant to interfere with
human affairs, has finally decided to intervene in order to rid human
beings of 'false gods and socialism' (BB 13), and that he has been
chosen 'to lead the world into a time of peace and prosperity under the
guidance of the One True God' (BB 13). After this, with the collaboration of the Unpronounceable, Noah starts working 'on a manuscript
that would be a kind of global history from the beginning of time
showing how the Lord had always been there, always would be there
and what a good thing this was, [. . . entitled] Genesis or How I Did It'
(O 14). The new doctrine, called 'Fundamental Religion' (BB 85), is
spread by strict capitalist methods. Echoing the American tycoon,
William Randolph Hearst, Noah buys a national newspaper and
founds the 'Glory Crusade' (BB 14) to carry out missionary work, touring 'all the major spots around Ur of the Chaldees' (BB 15).[60] The new
religion stresses the fact that there is 'no need, after all, to be
vegetarian, charitable and feminist' and enforces 'a return to real
values' (BB 14) by means of the sacrifice of 'convenience foods and
refrigerators' and the strict observance of a 'simple diet prepared by a
simple wife' (BB 15), regulated by the official Good Food Guide (BB
16). In an ironic travesty of the feminist motto, 'the personal is political', the male-chauvinistic element in this religion is the result of
Noah's hate of his late wife Grace, on whom he puts the blame for his
tendency 'to invent things', after she kills herself: 'An idea occurred to
Noah [. . .] when he sat down to re-draft Genesis, he'd make sure everyone knew where the blame lay. Women; they're all the same'. (BB
117). The prohibition to eat frozen food and use refrigerators has a
darker purpose, since it stems from Noah's fear that someone might
strike on the same formula that brought about the creation of the
Unpronounceable out of 'a slab of Black Forest Gâteau and a scoop of
ice cream [. . .] in a state of nauseating decomposition' (BB 83), thus
putting an end to his privileged position as interlocutor between 'the
Only True God' and humankind.

After *Genesis* or *How I Did It*, which 'had sold out over and over again', Noah writes a second volume, entitled *Exodus* or *Your Way Lies There* (*BB* 15). At this stage, Noah's wealth acquires fabulous proportions, as he becomes the owner of a monopolistic net controlling the business carried out in the whole of Nineveh, with the help of his three sons: 'Japeth the jeweller king, Ham the owner of that prestigious pastrami store, More Meat, and Shem, once playboy and entrepreneur, now a reformed and zealous pop singer' (*BB* 21). As Ham tells Mrs Munde, the Unpronounceable played a fundamental role in their success: 'I own those stores for His Sake, not my own. He has guided me through the money markets and the loopholes in the Health and Safety Regulations because he is more than YAHWEH, the God of Love, he is YAHWEH the Omnipotent Stockbroker and YAHWEH the Omniscient Lawyer. (Praise Him)' (*BB* 30).

Equally versed in business is Bunny Mix, Noah's hack writer and fiancée, and the world-famous author of 'two and a half thousand books' (*BB* 130), all of them consisting of variations on the same plot, about 'the purity of love between men and women, the importance of courtship and the absolute taboo of sex before marriage' (*BB* 16).[61] Described by Emma Fisher as 'an exaggeration of Barbara Cartland, if that were possible',[62] Bunny Mix, or rather Bunny Mixomatosis, as the Unpronounceable mistakenly calls her (*BB* 90), has a deadly ascendancy over the thousands of women who read her novelettes and are ready to undergo all kinds of physical and spiritual sacrifices in order to attain the 'bunny-girl' standards embodied by her perfectly objectified heroines.[63] With an eye for business comparable to that of Noah, Bunny has created Bees of Paradise (*BB* 74), the famous rest house and health spa, where all these dreams can be made real – for example, losing weight with a patent cure for the obese that involves being covered in a solution of honey and glycerine, and then having trained ants 'chew away the fat' (*BB* 77).

After the stupendous success of *Genesis* and *Exodus* Noah decides to dramatise the two books, bringing in his friend Bunny Mix 'to add legitimate spice and romantic interest' (*BB* 20). Noah's fabulous show project involves the construction of a gigantic ship for 'most of the Chaldees and the animals' which is to 'tour the heathen places of the world. As it happened, a film company would be putting the whole thing on camera, not just the play itself but the making of the play, because Noah claimed he was going to carry his ship over a mountain by a miracle' (*BB* 20). This is the project Noah and Bunny Mix are involved in when the Unpronounceable, following a whim, decides to change the script to include the Flood, and to transform the show into a real event (*BB* 90–1).

The Unpronounceable's unexpected intervention proves to be Noah's opportunity to 'rewrite *Genesis* and make it look like God did it all from the very beginning' (*BB* 110). That is, it gives Noah the opportunity to erase from the collective memory the knowledge of the cyclical nature of events and to impose on them a teleological myth of origins, with its prescribed beginning, middle and end. As he confides to his sons:

> If we've got a new world, we can tell them anything. They won't have any memory, any photo albums, any pressure groups or state-funded anarchy. We can say that God made the world, the air, the sea, and that it became so corrupt he had to flood it and start again. Who's to say we're lying? The girls'll keep quiet. (*BB* 110–11)

The 'girls' Noah alludes to are his sons' wives, Rita, Sheila and Desi. Like the males in Noah's family, they have a wonderful eye for business. They are the thriving owners of 'a kind of clinic, a place to help people who have problems, personal problems with their bodies and themselves' (*BB* 27). However, unlike Noah's Fundamental Religion, which aims at repressing sexuality and fosters the bland romanticism epitomised by Bunny Mix's novelettes, their clinic specialises in psychological therapy to liberate women's sexuality and in change-of-sex surgery. As Desi tells Gloria: 'We handle people who can't come to terms with either their sexuality or their chosen expression of it [. . . .] we tell them that *we're all God's children* and they can have a great time just as they are' (*BB* 33, emphasis in the original).

When Rita, with her red hair and leopardskin dress, Sheila, with her fat body covered from head to foot in solid gold and dangling snakes, and Desi, in her designer-cut suede catsuit, appear to Gloria for the first time, they make such an impression on the purblind protagonist that she describes them as the materialisation of a miracle (*BB* 26).[64] As the narrator explains, at that point, Gloria is in one of her 'dangerously emotional moments', so that, if she 'had been left unattended a moment longer the effects of that first wave of social rapport might have drowned her for good' (*BB* 26). The three wives, then, miraculously appear to save the heroine from the evils of emotionalism fostered by Fundamental Religion and immediately enrol her as helpmate in their clinic, where she is initiated into the mysteries of female sexuality, thus triggering off the beginning of her maturation process.

The three wives' splendid aspect and their miraculous intervention to save the heroine point to their condition as Mother earth or Mother nature goddesses, the pagan deities associated with spring and autumn rituals of archaic agricultural societies described by Sir James Frazer in *The Golden Bough*.[65] The poet Robert Graves, in a later adaptation of the myth, transformed Frazer's dual mother-daughter corn figure into a threefold matriarchal deity, the White Goddess of Birth, Love and Death.[66] In his 500-page book, Graves explored what he considered to be the inseparable connection between the ancient cult-ritual devoted to this ambiguously pleasant/horrifying pagan divinity and 'true' or 'pure poetry'. In this sense, Graves's muse/goddess may be said to constitute a female equivalent of Blake's male poet/prophet. Noah makes explicit this association when he asks his three daughters-in-law 'to interpret the characters of the overthrown goddesses, collectively described as The Trivia' (*BB* 21) in the film version of Genesis.

Both Frazer and Graves believed that the worship of this matriarchal goddess was the prototypical religion, eventually displaced by the advent of patriarchal monotheism. Therefore, Noah's in-laws symbolise the Nature-abiding, matriarchal values Noah is trying to destroy. In Frazer's version of the myth, the golden bough, the symbol of the magician-king's all-encompassing knowledge and power, is torn from an ash-tree. In Winterson's parodic matriarchal version of this, the three wives appear at the shooting of the film, standing 'arrogantly under the orange tree that was to symbolise their womanhood' (*BB* 50). Noah is so discomfited by this sight that he 'went over to the orange tree and set about making Rita, Sheila and Desi as ugly as possible' (*BB* 51), in a desperate attempt to transform the Mother-earth goddesses into witches, as is suggested by a remark by one of the art people overheard by Gloria: 'I see a lot of similarities here to *Macbeth*, don't you?' (*BB* 52).

Like Frankenstein and Noah, Rita, Sheila and Desi have the godlike capacity to create human beings by sewing together parts of different human bodies. Thus, when Marlene, the transvestite, repents of her former change-of-sex operation and wants her penis back, they provide her with one removed from someone else in a similar operation (*BB* 37). However, unlike Noah, who uses his knowledge to feed his *hybris* and who exerts power on other human beings by prescribing total sexual repression, and more in line with contemporary feminist and lesbian critics, the three wives advocate total sexual freedom – as Desi tells Gloria, 'Sex [. . .] is the only thing in life you should pursue with all your resources' (*BB* 35) – and use their knowledge to allow people to gather their sense of identity unbound to the specificities of their bodies. As Desi further explains, 'There are always people who . . . whatever you can think of. Whatever combination, innovation or desperation, there are always people who . . .' (*BB* 37).

When Noah's daughters-in-law meet Gloria for the first time, she is a timid eighteen-year-old girl with a strong mother, who, like many contemporary teenagers (and also like the Jeanette of *Oranges*), loves pets, has archetypal 'dreams of martyrdom [. . . and] of stardom' (*BB* 10), and is trying to 'understand the Meaning of Life' (*BB* 24). However, instead of a dog, Gloria's pet is an elephant called Trevor; she thinks nothing of taking care of carnivorous animals like crocodiles and hoopoes; and when she comes down from her bedroom, she slithers down a rope (*BB* 72). Further, she can swim and fish like a siren: the day she went for a swim in a river 'green and cold and slippery with fish[, s]he caught a fat one between her teeth, beat it to death on a stone, and took it back to her mother' (*BB* 54). This incongruous combination of traits shows Gloria as a character in perfect communion with Mother nature and as an archetypal quester enjoying the virgin/whore duality of the Jungian anima, as her friend Doris, Noah's cleaner-cum-organic philosopher, suggests when she calls her 'a fool' (*BB* 28) the first time they meet.[67]

In *Oranges*, Jeanette's individuation process was presented as an Oedipal struggle involving the heroine's separation from her monstrous mother.[68] Similarly, Gloria's development as a subject can only be achieved by outgrowing her mother's psychological and ideological control over her. Like Gloria's mother, Mrs Munde loves romantic fiction (*BB* 16), divides people into 'friends and enemies' (*BB* 98), and has a wholly black-and-white vision of the world. She is a militant member of Noah's 'Glory Crusade' (*BB* 14); she daydreams of being 'an Evangelist in the kitchen of the world' (*BB* 31); and she delivers passionate street harangues against sinful consumption of frozen food (*BB* 102–5). Her faith in Fundamental Religion remains unshaken when she loses an arm in Ham's Hallelujah Hamburger machine (*BB* 86), and continues to be undisturbed even after she has been left out of the Ark to drown and is being 'swept away into the darkening tide' (*BB* 153), just as Louie's faith survives the scandals surrounding the Society for the Lost and the Morecambe guest house at the end of *Oranges*. In short, like Jeanette's mother, Mrs Munde is a religious zealot, who cherishes the simplicity of a life without uncertainties, in 'a world where men and women knew exactly what they were doing and who they were doing it for' (*BB* 15). However, Mrs Munde also has an Evelike side, since she fell in love with Gloria's father in a garden, with her pet snake playing a decisive role: 'I was lying face-down in the soil crying my eyes out because I'd lost my grass snake. [. . .] He spent all day with me trying to find that snake, and at about half past three, I knew I had fallen in love' (*BB* 10–11).

With the help of Rita, Sheila and Desi, as well as of Doris and Marlene, Gloria will learn 'to separate what she felt and what she thought' (*BB* 44), will discover that women can have orgasms without men in places like supermarkets (*BB* 45), and will realise the beauties of vegetarianism, as she is revolted to discover that the penises discarded in change-of-sex operations were turned into sausages by 'a chain store called Meaty Big And Bouncy' (*BB* 46), a step in her maturation process that has all the satiric force of Swift's mincemeat pies in 'A Modest Proposal' (1729). After Gloria's reliance on received ideas is thus shattered, the heroine suddenly realises that she is no longer interested in 'fall[ing] in love with the right man' and participating in 'the Bunny Mix Romance Show' (*BB* 45). This realisation is a milestone in the heroine's maturation process, which she significantly compares with the three stages in the development of language postulated by Northrop Frye in *Anatomy of Criticism*: 'the metaphoric', 'the didactic' and 'the prosaic' (*BB* 44).

Gloria's wish is to reach the third stage, when her understanding of the world will be as fluent and fluid as that of 'Continuous Prose' (*BB* 98–9). However, as soon as she moves 'towards reason, the loss of wonder, the empty place in the heart' (*BB* 71), she starts having hallucinatory visions and dreams. Like Jeanette at a similarly crucial stage in her evolution, she dreams of an 'orange demon', who comes to teach her a lesson in 'plural reality' (*BB* 67). Once created by Gloria, the demon also becomes visible to her female friends, thus suggesting a kind of collective female identity among them similar to that enjoyed by The Trivia, the triadic Mother-nature goddess impersonated by Noah's trio of daughters-in-law.

The orange demon tells Doris that the 'impulse to worship is impossible to eradicate' and that he has come to teach Gloria 'to be poetic while she teaches herself to be analytic' (*BB* 71). However,

Doris complains about the demon's intervention, accusing it of spoiling the plot of the only novel in which she has a role: 'This may be my one appearance in print. I may never occur in another novel. You appear all the time; you can afford to be relaxed' (*BB* 71). Doris's words trigger off the external narrator's comment:

> It was true. The orange Thing turns up everywhere as a demon, a sprite, omnipotent author, flashes of insight. It is there in *Jude the Obscure, The Little Foxes*; it probably impersonated Scarlett O'Hara in most of *Gone with the Wind*. Whenever something other than the plot drops in, it is really the orange demon adding an extra dimension. (*BB* 71–2)

The narrator's contention that the orange demon is an 'omnipotent author' appearing in any fictional text to provide 'flashes of insight' whenever the development of the plot is arrested, associates it with Wayne Booth's 'implied author', the flesh-and-blood author's fictional persona leaving its ideological imprint on the text. But it is also, literally, a *deus ex machina*, since, like the god in Greek and Roman drama who was lowered by stage machinery to resolve the plot or extricate the protagonist from a difficult situation, the orange demon makes its unexpected entrance into the plot of *Boating* at a crucial moment, to help Gloria and her female friends disrupt Noah's totalitarian attempt to 'rewrite the world' (*BB* 124). As it confides to them: 'unless you lot do your best to stay alive there won't be anyone left to spread the word about what really happened' (*BB* 123–4).

Just as the Unpronounceable turned out to be superior to Noah, so the orange demon created by Gloria is superior to her and her friends, since: 'Unlike the rest of you, I'm not bound by the vagaries of this plot. I can move backwards and forwards and I can tell you [the future]' (*BB* 123). However, unlike the Unpronounceable, who is a transcendental god made by 'priestly' Noah as his instrument of power, the orange demon is the product of Gloria's imagination and, as such, can only exist within the metaphoric world created by her. As is suggested by Gloria's comparison of the stages in her maturation process with the three stages in the development of language postulated by Northrop Frye, the heroine's own identity is wholly fictional, a possibility that occurs to Gloria herself when, after telling Marlene that 'Art shows us how to transcend the purely physical', she finds herself 'wondering for a moment who was feeding her her lines' (*BB* 99, 100).

The heroine's imaginative capacity to create the orange demon points to Gloria's paradoxical nature, both as a fictional character existing in the textual world of *Boating* and as a fully visionary poet/prophet with the power to create selves and worlds within the realm of language. In this sense, Gloria's creativity may be said to stand in diametrical opposition to that of Noah. As a poet/prophet, she has the 'titanic' task of imagining an alternative to his 'priestly' version of events. As the orange demon makes clear, the truthfulness or falsehood of this imaginary alternative to Noah's official version is immaterial: 'It doesn't even matter if you forget what really happened; if you need to, invent something else. The vital thing is to have an alternative so that people will realise that there's no such thing as a true story' (*BB* 124).

In the 'Deuteronomy' chapter of *Oranges*, the external author-narrator defended a similar relativistic outlook on history and truth and asked the readers to make their own historical 'sandwiches' (*O* 95). Echoing this, *Boating* closes with an epilogue entitled '*A word from our sponsors*', which, sandwichlike, alternates fragments from the Book of Genesis containing God's instructions to Noah about how to make the Ark and the description of the effects of the Flood, with fragments from a supposedly historical account of the reaction of the American archaeologists Gardener and Soames on finding the remains of the Ark on mount Ararat.[69] Soames admitted to Gardener that 'he believed in the Bible' (*BB* 156). However, his faith received a deadly blow after finding a message in an ancient-looking bottle that read: 'Hey girls, I made it', signed 'love D . . .' (*BB* 159). The following day, Gardener was equally puzzled by the unearthing of 'a book, clearly thousands of years old, bound in a tough animal skin unlike anything [he] had seen before' and written 'in a recognisable combination of languages', which seemed to him to be 'part of a romantic novel' (*BB* 160). As a result, the archaeologist will be obsessed to the end of his life with the questions: 'Where did it come from? Who wrote it? And Doris, who was she?' To which he can only answer: 'God knows' (*BB* 160).

The fact that we readers 'know' the answer to these questions situates us at a higher ontological level than the archaeologist, on a par with the god invoked by Gardener. This god can only be Jeanette Winterson, the flesh-and-blood author of *Boating for Beginners*, whose fictional *alter ego* is the omniscient narrator we have encountered in the text making authorial comments. Still, the revelation that the ultimate creator of *Boating* is not a historian or an archaeologist but a fiction writer does not diminish the shattering effect that Jeanette

Winterson's fictional version of Genesis has on the biblical account, since, as the orange demon told Gloria and her friends, what is shattering for the believer's faith is not the truthfulness or falsehood of the alternative version, but the possibility of imagining a different history of the world.

This possibility is given a further turn of the screw in the next two novels, *The Passion* and *Sexing the Cherry*, two splendid historiographic metafictions that show Winterson moving away from what David Lodge has described as 'the Monty Pythonesque surrealism of *Boating for Beginners*', towards romantic 'high seriousness' and 'full-bloom magic realism'.[70]

Notes

1 Jeanette Winterson, 'Introduction' to *Oranges Are Not the Only Fruit*. London: Vintage (1991) [1985]: xi–xv; xii, xi.
2 Patricia Duncker, 'Jeanette Winterson and the Aftermath of Feminism', in Grice and Woods (eds), *'I'm telling you stories'* (77–88), 77.
3 *Ibid.*, 77.
4 Winterson, 'Introduction' to *Oranges*, xiii.
5 This is also the subject matter of 'Psalms' (*WOP* 219–30), a short story originally written for the *New Statesman* shortly after *Oranges*.
6 Roz Kaveney, 'Jeanette Winterson: *Oranges Are Not The Only Fruit*', *Times Literary Supplement* (22 March 1985): 326.
7 Winterson, 'Introduction' to *Oranges*, xiv.
8 *Ibid.*, xiii.
9 Some episodes in Jeanette's life have a distinct Dickensian flavour, as when, after being alienated from home and religious community, Jeanette finds herself in the street on Christmas Eve, chilled and lonely, looking through a window and envying the family warmth she has been excluded from: 'For a moment I leaned on the wall; the stone was warm, and through the window I could see a family round the fire. Their tea table had been left, chairs, table and the right number of cups. I watched the fire flicker behind the glass, then one of them got up to close the curtains' (*O* 133).
10 Rebecca O'Rourke, 'Fingers in the Fruit Basket: A Feminist Reading of Jeanette Winterson's *Oranges Are Not the Only Fruit*,' in Susan Sellers (ed.), *Feminist Criticism: Theory and Practice*. Hemel Hempstead: Harvester Wheatsheaf (1991): 57–70; 66.
11 D. H. Lawrence, *Sons and Lovers*. Harmondsworth: Penguin Classics (1987) [1913]: 36.
12 *Ibid.*, 36.

13 *Ibid.*, 37.
14 This episode is the germ of Winterson's 'The Green Man' (*WOP* 131–48),
    a short story that combines the *topoi* of the fair, the fortune-teller and 'the
    virgin and the gipsy' with another central *topos* in Lawrence's fiction in
    general, that of the horse as a symbol of male sexuality.
15 From Blake's perspective, the existence of 'contrary' versions of the same
    myth is essential, since it is what makes artistic activity possible: 'With-
    out Contraries is no progression. Attraction and Repulsion, Reason and
    Energy, Love and Hate, are necessary to Human existence. / From these
    contraries spring what the religious call Good and Evil. Good is the pas-
    sive that obeys Reason. Evil is the active springing from Energy. / Good
    is Heaven. Evil is Hell'. William Blake, *The Marriage of Heaven and Hell*
    (*c.* 1790), in John Sampson (ed.), *The Poetical Works of William Blake*. New
    York and Toronto: Oxford University Press (1956): 248.
16 A lesbian symbolism is implicit in this sea metaphor, since, as Cath Stow-
    ers, quoting Nasatir Shaktini, has pointed out, 'metaphors for "embarka-
    tion" for "lesbian islands" [are] image[s] of "displacement" from Freud's
    "dark continent" of femininity'. Cath Stowers, '"No legitimate place, no
    land, no fatherland": Communities of Women in the Fiction of Roberts
    and Winterson', *Critical Survey* 8.1 (1996): 139–59; 74.
17 Salman Rushdie, *Midnight's Children*. London: Picador (1981): 161.
    Margaret Reynolds has pointed out as another possible intertext the
    episode in Robert Louis Stevenson's *Treasure Island* (1883) in which 'Jim
    Hawkins is similarly hidden in an apple barrel on board the ship travel-
    ling in search of treasure when he overhears a conversation between
    Long John Silver and the other members of the crew, which makes him
    [. . .] aware of Silver's duplicity'. In Reynolds and Noakes (eds), *Jeanette
    Winterson*, 45.
18 This episode is further parodied in Winterson's short story, 'O'Brien's
    First Christmas' (*WOP* 75–86), where after a Christmas fairy in a tutu
    visits her in her dreams, O'Brien 'abandoned herself to chaos and decided
    [. . . to be] herself' (*WOP* 85). In 'A Green Square' (*WOP* 187–203), the
    protagonist, similarly confronted with the choice between '[f]reedom or
    protection', jubilantly decides to cast away her fears and 'ride the storm
    for no better reason than I need the storm' (*WOP* 201). By contrast, in
    Winterson's latest novel, *Lighthousekeeping* (2004), Babel Dark rejects
    freedom for the straitjacket of Victorian convention.
19 The allusion to the four cardinal points foreruns the description of the
    four islands in Winterson's short story, 'Turn of the World' (*WOP*
    149–60), where each island, situated at the far end of each cardinal point,
    is associated with one of the four basic elements: Fire (the island of Fyr),
    water (the island of Hydor), earth (the island of Erde), and air (the island
    of Aeros). In alchemical terms, they form the *quaternarivs* that has to be

'decoded' in order to find the Philosopher's Stone.

20 T. S. Eliot, 'Little Gidding' (1942), *Four Quartets*, in *Collected Poems 1990–1962*. London: Faber and Faber (1974): 214–23; 222.

21 Eliot, 'East Coker' (1940), *Four Quartets*: 196–204; 196.

22 See Susana Onega, "'I'm Telling You Stories. Trust Me": History / Story-telling in Jeanette Winterson's *Oranges Are Not the Only Fruit*', in Onega (ed.), '*Telling Histories': Narrativizing History; Historicizing Literature* (Costerus, 96). Amsterdam and Atlanta, GA: Rodopi (1995): 135–47.

23 Ihab Hassan, *The Right Promethean Fire: Imagination, Science and Cultural Change*. Urbana: University of Illinois Press (1980): 190. See also H. Aram Veeser (ed.), *The New Historicism*. New York and London: Routledge (1989).

24 See Susana Onega "'A Knack for Yarns": The Narrativization of History and the End of History', in Onega (ed.), '*Telling Histories'*: 7–18.

25 Patricia Waugh, *Practising Postmodernism: Reading Modernism*. London: Edward Arnold (1992): 3.

26 In Hazard Adams, *Philosophy of the Literary Symbolic*. Tallahassee: University Presses of Florida (1983): 111.

27 'Such warm tender flesh. / Her flesh now, sprung from her head' (*O* 10).

28 Mónica Calvo, 'A Feminine Subject in Postmodernist Chaos: Jeanette Winterson's Political Manifesto in *Oranges Are Not the Only Fruit*', *Revista Alicantina de Estudios Ingleses* 13 (2000): 21–34; 26.

29 The narrator alludes to this possibility at least on three occasions. First, when she finds 'a yellowy picture of a pretty woman holding a cat' in the section of her mother's photograph album devoted to her 'Old Flames', which subsequently disappears (*O* 36). Secondly, when Miss Jewsbury tells Jeanette that her mother 'is a woman of the world, even if she'd never admit it to me. She knows about feelings, especially women's feelings', and Jeanette comments: 'This wasn't something I wanted to go into' (*O* 106). And thirdly, when, after coming to terms with her own homosexuality, Jeanette reflects: 'my mother had painted the white roses red and now she claimed they grew that way' (*O* 136).

30 Blake, *The Marriage of Heaven and Hell*, 252–3. In 'The Book of Urizen' (1794), the correlation between Urizen, the archetype of the 'Priest' (among other things), and Los, 'the Eternal Prophet', provides the poem's central and recurrent theme. See especially Plate 20, Ch. IV. 2. Blake's conception of the poet-as-prophet was further thematised and explored by the Romantic poets. For example, Shelley discussed it in 'A Defence of Poetry' in terms that recall Blake's conception. Percy Bysshe Shelley, 'A Defence of Poetry' (1821), in Harold Bloom and Lionel Trilling (eds), *The Oxford Anthology of English Literature IV. Romantic Poetry and Prose*. Oxford: Oxford University Press (1973) [1840]: 748. The origins of this figure may be traced back to Sir Philip Sidney's 'The Defence of Poesie',

and further back to Plato's description of the poet as 'a light and winged and holy thing' with 'the oracular gift of poetry' (*Ion* 15).

31 Waugh, *Practising Postmodernism: Reading Modernism*, 13.

32 *Ibid.*, 13.

33 However, the Nietzschean 'mode of the liar' is not exclusively theirs. We have seen how Jeanette's schoolteachers were equally incapable of accepting her divergent outlook on things, what she herself described as a 'tendency towards the exotic [which] has brought me many problems, just as it did for William Blake' (*O* 42). What is more, the protagonist herself originally enjoyed a similarly monolithic certainty: 'Uncertainty to me was like Aadvaark to other people. A curious thing I had no notion of, but recognised through second-hand illustration' (*O* 100). Thus, when Melanie told her that she intended to go to university to read theology, because she thought 'she should understand how other people saw the world' (*O* 103), she curtly retorted: 'But you know they're wrong' (*O* 103).

34 Calvo, 'Jeanette Winterson's Political Manifesto', 27, 25.

35 *Ibid.*, 23.

36 *Ibid.*, 23.

37 *Ibid.*, 31.

38 Echoing Virginia Woolf, Maureen Duffy said in *The Microcosm*: 'in using these earlier forms of fiction she hoped to subvert the received literary doctrine that the novel was a form developed for the amusement of "a middle-class female reader with time on her hands"'. Quoted in Anira Rowanchild, 'The State of the Heart: Ideology and Narrative Structure in the Novels of Maureen Duffy and Caeia March', in Elaine Hutton (ed.), *Beyond Sex and Romance? The Politics of Contemporary Lesbian Fiction*. London: The Women's Press (1998): 29–45; 31.

39 Pykett, 'A New Way With Words?', 58.

40 Northrop Frye, *Anatomy of Criticism: Four Essays*. Princeton: Princeton University Press (1957): 314.

41 *Ibid.*, 314.

42 Gérard Genette, *Figures III*. Paris: Éditions du Seuil (1972): 245.

43 Lucien Dällenbach, *The Mirror in the Text*, trans. Jeremy Whiteley and Emma Hughes, Cambridge: Polity Press (1989) [1977]: 175–208.

44 According to Blake, poet/prophets like Isaiah, Ezekiel or Los enjoyed 'fourfold vision' or enlarged consciousness. Opposed to it is the 'Single vision & Newton's sleep' brought about by the advent of rational materialism. William Blake, 'Letter to Butts' (22 November 1802), in Geoffrey Keynes (ed.), *The Complete Writings of William Blake*. London: Nonesuch; New York: Random House (1957): 818.

45 Frye, *Anatomy of Criticism*, 322.

46 *Ibid.*, 323.

47 *Ibid.*, 323.

48 Jorge Luis Borges, 'La Biblioteca de Babel', *Ficciones* (1944), in *Obras completas* I (1923–49). Barcelona: María Kodama y Emecé editores (1989): 465–71.

49 Alan Cheuse and Phyllis A. Nagy refer to *The Passion* as Winterson's second instead of her third novel. Alan Cheuse, 'Sating a Passion for High Romance', *Chicago Tribune* (5 July 1988): 3c; Phyllis A. Nagy, 'Fiction Set in the Fury of Napoleon's Wars', *Philadelphia Inquirer* (5 November 1998): F03. *Boating* is not mentioned in the Penguin edition of *The Passion* (1987), the Vintage edition of *Sexing the Cherry* (1989), the script of *Oranges* (1990) or the Vintage edition of *Oranges* (1991).

50 'Her novel *Boating for Beginners* was published by Methuen in 1986'.

51 David Lodge, 'Outrageous Things', *New York Review of Books* (29 September 1988): 25–6; 25.

52 Eileen Williams-Wanquet, 'Jeanette Winterson's *Boating for Beginners*: Both New Baroque and Ethics', *Études britanniques contemporaines* 23 (2002): 99–117; 101.

53 Julian Barnes, *A History of the World in 10½ Chapters*. London: Jonathan Cape (1989): 3–30. 'The Stowaway' is the 'truthful' account of the Flood narrated by an unsuspected eye witness, a woodworm who managed to get on board the Ark without Noah's knowledge. *Boating* also recalls feminist versions of Genesis like Michèle Roberts's *The Book of Mrs Noah*, in which the ark is the womblike space where women can 'come [. . .] to free their imaginations' and find a 'home at last'. Michèle Roberts, *The Book of Mrs Noah*. London: Minerva (1993): 21, 274. See also Sara Maitland's reworking of Old and New Testament stories, in particular her feminist versions of the creation myth in *Telling Tales* (1983) and, with Michelene Wandor, in *Arky Types* (1987).

54 Emma Fisher, '". . . and before": Jeanette Winterson. *Boating for Beginners*', *Times Literary Supplement* (1 November 1985): 1228.

55 Eliot, 'Little Gidding', 222.

56 Jonathan Swift, *Gulliver's Travels*, eds Peter Dixon and John Chalker, Introduction by Michael Foot. Harmondsworth: Penguin (1967) [1726]: 75.

57 Quoted in Reynolds and Noakes (eds), *Jeanette Winterson*, 177.

58 Fortunata's description of the dancing and 'weightless city' in *Sexing the Cherry* (95–9) may also be read as an accurate though less satiric version of Swift's floating island.

59 'So God created man in his own image, in the image of God created he him; male and female created he them' (Genesis, 1. 27).

60 'Glory Crusade' is also the name of Pastor Spratt's mission (*O* 8).

61 Although the product of parodic exaggeration, these figures accurately point to a real enough situation in the 1980s: the unprecedented boom of romance fiction publishing houses like the giant Harlequin and its

rivals, Dell's Candlelight Romances, Bantam's Loveswept, and Simon & Schuster's Silhouette Romances. See Leslie W. Rabine, 'Romance in the Age of Electronics: Harlequin Enterprises', in Judith Newton and Deborah Rosenfelt (eds), *Feminist Criticism and Social Change*. New York and London: Methuen (1985): 249–67.

62 Fisher, '". . . and before"', 1228.

63 In the introduction to Elizabeth Inchbald's *A Simple Story*, Jeanette Winterson contends: 'Unhappiness between the sexes is a commonplace of our lives and literature but not many writers are brave enough to suggest that much of this unhappiness could be alleviated if men could learn to give women some head-room. Indeed, the current literary trend from Mills & Boon to Kingsley Amis is to suggest that this unhappiness is precisely because women want head-room'. Jeanette Winterson, 'Introduction' to *A Simple Story by Elizabeth Inchbald*. London: Pandora (1987): vii–xi; x.

64 Gloria's reaction brings to mind that of Paul Pennyfeather on seeing Margot Best-Chetwynde get out of a car, with her 'two lizard-skin feet, silk legs, chinchilla body, a tight little black hat with platinum and diamonds', in Evelyn Waugh, *Decline and Fall*. London: Penguin (1940) [1928]: 75.

65 Sir James George Frazer, *The Golden Bough* (1922): Ch. 45 www.bartleby.com/196/100.html. Consulted on 24 February 2005.

66 Robert Graves, *The White Goddess: A Historical Grammar of Poetic Myth* (1948). Revised and enlarged edn. New York: Farrar, Straus and Giroux (2000) [1966].

67 In the Tarot, the Fool is the quester who undertakes the journey through life. Alfred Douglas, *The Tarot: The Origins, Meaning and Uses of the Cards*. Illustrated by David Sheridan. Harmondsworth: Penguin (1982) [1973]: 13.

68 Jeanette's comment at the end of the novel that her mother 'had tied a thread around my button, to tug when she pleased' (*O* 176) may be read as an allusion to Freud's famous example, in 'Beyond the Pleasure Principle' (1920), of his infant grand-son's *fort-da* game, in which the child staged a fantasy of control over the disappearance and return of his mother, by discarding and retrieving a cotton reel attached to a piece of string. The comment evinces Jeanette's yearning for the bliss of completeness and oneness with her mother she enjoyed in her pre-gendered stage.

69 The names of Gardener and Soames do not appear among those of the participants in the numerous expeditions to Mount Ararat recorded by B. J. Corbin in *The Explorers of Ararat*. Highlands Ranch, CO: CGI Books (1999). Nor are they on the NoahsArkSearch.com website, consulted on 17 June 2005.

70 Lodge, 'Outrageous Things', 26.

2

History and storytelling

One year after the publication of *Oranges Are Not the Only Fruit* and *Boating for Beginners*, Jeanette Winterson published *Fit for the Future* (1986), a non-fictional book on fitness for women, which, as the author herself has noted, she wrote for money and because she was extremely fit at the time. As she humorously remarked in her column in the *Guardian*, this book might have led her career in an utterly different direction from the one it eventually took: 'Thankfully, this is out, and what a good thing it is that *Oranges* was a success, otherwise you would have had me setting up a studio in Covent Garden, and training the stars – yes, that was my plan.'[1] The following year the young writer published her third novel, *The Passion*. This book won the 1987 John Llewellyn Rhys Prize for fiction, thus confirming the opinion of most reviewers that it was the work of an innovative writer already at the height of her powers. This general opinion was summarised by Anne Duchêne when she said that *The Passion* is 'a book of great imaginative audacity and assurance [with which Jeanette Winterson] quite overwhelms talk of "promise"'.[2]

On the whole, the reviewers agreed that *The Passion* exemplified a tendency away from the autobiographical, realistically set comedy of the earlier fiction and towards a much more openly fantastic and lyrical kind of fiction. Thus, David Lodge aligned it with 'magic realism' and with the Romantic tradition of storytelling as developed by Poe, Mary Shelley and Emily Brontë.[3] Other critics compared its stylistic richness to that of Virginia Woolf,[4] described its tone as 'rhythmic and seductive' and likened its 'feel' to that of 'a villanelle, an elaborate [. . .] verse form in which words are repeated in a mesmerizing pattern'.[5] In short, they pointed to the novel's stylistic exuberance, its aspiration to the category of poetic prose.

In Chapter 1 we saw how *Oranges* combines realistic, fantastic, mythical and archetypal elements and how they are unified under the quintessential 'fifth' biblical form. In *The Passion*, a similar unifying role is played by the New Testament, since, as Tamás Bényei has pointed out, the definite article in the title transforms Winterson's third novel from 'a parable of passion' into 'a retelling of *the* passion', that is, into a novel 'about the way in which every trajectory of passion is inevitably a repetition of what our culture knows as the "original" passion'.[6] The definite article in the title, then, gives the life stories of the protagonists a representative, archetypal character, just as the noun justifies its stylistic repetitiveness, since, as Bényei, following Roland Barthes, acutely notes, any discourse on passion is inevitably surrounded by silence and it is only through repetition that the writer can aspire to express 'the difficulty of talking and telling stories about passion'.[7] Bényei's interesting contention is that the text incessantly veers towards its own discursive limit, managing, through repetition and excess, to express 'a beyond of passion, of madness that can never be spoken of, but which always already speaks in the very language that is unable to speak about it'.[8]

Considered from a realistic perspective, *The Passion* may be said to combine the parallel stories of two marginal witnesses to the Napoleonic wars, at the crucial moment in Hegelian World History when it was approaching its apocalyptic synthesis.[9] One is Henri, a French soldier who joined the *Grande armée* because he wanted to be a drummer and ended up as chicken-neck wringer and personal cook to Napoleon. The other is Villanelle, a Venetian boatman's daughter who worked at the casino as a croupier until she was sold by her husband as *vivandière*, or army prostitute. Henri is a sensitive and romantic young man from a peasant family, who has been brought up by a pious mother, Georgette, and a Roman Catholic priest with a taste for drinking and card-playing. Like the tender-hearted eponymous hero of Thomas Hardy's *Jude the Obscure*, Henri abhors pain inflicted on animals. His friend Domino says that he 'can't pick up a musket to shoot a rabbit' (*P* 28) and he himself admits that he can only bring himself to kill the moles that destroy the family crops 'by looking the other way' (*P* 31). By contrast, Villanelle is a resourceful and witty bisexual woman with sparkling blue eyes and flashing red hair (*P* 51) and a taste for transvestism (*P* 54), who can literally live without a heart (*P* 115–16) or walk on water with her webbed feet (*P* 69), the result of a mistake made by her pregnant mother while carrying out a propitiatory magic rite (*P* 49–50). The refocusing of World History from the perspectives of these two irrelevant individuals brings to mind the New Historicists' contention that history is always written by the dominant culture on top of the unwritten histories of the smaller cultures it defeated, so that it necessarily leaves out of its account many facts that remain ungraspable.[10] The combination of history with fantasy aligns *The Passion* with 'historiographic metafiction', the type of novel characterised by intense self-reflexivity and a relish in storytelling which Linda Hutcheon considers to be the best expression of the contradictory nature of the postmodernist ethos.[11]

The Passion begins with an epigraph which reproduces the words spoken by the Chorus to Medea in Euripides' tragedy *Medea* (ll. 432–5), after she discovers Jason's infidelity. They allude to how Medea renounced family and home for Jason's sake when she helped him and the Argonauts run away with the Golden Fleece. Thus, the epigraph points to two parallel quests, equally motivated by an all-consuming passion to possess something unique – in Jason's case the Golden Fleece and in Medea's case Jason's heart. Jason's perilous journey in search of the Golden Fleece is repeated by Henri's soldier travels across Europe, triggered off by his passion for Napoleon.[12] Medea's exile from home and her psychological breakdown caused by Jason's betrayal and abandonment is repeated by Villanelle's loss of her heart to a married lady nicknamed 'the Queen of Spades', and her ensuing marriage to Napoleon's former cook, nicknamed 'the Jack of Hearts'.

The double quest pattern alluded to by the epigraph is replicated by the alternation and intertwining of narrative voices. In the first chapter, Henri begins to narrate his life story in retrospect to an addressee simply identified as 'you', of whom he asks questions such as: 'What would you do if you were an Emperor?' and 'Do you ever think of your childhood?' (*P* 25); and to whom he confidentially says: 'I'm telling you stories. Trust me' (*P* 12),[13] or 'Don't believe that one' (*P* 23). This chapter begins at the moment when Henri volunteers as a recruit to join 'the army of England at Boulogne' (*P* 8) in 1797 (*P* 86) and ends on New Year's Day, 1805, when he is twenty years old, but also includes a series of flashbacks recalling episodes of his childhood and youth as well as episodes from his parents' lives, especially his mother's. Likewise, in the second chapter, Villanelle narrates her life story to an unidentified 'you', whom she also tells: 'I'm telling you stories. Trust me' (*P* 69). Her narration begins at the moment when

Bonaparte invaded Venice, also in 1797 (P 52) and, like Henri's, includes a series of flashbacks recalling episodes in her parents' lives and her own birth and early years. It also ends on 'New Year's Day, 1805' (P 76). The meeting of Henri and Villanelle in Russia is reflected structurally in the alternation of narrative voices in Chapter 3, where Henri acts as first-level narrator and Villanelle as second-level narrator – that is, at a certain moment, Henri hands over the narrative role to Villanelle, who starts narrating her life story to Henri and his two friends, Patrick and Domino. Henri's narration begins after he lost an eye at the battle of Austerlitz (P 79), that is, after 2 December 1805, and covers the Russian campaign and his desertion with Patrick and Villanelle, travelling on foot from Russia to Venice. Only Henri and Villanelle arrive in Venice, however, since Patrick dies on the way. The chapter ends with Henri's murder of Villanelle's husband, on an unrecorded date, and his incarceration in 'the madhouse on the island' of St Servelo (P 140). The fourth chapter begins again near 'Christmas and New Year' (P 158). It is 'more than twenty years since we went to church at Boulogne' (P 160), that is, more than twenty years after 1789, thus providing the present from which the events in the other three chapters are narrated. In this chapter, Henri's and Villanelle's narrations again alternate, but now Villanelle's status as narrator is not subordinated to Henri's, since she directly addresses the reader, as in the second chapter. However, it is Henri who opens and closes the narration in the novel and, in this sense, Villanelle's narration is psychologically contained within that of Henri.

The striking complementarity of the two characters' narrations is enhanced by the similarity of what they narrate: they often use the same words, expressions and refrains, share the same or complementary thoughts and do the same or similar things. Thus, for example, in the first chapter, Henri tells the story of a man in his village 'who liked to think of himself as an inventor' and wasted his time making useless and ruinous experiments while his wife tilled the fields, kept house and brought up their six children (P 26–7), and in the second chapter Villanelle tells the legend of the 'weak and foolish man whose wife cleaned the boat and sold the fish and brought up their children' (P 50), who is then revealed to be Villanelle's own father. In another example of complementarity, Henri says that he first encountered Joséphine 'over the billiard table [. . .] playing Monsieur Talleyrand' (P 34), and then Villanelle tells how she lost an unusual wager at billiards and had to pay with sex in a way that she explicitly compares to a crucifixion.[14] In this chapter, Villanelle compares her attachment to the Queen of Spades to that felt by the disciples for Jesus Christ: 'Christ said, "Follow me", and it was done' (*P* 64). Her blasphemous identification with Christ refracts the episode in the first chapter in which Henri is having communion and suddenly tastes in the host and wine the suffering and the blood of the 2,000 men who have just drowned in the Channel (*P* 42). Formally as well as thematically, then, Henri's and Villanelle's lives form an intricate pattern, suggesting a shared identity comparable to that of the man and woman in William Blake's poem, 'The Mental Traveller', whose opening stanza strikingly recalls Henri's travels across Europe:[15]

> I travell'd thro' a land of men,
> A land of men and women too;
> And heard and saw such dreadful things
> As cold earth-wanderers never knew. (*c.* 1801–3, ll. 1–4)

As the title of the poem suggests, the journey undertaken by Blake's traveller has the duality of an archetypal hero's quest: it is both a perilous journey across the waste land and a process of psychological maturation.

In classical mythology there are two basic versions of the archetypal hero's quest: Ulysses's journey on water and land takes place in the open air; Theseus's quest occurs in the enclosed and subterranean darkness of the Minotaur's labyrinth. Like Ulysses, with whom he compares himself (*P* 83), Henri is constantly associated with daylight and open air. However, this identification is often mediated through Eliot's modern equivalent of Homer's hero, J. Alfred Prufrock, thus giving a further parodic turn to Eliot's allusion. Prufrock is a common man, 'glad to be of use', who compares himself with 'the Fool' in the Tarot and likes going out at twilight.[16] Henri is also a common man, glad to be of use to Napoleon, who likes walking at twilight: 'I like the early dark. It is not night. It's still companionable. No one feels afraid to walk by themselves without a lantern' (*P* 32). However, he is very much afraid of the dark: 'Walking in the Dark is like swimming underwater except you can't come up for air' (*P* 33). In *The Odyssey*, Ulysses managed to listen to the alluring sirens' song without drowning by tying himself to the ship's mast; Prufrock has also 'heard the mermaids singing, each to each', and has 'seen them riding seaward on the waves', but he does not think that they sing for him or try to precipitate his death. His fear is that his vision will only last 'Till human voices wake us, and we drown'.[17] In contrast both to Ulysses, who has seen and heard them, and to Prufrock, who has imagined them, Henri's knowledge of the sirens is second hand and devalued, an old wives' tale told him by his friend, the defrocked Irish priest, meant to provide a comforting explanation for the overwhelmingly irrational and unjustifiable death by drowning of thousands of French soldiers.[18]

Unlike Henri, Villanelle is constantly associated with darkness and water. For all her mother's efforts to postpone her delivery, she was born in the total darkness of an eclipse of the sun (P 51), and her natural element is Venice, a watery and uncanny world with mysterious dark lanes and apparently dead-end canals, which recall the dark and claustrophobic wanderings of Theseus along the Cretan labyrinth. Her inborn ability to find her way in this watery maze links her to Ariadne, the daughter of Minos, the king of Crete and of the moon goddess, Parsiphae. Ariadne fell in love with Theseus and helped him slay the Minotaur by providing him with a reel of golden magical thread to find his way out of the monster's labyrinth. Theseus took Ariadne with him when he sailed for Athens but soon abandoned her, leaving her asleep on the island of Naxos, where Dionysus, the god of vegetation and wine, wooed and later married her. As Dionysus's wife, Ariadne led novitiates through the mazes for the Eleusinian mysteries, a role suggested by Villanelle's promiscuity and her initiation of Henri/Theseus into sex, as well as by her fascination for carnival and open-air entertainments. From this mythical perspective, Villanelle's husband, the brutal and disgusting cook who made his fortune 'supplying the French army with meat and horses' (P 63), would fit into the role of Minotaur, the half man/half beast Theseus must kill in order to get out of the labyrinth. This role is suggested by Henri's description of the cook's dark figure, just before killing him, as 'a great expanse like a matador's cloak' (P 125).

In 'A Psychological Approach to the Dogma of the Trinity', Carl G. Jung pointed out how the will to be different and contrary is characteristically evil, just as disobedience was the hallmark of original sin. Therefore, the Son who revolts against the Father has a 'light' side (the 'conscious' or 'ego') and a 'dark' emanation (the 'unconscious' or 'shadow') and contains in himself the principles of both good and evil. Consequently, the archetypal hero's quest for individuation of the self is not accomplished until the conflict created by his own duality is resolved in a fourth principle, the 'spirit' or 'soul' (the Christian Holy Spirit, the alchemical *lumen lumini* imprisoned in matter, the 'Mother Earth', the female principle embodied in the anima, etc.).[19] With Jung's ideas in mind, the three characters can be regarded as the fragmented facets of a single individual striving for self-individuation, with Henri playing the role of 'conscious' or 'ego', Villanelle that of 'spirit' or 'anima', and the cook that of 'unconscious' or 'shadow', as is suggested by his unfettered lasciviousness and his association with horses.[20]

In keeping with *The Passion*'s baroque economy of repetition and excess, Henri's maturation process is simultaneously expressed by means of Jungian, Freudian, Lacanian, mythical and Tarot imagery. Freud divided the psychological evolution of the self into three basic stages, according to the object of instinctual desire: the first one is the child's narcissistic stage of self-love. During this stage the child knows only itself and cannot tell the difference between 'self' and 'other' and so cannot develop the notion of 'self' as opposed to the rest of the world. The second one is the stage of attachment to love objects. During this stage the child loses the reassuring unity with the mother characteristic of the pre-Oedipal phase and tries to identify with the father, who, according to Freud, is the primal 'other', since it is the father who forbids incest, threatens with castration and, by placing an absolute prohibition upon the child's desire for the mother, becomes the inhibiting agent of external law. The third stage is achieved when the adult subordinates 'the pleasure principle' to the requirements of 'the reality principle', that is, the necessity to come to terms with the world, accepting the need to postpone pleasure without, however, relinquishing its eventual attainment.[21] As Malcolm Bowie has pointed out, one of Jacques Lacan's most fruitful additions to Freud's theory of the self is his analysis of the transitional stage between primary narcissism (love for self) and attachment to loved objects (love for others), which he calls '*le stade du miroir*', or 'mirror stage'.[22] This stage is reached by the child between the ages of six and eighteen months, when, despite its imperfect control over its own body, it is first able to imagine itself as a coherent, self-governing entity, as it contemplates its own reflection in a mirror. Appositely following Lacan's 'mirror stage' imagery, Henri points to his fragmentation of the self, when, speaking of himself in the third person, he recalls how, as a child, he refused to watch himself in the mirror held up for him by his father:[23]

I see a little boy watching his reflection in a copper pot he's polished. His father comes in and laughs and offers him his shaving mirror instead. But in the shaving mirror the boy can only see one face. In the pot he can see all the distortions of his face. He sees many possible faces and so he sees what he might become. (P 26)

The mirror stage is the crucial phase in the evolution of the child when it feels for a brief moment the exhilarating experience of identification of the '*je*' (Freud's '*ich*' or 'ego') with the '*je-idéal*' (Freud's 'ideal *ich*' or 'superego'). Therefore, Henri's refusal to identify with the image offered to him by his father is crucial: if he is to mature he will have to find a substitute 'ideal-I' figure. Like many other French youths, Henri finds it in the figure of Napoleon. Reflecting on his passion for him, Henri explicitly uses Lacanian mirror imagery:

When I fell in love it was as though I looked into a mirror for the first time and saw myself [. . .]. And when I had looked at myself and grown accustomed to who I was, I was not afraid to hate parts of me because I wanted to be worthy of the mirror bearer.
    Then, when I had regarded myself for the first time, I regarded the world and saw it to be more various and beautiful than I thought. (P 154–5)

Passionately in love with his Lacanian *je-idéal*, then, Henri, like so many other adolescent French soldiers, endured without a word of reproach eight terrible years of imperialist wars, never attempting to question Napoleon's orders, no matter how dangerous or how wrong, brutal or unnecessary. In keeping with his role of self-centred and all-powerful father figure, Napoleon is happy to send his adoring men to the slaughter-house at the same rate as that with which he devours fowl like an ogre in a fairytale: 'He wishes his whole face were mouth to cram a whole bird. In the morning I'll be lucky to find the wishbone' (P 4). As the symbology of the *coq gaulois*, emblem of the French nation, makes clear, Napoleon's passion for chicken symbolises the all-consuming, never satisfied *hybris* of this Saturnlike law-giver, devouring his own children in order to satisfy his ego. The sight of the fowl Napoleon's cook keeps in cages in great numbers, 'beaks and claws cut off, staring through the slats with dumb identical eyes'(P 5-6), produces in Henri the same horror a child might feel imagining Hansel and Gretel waiting in the cage to be eaten by the witch, for it confirms his fear that his love for Napoleon will never be returned: 'He was in love with himself and France joined in. It was a romance.

Perhaps all romance is like that; not a contract between equal parties but an explosion of dreams and desires that can find no outlet in everyday life' (*P* 13).

Like Henri, Villanelle admits her self-fragmentation and the resulting need for an 'ideal-I' with whom to identify when she says, echoing Narcissus, that she has a preference for the distorted reflection of her face as it appears on the glistening water of the lagoon: 'I catch sight of myself in the water and see in the distortions of my face what I might become' (*P* 62). Like Henri, Villanelle falls in love at first sight, in her case with the unknown lady who wins a game of cards with the trump called 'the Queen of Spades' (*P* 59). After the game, the lady invites Villanelle to a bottle of French champagne:

> She held the glass in a silent toast [. . .]. Still she did not speak, but watched me through the crystal and suddenly draining her glass stroked the side of my face. Only for a second she touched me and then she was gone and I was left with my heart smashing at my chest and three-quarters of a bottle of the best champagne. (*P* 59)

The scene, with its emphasis on sight through glass, materialises the symbology of Lacan's mirror stage. The young croupier is instantly seduced by the beautiful face she sees on the other side of the glass, which is that of a woman with 'grey-green eyes with flecks of gold' and hair 'darker and redder' (*P* 59) than Villanelle's own 'crop of red hair and a pair of eyes that made up for the sun's eclipse' (*P* 51); that is, she falls in love with a mature, improved version of herself.

As Villanelle soon learns, the lady is married. Therefore, a triangular relationship is established which conforms to the medieval tradition of courtly love. In this tradition, 'the beautiful women that inspire courtly love and devotion are beyond the threshold of the norm set by their husbands and suitors: Courtly ladies are objects that approach divinity, one serves as one would a goddess (imagined as an icon)'.[24] Clearly, this is the reverential attitude Villanelle has for her *je-idéal*, whose superiority and quasi-divinity are constantly suggested, like the superiority and quasi-divinity of Napoleon. Central to this courtly love tradition is the motif of the heart, developed in the conceits of sixteenth-century poets such as Sir Philip Sidney and John Donne. As Paulina Palmer has pointed out, this tradition is alluded to, for example, when Villanelle tells the Queen of Spades 'in a manner reminiscent of Donne': 'If you should leave me, my heart will turn to water and flood away' (*P* 76)[25]. But the courtly love tradition is given an ironic turn when Villanelle literally loses her heart and, like Edgar Allan Poe's 'Tell-Tale Heart', it keeps on beating in the lady's palace in Venice while she is far away in Russia.[26] Henri gives the courtly love tradition a similar ironic turn when, after strangling Villanelle's husband, he insists, like Shylock, on carving out the cook's heart (P 128).[27] Further, the fact that it is the two women who fall in love with each other, instead of two men with a lady, transforms the original *amour courteois* triangle into a characteristic Wintersonian lesbian triangle.

Paulina Palmer has pointed out how, in *The Passion*, homosexual love is recurrently associated with the carnivalesque and with the grotesque body, 'described by Bakhtin as a body in "the act of becoming", in the process of being "continually built, created"' and, therefore, associated with movement.[28] In keeping with this, just before meeting the Queen of Spades, Villanelle notices an open-air attraction provided by acrobats who swing above the square in a series of nets and trapezes 'and snatch a kiss from whoever is standing below', and reflects:

> I like such kisses. They fill the mouth and leave the body free. To kiss well one must kiss solely. No groping hands or stammering hearts. The lips and the lips alone are the pleasure. Passion is sweeter split strand by strand. Divided and re-divided like mercury then gathered up only at the last moment. (P 59)

As Palmer acutely notes, '[t]his description of the acrobats and the kisses they steal anticipates and acts as a metaphor for Villanelle's love affair with the Queen of Spades',[29] the sexual climax of which is reached when they exchange a kiss: 'She lay on the rug and I lay at right angles to her so that only our lips might meet. Kissing in this way is the strangest of distractions [. . .], the mouth becomes the focus of love and all things pass through it and are re-defined' (P 67). Thus, Winterson incorporates into *The Passion* a key motif in lesbian culture: the treatment of the mouth as a lesbian signifier, 'fusing two taboo activities, female speaking and lesbian sexuality'.[30]

As Malcolm Bowie has pointed out, whereas for Freud identification with a father figure would represent a stage in the way towards adulthood, or 'genital maturity', and so towards the acceptance of the 'reality principle', for Lacan the mirror stage represents a permanent tendency of the individual to seek and foster the *imaginary* wholeness of an ideal ego. Consequently, the 'unity invented at these moments,

and the ego that is the product of successive inventions are both
spurious: they are attempts to find ways round certain inescapable
factors of lack, absence and incompleteness in human life'.[31] As a
mirror-stage infatuation, then, Henri's passion for Napoleon and
Villanelle's passion for the Queen of Spades are similarly bound to
remain unrequited, establishing a triangular pattern of passion,
jealousy and neglect that, in keeping with the novel's economy of
repetition and excess, seems to reproduce itself *ad infinitum*:
Napoleon ignores Henri because he is too much in love with himself
and with Joséphine. Henri then falls in love with Villanelle, but she is
in love with the Queen of Spades. In her turn, the Queen of Spades
cannot respond adequately to Villanelle's love because she has a husband she loves, while she herself is neglected by him, obsessed as he
is with his futile search for the Holy Grail. Villanelle's mother was
likewise neglected by her first husband, as was the inventor's wife in
Henri's tale. . . . With impeccable symmetry, the novel presents
Napoleon collecting the hearts of the French soldiers, while the
Queen of Spades collects the hearts of her lovers in coloured glass
phials kept in ebony boxes (*P* 120) that recall the 'vials of ivory and
coloured glass' of the lady in the second section of *The Waste Land*,
'A Game of Chess'.[32]

The archetypal, *je-idéal* complementarity of Napoleon and the
Queen of Spades is neatly pointed up by a series of significant paral-
lelisms. At the beginning of the novel, Henri describes Napoleon 'sitting alone with a globe in front of him [. . . .] turning the globe round
and round, holding it tenderly with both hands as if it were a breast'
(*P* 4). This scene symbolises the extent of the emperor's consuming
passion to conquer the world. Years later, during his inspection of the
Queen of Spades's palace in search of Villanelle's heart, Henri finds
a room with a map of the world covering the whole of one wall: 'A map
with whales in the seas and terrible monsters chewing the land' (*P*
119). This map, with 'roads marked that seemed to disappear into
the earth and at other times to stop abruptly at the sea's edge' (*P* 119),
contains the mazelike contours of 'the inner city' of Venice, whose
'[s]treets appear and disappear overnight, new waterways force themselves over dry land' (*P* 97). That is, this map represents the fantastic,
dreamlike counterpart of the material world represented by
Napoleon's globe: in psychological terms, the visionary world of
dreams and the unconscious and, in mythical terms, the underworld.
The association of Venice with the underworld is made explicit by

Villanelle's description of the inner city as a 'shadow-land' of 'darkness and death' (*P* 97), and by her remark that 'you may lose your soul or find it here' (*P* 57). Therefore, the possession of this map signals the Queen of Spades and her husband both as Jung's 'syzygy' or 'divine couple' – the king and queen of the enchanted castle whose matrimony symbolises the wholeness and integration of the outer and the inner life[33] – and as the gods of the underworld. This identity is suggested by the fact that the Queen of Spades collects insects (*P* 66), and so is associated with Satan as the Lord of the Flies.[34]

Next to the room with the map Henri finds 'a tapestry some three quarters done [lying] in its frame. The picture was of a young woman cross-legged in front of a pack of cards. It was Villanelle' (*P* 117). The lady's tapestry, then, presents Villanelle as one of the insects in the lady's collection, caught up in her textile net.[35] As she tells Henri: 'if the tapestry had been finished and the woman had woven in her [Villanelle's] heart, she would have been a prisoner for ever' (*P* 121). This remark points to the Queen of Spades as the evil *alter ego* of Villanelle-as-Ariadne, that is, as voracious Arachne, patiently weaving her invisible spider's web around her prey. As a complex design made up of apparently singular fibres woven together in a self-contained tapestry, the spider's web is associated with the Fates, the three Greek goddesses, also called by the collective name of Moirai (or Parcae, in Latin), who spin the strands of human destiny and 'give mortals their share of good and evil' (Hesiod, *Theogony*, 905–6). In this myth, human destiny is closely bound to hazard and death, as is implied by the roles of the Fates: Clotho is the spinner, Lachesis is the drawer of lots, and Atropos represents the inevitable end to life. The tapestry proves that the Queen of Spades has Clotho's ability to spin. Her mastery at playing cards matches that of Lachesis at drawing lots. And, like Atropos, she is associated with death and even with vampirism, as is suggested by the fact that the boat Villanelle borrows to take Henri to her palace is 'a funeral boat' (*P* 118) and that Henri finds in their palace, instead of beds for her and her husband, only 'two coffins, their lids open, white silk inside' (*P* 119). This association becomes more evident if we recall that in Homer's *Iliad* (24.49) the three goddesses are described as a single Moira who spins with her thread a particular human fate.

The association of the lady with hazard and death points to the central motif in the novel: existence as a wager. At the beginning of his narration Henri tells the reader that he was educated by a priest

who 'had a hollow Bible with a pack of cards inside' and that the priest
had taught him 'every card game and a few tricks' (*P* 12). After joining the army, Henri continued to play cards regularly with Patrick and
sometimes with Domino (*P* 22–3), and one day, watching a game of
noughts and crosses scrawled on the floor, he found himself reflecting on the meaning of life in terms of play: 'You play, you win, you
play, you lose. You play. It's the playing that's irresistible [. . . .] what
you risk reveals what you value' (*P* 43). Villanelle, who repeats these
words (*P* 73, 91),[36] is not only a gifted card player, she is a professional
player of cards, billiards and other games. She works double shifts as
a croupier, dressed as a woman by the day and as a man by the night,
in a casino that constitutes the social and symbolic centre of Venice.

Villanelle and the Venetians' passion for gambling echoes that of
the citizens of Babylon in Jorge Luis Borges' tale 'The Lottery in Babylon',[37] where each individual's position in the social scale, the kind of
jobs, entertainments and even rights over life and death are exclusively ruled by lottery. Borges' tale takes to extremes the principle that
life is ruled by hazard and dramatises the logical consequences of the
gamblers' pleasurably tormenting knowledge that their skill – that is,
their ability to orient their own lives in a particular way – is always
threatened by chance and consequently cannot be predetermined or
directed in any desirable way. A more obvious intertext of the chapter
entitled 'The Queen of Spades' is Pushkin's 'The Queen of Spades', a
fantastic tale about the irrepressible passion for gambling of a young
officer called Hermann, whose soul is compared to that of
Mephistopheles and whose profile reminds Tomsky and Lisavieta
Ivanovna of Napoleon.[38] Pushkin's 'The Queen of Spades' is the story
of a 'Devil's gambler' who tries to behave as an 'astute gambler' only
to be destroyed in the attempt. Like Pushkin's, Villanelle's story of
'the Devil's gambler' has the Faustian overtones of a satanic pact: a
tradesman agrees to wager his life against that of a mysterious old
man who is openly associated with the devil (*P* 92). When, inevitably,
the tradesman loses, he is sentenced to die through 'dismemberment
piece by piece beginning with the hands' (*P* 93), a death that re-enacts
the mythical hero's ritual phase of *sparagmos*, or death by dismemberment, prior to his triumphant rebirth, whose Christian equivalent
is the crucifixion and resurrection.

In *The Passion*, as in Borges' 'The Lottery in Babylon', Peter Carey's
Oscar and Lucinda, Julio Cortázar's *Hopscotch* or Thomas Pynchon's
The Crying of Lot 49, the gambler's painfully pleasing knowledge that

the thing at stake is his or her own life functions as an apt metaphor for an existentialist conception of life that goes back to Pascal's conception of faith in God as a Wager on human destiny. As Borges' tale suggests, the idea of life as a wager can be retraced further back to Greek gnosticism and even further back to the Babylonian conception of hazard and of human life as an ever-changing flux ruled by fortune's wheel. This idea is also present in the Bible, in the Book of Job, where God engages in a bet with the devil about whether an unjustly punished Job would rebel or not. At the same time, Villanelle's story of the Devil's gambler, with its central idea that 'Pleasure on the edge of danger is sweet' (P 137), may be said to synthesise iconically the Freudian ambivalent pattern of repression and satisfaction of the individual's primal pleasure-seeking instinctual drive as described in 'Totem and Taboo' (1912–13), expressing the Venetians' and the protagonists' belief in the possibility of realising their most urgent needs and desires and confirming the validity of their quest.

Further, the Venetians' passion for gambling gives Venice mythical centrality, for the climax in the classical Greek versions of the quest myth is the *katabasis* (the descent to Hades), or what Homer called in *The Odyssey* the *nekya* (the visit to the underworld). The heroes who visit the underworld are many (from Persephone, Odysseus, Tiresias, or Hermes to Dante's Virgil) and, as Evans Lansing Smith has pointed out, the underworld has four main functions: as ancestral crypt of the dead, containing the accumulated knowledge of the human race; as granary, or repository of the archetypal forms of the imagination; as *temenos*, or sacred site of initiatory transformation; and as inferno.[39] Villanelle alludes to Venice as crypt, granary and *temenos* when she tells Henri: 'Here, there are mysteries that only the dead know' (P 118), and as inferno when she describes its ever-changing and watery lanes as the intestines of 'a living city' (P 113), feeding on and pouring out the human detritus of the war: 'the exiles, the people the French drove out. These people are dead but they do not disappear' (P 114). Just as Eliot's London in *The Waste Land* is both a contemporary metropolis and an 'Unreal City, / Under the brown fog of a winter dawn', where the dead flow in a crowd,[40] so Venice is simultaneously real and unreal, a cosmopolitan and affluent city swarming with multiracial gamblers and pleasure-seekers, and a Hermetic underworld, populated by the living dead, as Henri does not fail to realise when he admires Villanelle's easy way with the inhabitants of 'the inner city' on New Year's Eve: 'Tonight the spirits of the dead are abroad speaking in tongues. Those who may listen will learn. She is at home tonight' (P 75). Unlike Eliot's 'hollow men', then, these living dead can teach their secret wisdom to those, like Villanelle, who are ready to listen. The crowned queen of these living dead is 'the Lady of Means'(P 115), a weird old lady who wears a crown 'made out of rats tied in a circle by their tails' (P 74), that is, a witch's quincunx or mandalic circle, evoking the Hermetic occultism of the Tarot, and thus pointing to her condition of chthonic mother, Carl G. Jung's female equivalent of the Old Wise Man. This haggish creature is always asking the passers-by, in words that recall the opening section of 'Burnt Norton', 'what time it might be' (P 49, 54, 74, 114).[41] Villanelle explains to Henri, in words that are close to Eliot's description of Madame Sosostris, 'the wisest woman in Europe, / With a wicked pack of cards',[42] that this repulsive soothsayer was 'one of the wealthiest women in Venice' (P 115) before Napoleon seized her fortune. Therefore, this hag with the black magic crown gives a further turn to the symbolism of Madame Sosostris in The Waste Land, who used the ancient and powerful magic of the Tarot in a devalued and meaningless way in order to earn her living by casting horoscopes, thus pointing to the Tarot as yet another source of symbolic imagery in the novel.

While stylistically and thematically the first two chapters echo the first and second sections of Eliot's Prufrock ('The Love Song of J. Alfred Prufrock' and 'Portrait of a Lady') respectively, their titles, 'The Emperor' and 'The Queen of Spades', correspond to two trumps in the Tarot. The Emperor is the fourth card of the greater arcana and The Queen of Spades one the four court cards in the lesser arcana. According to Alfred Douglas, the Emperor 'indicates reason, will power, and the world of mankind on earth [. . .]. He is the symbol of the warlike patriarchal societies which superseded the primitive agricultural cultures of the Great Mother.'[43] The Queen of Spades, on the other hand, 'is highly intelligent, has a complex personality and is concerned with attention to detail and accuracy in all things. She is alert to the attitudes and opinions of those around her, and is skilled at balancing opposing factions whilst she furthers her own schemes. She is self-reliant, swift-acting, versatile and inventive.'[44] The oppositional difference in temperament and symbolism between the figures in these two trumps echoes a similar difference between Bonaparte's patriarchal world, ruled by logic, and the much more irrational and uncanny world of Venice, pointing to the complementary physical/ psychological nature of their respective worlds.

The major arcana of the Tarot are derived from Hermetic occultism and were originally devised to represent grades or stages in a system of initiation. Therefore, of the twenty-two cards, only one, The Fool, is not numbered, for it represents the subject who undertakes the quest through the stages symbolised by the other cards. Both in the Tarot and in Jung's theory of the individuation process, the quest encompasses the whole of the subject's life and falls naturally into two halves. The first half is concerned with the individual's relationship to the world (Freud's *Umwelt*) and is directed towards the development of the conscious mind and the stabilization of the ego. The second half reverses this process and confronts the ego with the depths of its own psyche, seeking to establish links with the inner self, the true centre of consciousness (Freud's *Innenwelt*).[45] This double structure is represented visually by the arrangement of the cards in sequential order, from one to twenty-one, with the numberless card, the Fool, situated between the first and the last and forming two symmetric loops merging at the centre by the superposition of cards ten and twenty-one – that is, assuming the shape of a recumbent eight, the symbol of the infinite (∞), and also of Möbius strip.

This double-loop structure is alluded to in Henri's comment that he has been in the army for eight years (P 86, 125); in Villanelle's remark that she lost her heart 'eight years ago' (P 94); and, most clearly, in Henri's baffled realisation, soon after his arrival in Venice, that he and Villanelle had been rowing 'in a shape that seemed to be

Frontispiece by David Sheridan from Alfred Douglas, *The Tarot: The Origins, Meanings and Uses of the Cards*. Illustrated by David Sheridan. Harmondsworth: Penguin, 1982 (1973).

a figure of eight working back on itself' (*P* 113). The intertwining of Henri's and Villanelle's narrations may also be said to reproduce this convoluted structure at the narrative level.

The first phase in Jung's individuation process symbolised by the Fool's journey along the first loop in the Tarot is the child's appre- hension of the difference between the 'I' and the 'not I', between self and world. Henri expresses his awareness of this difference when he writes: 'when I had regarded myself for the first time, I regarded the world and saw it to be more various and beautiful than I thought' (*P* 155). The recognition of the world as different from the self signals the beginning of the child's maturation and often involves a sudden confrontation with the inevitability of death, which is usually accom- panied by the reversal of all the ideals and values cherished until that moment. In *The Passion*, this watershed is reached in the third chap- ter, 'The Zero Winter', whose title parodies the question that closes the first section of 'Little Gidding': 'Where is the summer, the unimaginable / Zero summer?'[46] For Eliot, the unimaginable zero summer is the season outside time's covenant that the traveller finds at the end of his journey, when the quester eventually realises either the futility of the purpose that had led him there, or that 'the purpose is beyond the end you figured'.[47] Eliot described this 'zero summer' with two opposed seasonal images: as 'midwinter spring', that is, as a brief moment when the 'sun flames the ice' in the middle of winter, and with the contrary image of springtime suddenly 'blanched for an hour with transitory blossom / Of snow'. In both cases the images are positive, for in the first one the icy cold of winter is unexpectedly warmed by the sun and in the second the hedges seem to bloom again 'with voluptuary sweetness'.[48] In accordance with Eliot's religious faith, the journey's end is not a place 'to verify, / Instruct yourself, or inform curiosity / Or carry report. You are here to kneel / Where prayer has been valid'.[49] Deprived of this metaphysical meaning and consolation, Eliot's 'zero summer' becomes Jeanette Winterson's 'zero winter' where the cosiness of Eliot's wasteland, in which 'Winter kept us warm, covering / Earth in forgetful snow, feeding / A little life with dried tubers',[50] has become the frozen Russian fields of war and the burnt-out and deserted Russian towns, offering neither shelter nor warmth. However, in Russia, Henri, like Eliot's quester, finds that the purpose he had in mind when he enrolled with Napoleon was 'beyond the end he figured'. Watching his enemies, he suddenly realises that 'I had been taught to look for monsters and devils and I found ordinary people' (*P* 105). After this, he rejects the anonymity imposed on him by Napoleon: 'I don't want to worship him any more. I want to make my own mistakes' (*P* 86).

The realisation of his own worth initiates the inward-looking movement in Henri's individuation process, away from the world and into the depths of his own psyche. This is suggested by the title of the fourth chapter, 'The Rock', which refers to the rocky island where Henri is secluded after he is convicted of the cook's murder. The title echoes Eliot's 'rock' in *The Waste Land*, especially in 'What the Thunder said', where the poet imagines the regenerating and fructifying effect of water on the dry rock,[51] while the name of the island, 'San Servelo', has been interpreted by Judith Seaboyer as 'a typographical error' for the real Benedictine monastery on the Venetian island of San Servolo.[52] Yet, it can also be read as an intentional misspelling meant as a (quasi)pun on the Italian word for brain, *cervello*, intended to underline the fact that Henri is now immersed in the inward-looking phase of his quest.

Soon after his enrolment in the army, Henri was taken to a brothel by his superior, the chicken cook. There, the purblind young soldier underwent a crucial traumatic experience, as he witnessed the cook's atrocious ill-treatment of a prostitute, whom he slapped violently across the face and forced to perform *fellatio* (*P* 14–15). This caused Henri to suppress similarly reprehensible sexual drives in himself and to project them onto the cook, thus bringing about the fragmentation of his ego and shadow. This is the original trauma Henri has to overcome if he is to mature, since the less aware of the shadow he is, the blacker and denser it becomes. In keeping with this interpretation, the episode ends with the cook's dismissal (he is found by Napoleon in a drunken stupor – that is, literally *unconscious*), followed by Henri's promotion to the same job. Their paths separate then, but their actions continue to affect each other. Henri, incapable of assuming his sexuality, takes Napoleon as his 'ideal I' and continues to be Oedipally attracted by his mother. When he meets Villanelle in Russia he is still a virgin, a deficiency she will help him overcome by teaching him how to combine love and sex. Still, the kind of love Henri feels for Villanelle is quite different from the narcissistic infatuation he felt for Bonaparte:

> Her. A person who is not me. I invented Bonaparte as much as he invented himself.
> My passion for her, even though she could never return it, showed me the difference between inventing a lover and falling in love.
> The one is about you, the other about someone else. (*P* 156)

Falling in love with Villanelle, then, Henri is freed from the self-absorption of the 'mirror stage': 'I think now that being free is not being powerful or rich or well regarded or without obligations but being able to love. To love someone else enough to forget about yourself even for one moment is to be free' (P 154). Henri conceives the fulfilment of this liberating, mature 'love for the other' in patriarchal terms as the building of a nuclear family. Villanelle, however, insists on offering him only pleasurable sex and brotherly love: '"I love you", I said. / "You're my brother", she said' (P 117). The suggestion of incest in her words enhances the psychological ego/anima complementarity of the two characters.

Villanelle nicknamed the cook 'the Jack of Hearts' after his lucky card (P 56). This playing card corresponds to The Knave of Cups in the Tarot. The figure represented in it is Narcissus, the beautiful young man who was not allowed to look at himself in a mirror, and so did not know his own identity. When Narcissus saw his own reflection on the water of a pond he fell in love with himself and when he could not bear any longer the agony of his impossible love, he stabbed himself to death. The suicide of the self-absorbed youth is unavoidable, since Narcissus/the Jack of Hearts must die in order to transform itself into the Knight of Hearts, where love can be projected outwards, to the other.[53] Similarly, in Jung's scheme, the shadow must sacrifice itself if ego and anima are to achieve their unification.

Villanelle's marriage to the cook perfectly fits into the mythical and psychological patterns, since Henri's spiritual love (*agape*) for Villanelle must be complemented by the carnal love (*eros*) the cook feels for her, which, significantly, is aroused by her androgyny (P 63), that is, by the very feature that symbolises her oxymoronic good/evil, innocent/corrupt anima nature. Thus, driven by a fatal compulsion 'to play' (P 65–6) comparable to that of a Devil's gambler, Villanelle agrees to marry the cook even though she is thoroughly repelled by him and feels like 'pulling a knife on him' when he is proposing marriage to her (P 62). Villanelle and the cook's first sexual encounter repeats the scene that traumatised Henri at the brothel: the cook hits, rapes and pays Villanelle with a token coin. But unlike Henri, who was incapable of helping the prostitute, Villanelle responds to the cook's violence with her own violence and makes light of the rape: 'He hit me then. Not hard but I was shocked. I'd never been hit before. I hit him back. Hard. [. . .] I didn't try to move, he was twice my weight at least and I am no heroine. I'd nothing to lose either, having lost it already in happier times' (*P* 64). The same climactic scene is re-enacted a final time when the cook unexpectedly reappears in Venice, in what Judith Seaboyer has fittingly described as 'a return of the repressed'.[54] Henri, who, Narcissuslike, is watching his own reflection in the glass pane of one of the casino's windows, looks beyond it and sees the cook blocking Villanelle's way and slapping her across the face (*P* 125–6); that is, in Jungian terms, he sees his shadow hurting his anima. Unlike in the brothel, however, this time Henri is not paralysed by shock and, opening the window, he 'jumped into the canal' (*P* 126). This Alice-through-the-looking-glass leap transports Henri from the realm of his imaginary ego to the realm of the real. As the cook attempts to strangle him, Henri stabs him dead with the knife Villanelle has put within his reach (*P* 128). Thus, in a pivotal, archetypal scene, ego and anima defeat the shadow and ritually sacrifice it. In keeping with the sacrificial nature of the cook's death, Henri observes at this point that his chest was '[h]airless and white, like the flesh of saints' and this observation leads him to ask himself the crucial question: 'Can saints and devils be so alike?' (*P* 128). Thus, Henri finally comprehends that the violence he had always restrained in himself and projected onto the cook in fact formed part of himself. This is the vital insight the Venetians had always lived by – 'the Venetians are a philosophical people, [. . .] holding hands with the Devil and God' (*P* 57) – and the lesson Villanelle has been trying to teach Henri. However, instead of finding a balance between *agape* and *eros*, good and evil, love and hate, Henri at this point gives up rationality and lets loose all the violence he had forcefully repressed during his eight soldier years. In a frenzy of passion that has the excessiveness of baroque opera, he carves open the cook's chest and plucks out his heart with his own bloody hands. This is the second heart Henri offers Villanelle, but this time she 'shook her head and started to cry' (*P* 128). Henri's closing remark that 'the blue and bloody thing lay between us' (*P* 129), literally points to this unnecessary act of violence (rather than the necessary murder of the cook) as the watershed beyond which there is no possibility of reunification of ego and anima, the reason why Villanelle cannot marry Henri even though she is expecting a child of his.[55]

The episode ends with Villanelle walking on the water, pulling at a rope over her shoulder and dragging behind the cook's and her own boat with Henri and the corpse in them, in a scene that combines allusions to Jesus Christ and to the Fool in the Tarot carrying his heavy bag on his shoulder (as well as to Christian in John Bunyan's *Pilgrim's Progress*). It is then that Henri sees Villanelle's webbed feet and plunges into the chaotic wilderness of the unconscious: 'I was in the red forest and she was leading me home' (*P* 128).

Tamás Bényei has pointed out how 'the final section of the novel is an inversion of the Orpheus-Eurydice myth, with Eurydice feeling pity rather than love for her Orpheus'.[56] This is an accurate description, since Orpheus is prevented from rescuing Eurydice from Thanatos, and is himself condemned to stay in Hades because, forgetting the prohibition of the gods of the underworld, he turns his head to *look* at her walking behind him before they have both crossed the boundary separating the living and the dead.

Henri is soon after convicted of murder and confined to the madhouse of San Servelo, where he suffers terrible bouts of schizophrenia or post-traumatic stress disorder, during which he sees and hears the ghost of his dead mother, or, assuming the persona of the cook, tries to strangle himself with his own hands. Villanelle organises his escape from the madhouse, but he refuses to follow her instructions or to see her again. This behaviour might be read as evidence that Henri has succumbed to the pull of his unconscious and has regressed for ever to the 'red forest'. However, during his voluntary seclusion and isolation, Henri devotes his time and energy to two apparently trifling tasks with interesting symbolic connotations. The first is an attempt to transform the rocky yard of the madhouse into a 'forest of red roses' (*P* 160), that is, to transform the barrenness of his 'red forest' into an Eliotean 'rose garden', where he might achieve a 'condition of complete simplicity (costing no less than everything)' capable of granting him his 'shantih', 'The Peace which passeth understanding'.[57]

The other task Henri has set himself is the rereading and rewriting of the war journal (*P* 36) he kept in a notebook (*P* 159) during the eight years he was in the army. After working in the Burgholzli Psychiatric Hospital in Zurich from 1900 to 1910, Carl G. Jung concluded that this activity was the most important instrument he had for the treatment of schizophrenics:

> In many cases in psychiatry, the patient who comes to us has a story that is not told, and which as a rule no one knows of. To my mind, therapy only really begins after the investigation of that wholly personal story. It is the patient's secret, the *rock* against which he is shattered. If I know his secret story, I have a key to the treatment.[58]

Jung's words cast new light on our interpretation of Henri's future, for if the 'rock' against which he is shattered is 'the secret story' buried in the deepest recesses of his brain (his *cervello*), he still holds the key to his recovery. This surely is the intended meaning of his refrain 'I'm telling you stories. Trust me', which Henri significantly repeats in the last line of the novel (*P* 160). If telling secret stories is a therapeutic activity, then Henri is not a madman but a 'myth-maker', in Jung's sense of the word – that is, someone with the (Hermetic, or shamanistic) imaginative capacity to translate the deep, penetrating and meaningful events and experiences of his own life (*ego*) into archetypal stories that give sense to human existence at large (*eidos*).

Sitting still in the voluntary isolation of his brainlike cell, Henri (like the heroes of many other experimental writers, such as Kafka, Proust, Borges, Robbe-Grillet, Beckett, Golding, Durrell, Fowles, Lessing or Ackroyd) weaves the labyrinthine pattern of his own life into a journal, only to discover that, in Gabriel Josipovici's words: 'the writing *was* the travelling'.[59] In other words, Henri's journal is the path for his quest, and so, his world.[60] And as *The Passion* reveals its condition of textual labyrinth, Henri transforms himself from Theseus into Dedalus, both the mythical *builder* of the Cretan labyrinth and Joyce's Stephen Dedalus, who, like Henri, built his own textual labyrinth and begot himself as an artist by rewriting his diary as *A Portrait of the Artist as a Young Man*.

The association of Henri with Stephen Dedalus expands in various directions. Thus, where Henri's name can be read, as Bényei suggests, as an anagram of Christ's passion (I.N.R.I.),[61] Joyce's hero is named after the first Christian martyr, St Stephen. And where Stephen Dedalus's contemplation of a 'bird-girl' gave him the inspiration to write a 'villanelle', i.e. a short lyric poem of Italian-French origin, Henri falls in love with Villanelle, an Italian woman who works for the French.[62] The logical implication of this intertextual relation is that Villanelle and by extension the fantasy world she represents are only figments of Henri's imagination, a reading that enhances the psychological interpretation of Villanelle as a projection of Henri's ideal woman/anima.

The intertextual indebtedness of *The Passion* to Joyce's *Ulysses* is also evident, not only in that both are rewritings of the *Odyssey*, but primarily because both novels are built on the same baroque principle of repetition and excess, aiming towards the ineffable all-inclusiveness of Jorge Luis Borges' 'total library'. Thus, as was the case in the earlier novels, *The Passion* reveals itself ultimately as an all-encompassing (inter)textual world offering crucial insight into the meaning of human existence. Displaying the characteristic behaviour of Isaac Berlin's 'hedgehog' writer, Winterson will again delve into this and related issues in her next novel, *Sexing the Cherry*.

With the publication of *Sexing the Cherry* in 1989 Jeanette Winterson won the E. M. Forster Award from the American Academy and Institute of Arts and Letters in New York, confirming the reviewers' opinion that she was the talented representative of 'a new phase in lesbian fiction, one moving on from the themes of self-discovery and self-affirmation that have characterized the [lesbian] literature of the past twenty years, to engage a more complex reality'.[63] In keeping with this view, Charlotte Innes set Winterson on a par *both* with lesbian writers like Sarah Schulman and Margaret Erhart and with 'fantasists, like Donald Barthelme or Italo Calvino', and concluded that '*Sexing the Cherry* is Winterson's most ambitious creation so far'.[64] Although shared by many, this type of enthusiastic reaction was not, however, universal. Thus, Lewis Buzbee claimed that '"Sexing the Cherry" is a dangerous jewel. It is a novel of such fine writing and lofty imagination that it dazzles the reader, yet its underlying theme is an insistent rage against our impossible human condition, a rage that is both personal and political.'[65]

Buzbee's unrest at realising that *Sexing the Cherry* is both fully imaginative and ideologically charged brings to mind Linda Hutcheon's contention that the defining characteristic of postmodernist art is its paradoxical nature, its 'deliberate refusal to resolve contradictions' and to raise 'questions about (or render problematic) the common-sensical and the "natural"'.[66] Indeed, like *The Passion*, *Sexing the Cherry* may be said to belong to Hutcheon's category of 'historiographic metafiction', a paradoxical type of postmodernist novel that combines self-reflexivity with history. Thus, its main storyline is situated in the seventeenth century, at a time of extraordinary upheaval in English history, but, as happens in *The Passion* with Napoleon's imperialist campaigns, the historical events that take place in *Sexing the Cherry* are not focused from the generalist and totalitarian perspective required by World History, but rather from the subjective perspectives of two marginal narrator-characters, a huge dog-breeder who lives by the bank of the Thames, nicknamed the Dog Woman, and her foundling son, Jordan.

As the Dog Woman explains at the beginning of her narration, Jordan 'was something close to ten' in 1640 (*SC* 21), so that she must have 'fished' the newly born baby 'from the stinking Thames' (*SC* 10) around 1630. This year, then, may be said to provide the starting point for the Dog Woman's and Jordan's alternative narrations, which thus begin during the last years of Charles I's reign, run parallel to the Civil War and the Puritan Commonwealth, the king's trial and execution in 1649 and the restoration of the monarchy in 1660, and end with the Plague of 1665 and the Great Fire of London of 1666.

The novel is divided into three sections. In the first one, which has no title, the Dog Woman and Jordan alternate in the retrospective narration of their life stories, covering the years from 1630 to 1649. The second section, entitled '1649', is also narrated alternatively by the Dog Woman and Jordan. It begins with the Civil War and ends in 1661 with Jordan's return from the island of Barbados with the first pineapple. In the third, entitled 'Some Years Later', the Dog Woman and Jordan continue their alternating narrations, covering the period from 1661 to the Great Fire of 1666. But in this section their voices also interweave with those of two new narrator-characters: a nameless ecologist and a naval cadet called Nicolas Jordan, who are living in the novel's present, that is, in the late twentieth century.[67] These characters are strikingly similar to the Dog Woman and Jordan, sharing with them vital attitudes, thoughts and even turns of phrase. Like their ancestors, they lead solitary lives and are perfectly aware of their difference and marginality with respect to the predominant social order. Nicolas Jordan feels immediately attracted by the ecologist when he reads in the newspapers that she is leading an unequal, solitary struggle against a factory that is poisoning a river with mercury. And the rage the ecologist feels against such emblems of patriarchal power as 'the World Bank', 'the Pentagon' and 'the world leaders' (*SC* 121), on whom she puts the blame for destroying the planet with their policy of unmitigated capitalism, is comparable to the solitary struggle the Dog Woman wages against the Puritans and the rage she feels for their life-denying and hypocritical policy of physical and spiritual repression.

The fact that Jordan can cross the boundary separating the world of common day from the world of fantasy suggests the complementarity and reversibility of the real and the unreal, of the imagined and the actually lived. Further, the merging of events and characters widely separated in time in what appears to be an atemporal present effectively undermines the chronological notions of past, present and future in favour of the cyclical temporality of myth. Mythically, time is linear and finite in that it is conceived as a succession of 'nows' existing between two atemporal eternities. But these present moments are also cyclical in that they repeat themselves in an endless pattern of recurrence. As Eliot put it in 'Burnt Norton':

> Time present and time past
> Are both perhaps present in time future
> And time future contained in time past.
> If all time is eternally present
> All time is unredeemable.
> What might have been is an abstraction
> Remaining a perpetual possibility
> Only in a world of speculation.
> What might have been and what has been
> Point to one end, which is always present.[68]

Eliot's assertion that 'What might have been and what has been / Point to one end, which is always present' may be said to provide the structuring principle for the novel, as the author herself suggests in *Art Objects* when she says that '*Sexing the Cherry* is a reading of *Four Quartets*' (*AO* 118). The importance given to the related notions of time and space in *Sexing the Cherry* is already hinted at in the double epigraph, which makes reference to the language of the Hopi, with 'no tenses for past present and future', and to the definition of matter as '[e]mpty space and points of light' (*SC* 8). The reference to the Hopi prefigures a story Jordan tells his mother about a visit he paid to an Indian tribe known as the Hopi. As he tells her, when he asked a Spaniard who lived with them if their language had some similarity to Spanish, the old man laughed and said that 'their language has no grammar in the way we recognize it. Most bizarre of all, they have no tenses for past, present and future. They do not sense time in that way. For them time is one' (*SC* 134–5). The epigraph and Jordan's story echo the Sapir-Whorf hypothesis that time is an effect of language and that, consequently, as Edward Sapir contended, the real world is to a large extent unconsciously built up on the language habits of the group.[69] His disciple, Benjamin Lee Whorf, tried to demonstrate the validity of Sapir's hypothesis by studying the language of the Hopi Indians of Arizona.[70] Although no longer tenable as a demonstration of linguistic determinism, this hypothesis rightly points to the decisive role of language in the burgeoning of consciousness, adding a linguistic perspective to Freud and Lacan's central notion that it is through the construction of verbal images that the contents of the unconscious become conscious.

The Hopi concept of time also points to Maureen Duffy's *The Microcosm* (1966), a novel that begins with an ironic anthropological account of an obscure and isolated social group, whose most interesting feature is 'that their language has no form of the verb to be nor any way of expressing past or future time. The philosophical concept of existence or being is quite beyond their grasp. Everything simply happens in an eternal present.'[71] As Anira Rowanchild has pointed out, '[t]he group is an analogy for the microcosmic world of the lesbian [. . . . living in] an era in which feminist energy is concentrated on personal survival, where "everything happens in an eternal present"'.[72]

The second paragraph in the epigraph of *Sexing the Cherry* points to the tenet of the New Physics that the traditional definition of matter as solid and indestructible is a myth, 'built on the fiction that the physical Universe consists of nothing but a collection of inert particles pulling and pushing each other like cogs in a deterministic machine'.[73] As early as 1905, Albert Einstein theorised that the conservation of energy is not distinct from the conservation of mass, and he demonstrated the existence of force without the interaction of bodies. His analysis of the strange behaviour of light and its constant speed led him to postulate the Theory of Relativity, summarised in the famous formula: $E=MC^2$. According to it, mass and energy are equal and all elementary particles consist of energy. However, Einstein also demonstrated that light energy can manifest itself in discreet units which he called quanta. This discovery led Werner Heisenberg to postulate his path-breaking 'indeterminacy principle' (1929), which states that pairs of quantities (for example, the position and momentum of a particle) are incompatible and cannot have precise values simultaneously, so that the more precisely one quantity is measured the less precise the other becomes. Einstein's equation of mass and energy and Heisenberg's demonstration that objective measurement is not possible transform the static image of the universe into a network of ever-changing interactions, where all activities in the cosmos are intimately and immediately connected with each other. Thus, the New Physicists provide striking scientific confirmation of the mythical belief in the unitary wholeness of the universe.[74]

Jordan tackles these ideas in an entry entitled 'The Nature of Time', where he distinguishes between chronological and mythical time; he points out the apparent paradox that the earth appears to be both flat and round; and underlines the coincidence between the religious (or mythical) outlook on the universe and the findings of the New Physics: 'Until now religion has described it better than science, but now physics and metaphysics appear to be saying the same thing' (SC 90). Jordan then describes Ucello's painting 'A Hunt in a Forest'. As he notes, this medieval painting, with its colourful riding hunters and fierce dogs in full chase progressively becoming smaller and smaller until they vanish in the distance, heralds 'the coming of perspective' (SC 92). The painting, then, may be said to provide an artistic equivalent for Heisenberg's indeterminacy principle and, as Jeanette Winterson has pointed out, for the way in which memory operates: 'Memory, I think, plays similar tricks with the eye. We try and see things clearly but find the foreground distractions too big and noisy. Then we discover that whatever is further away has already begun to merge with the trees and the night. The past cannot be recorded, it can only be retold.'[75]

In summary, Jordan and Winterson's comments on the painting, like the epigraph's double assertion that language determines the shape of reality and that matter is only empty space and points of light, may be said to provide the theoretical frame for the novel's structure, justifying the coexistence of 'real' and 'unreal' worlds and characters in what can be described as an ever-changing and fluid post-Newtonian multiverse existing in the space-time continuum, whose shape can only be provisionally and partially determined by each narrator's act of retelling. As Jordan puts it, parodying the opening of 'Burnt Norton': 'If all time is eternally present, there is no reason why we should not step out of one present into another' (SC 90).

Myth considers human beings as microscopic replicas of the macrocosm. In keeping with this, the uncanny coexistence of real and unreal worlds is reflected in the paradoxical characterisation of the Dog Woman and Jordan. While the young man has a perfectly normal physical appearance, his narration is wholly concerned with his travels to unreal cities and his relationship with fantastic characters. By contrast, the Dog Woman, who is a resilient materialist and has never travelled beyond London, is a fantastically huge giantess, who, like the awe-inspiring ogres in fairytales, has murdered or maimed thousands of men, including her own father (SC 107). The critics have compared her to Rabelais's Gargantua;[76] to Jaba the Hutt, the alien monster in

The Return of the Jedi; and to Fevvers, the bird-woman in Angela Carter's *Nights at the Circus*;[77] she has also been described as a grotesque reincarnation of Moll Flanders.[78] As I have pointed out elsewhere, she herself constantly alludes to her grotesque Swiftean parentage.[79] For instance, she refers to her body as 'the mountain of my flesh' (*SC* 14), thus echoing the name given by the Lilliputians to Gulliver: 'the Man-Mountain'.[80] And when a frustrated lover complains that she is too big for sex, she retorts, like Gulliver to the king of Brobdingnag,[81] that her bodily parts are 'all in proportion' to each other (*SC* 107). Her huge body and her ugly face with a flat nose, a few broken black teeth and skin covered with pock marks as big as caves where fleas live (*SC* 24) provoke in male onlookers the same misogynist nausea that Gulliver felt when, reduced to one twelfth of his normal size, he was allowed to watch the Brobdingnagian Maids of Honour in their nakedness.[82] Needless to say, all these features conform to Mikhail Bakhtin's description of the grotesque body characteristic of carnival imagery, as found in writers like Shakespeare, Cervantes, Diderot, Voltaire, Swift and Rabelais.

According to Bakhtin, grotesque imagery, with its emphasis on the life of the belly and the reproductive organs, symbolises contact with the earth. Symbolically, the earth has a paradoxical double nature: '[it] is an element that devours, swallows up (the grave, the womb) and at the same time is an element of birth, of renaissance (the maternal breasts)'.[83] The Dog Woman fully displays this paradoxical duality. Her love for Jordan and her mountainous shape clearly identify her with the earth, with its connotations of maternity, cyclical renewal and cosmic regeneration. And she herself describes her finding of Jordan as, literally, a present from Mother earth: 'When I found Jordan, [he was] so caked in mud I could have baked him like a hedgehog' (*SC* 14). Jordan loves his huge mother because she has the solidity of a rock and makes him feel secure and protected. Therefore, he is not afraid or revolted by her enormous ugly body. A similarly symbolic blindness seems to affect Jordan's protector, John Tradescant Jr, the royal gardener, who always treats her like a lady, provoking many a humorous episode, as when he gallantly tries to carry her bundle, 'which immediately flattened him to the ground' (*SC* 29). The Dog Woman shows a most benign and protective side towards them and towards her numerous female friends, including nuns, prostitutes and the wives of the Puritan men she loathes. Indeed, it is only with men, especially Puritans with a double standard of morality, that she displays the all-devouring and deadly facet of her Mother-earth personality. A clear case in point is the killing of Preacher Scroggs and Neighbour Fire-brace with an axe in a scene that parodies the orgies of the Marquis de Sade's libertines (*SC* 86–9). To this type of man, the Dog Woman appears to be, literally, a monster. Thus, her parson has forbidden her to enter the church on the contention that 'gargoyles must remain on the outside' (*SC* 14). And, on seeing her for the first time, the half-wit who kept the gate of the royal gardens tells Tradescant in utter discomfiture that the 'garden had been invaded by an evil spirit and her Hounds of Hell' (*SC* 29), thus comparing her, as Patricia Waugh acutely notes, 'to Milton's Sin with her brood of hungry dogs'.[84]

Sandra M. Gilbert and Susan Gubar have pointed out how the monstrosity of mythical female hybrids such as sirens, harpies and sphinxes is invariably located in the lower half of their bodies, thus symbolising men's fear of female sexuality and power.[85] Milton's description of Sin, Satan's incestuous daughter, leaves no doubt about where the monstrosity of the 'Snakie Sorceress' lies:

> The one seemed woman to the waist, and fair,
> But ended foul in many a scaly fold
> Voluminous and vast, a serpent armed
> With mortal sting: About her middle round
> A cry of Hell-hounds never-ceasing barked[86]

Similarly, the Dog Woman's monstrosity is located in her lower half and is associated with her sexual power. The day she lifts her skirts over her head to show the public that she is not hiding any weights, before competing with an elephant in a fair attraction, she provokes 'a great swooning amongst the crowd' since she is 'wearing no under-clothes in respect of the heat' (*SC* 25). On another occasion, when an exhibitionist asks her to put his member in her mouth 'as a delicious thing to eat', she does 'as he suggested, swallowing it entirely and biting it off with a snap' (*SC* 41). Further still, the only time she finds a man brave enough to attempt to have sex with her, she literally swallows him with her vagina, 'pull[ing] him in, balls and everything' (*SC* 106). These actions, as well as the fact that she sings as beautifully as a siren (*SC* 14) and sleeps on a bed made of watercress and the 2,000 teeth she has torn form the skulls of numberless Puritans she has murdered (*SC* 85), present the Dog Woman as the embodiment of Freud's *vagina dentata* and her counterpart, Joseph Campbell's 'phallic mother', the castrating mother of primitive male fears.[87]

Also in keeping with this all-devouring, womblike facet of her Mother-earth personality, the Dog Woman is constantly associated with dirt, excrements, waste, rottenness and death. She considers 'rotting a common experience' (*SC* 105), thinks nothing of helping to collect hundreds of corpses during the Plague of 1665, and when she finds that one of the deceased is a friend of hers, she carries her body on her shoulder to the bottom of the infernal pit where the corpses are being burned, on the simple reflection that it is an 'indignity to be tossed aside' (*SC* 140). When, in order to gain admittance to the king's trial, she has to disguise herself, she sits on a wheelbarrow 'like a heap of manure' (*SC* 68), and gains immediate access by telling the horrified soldier at the door that she cannot stand up, 'for I have the Clap and my flesh is rotting beneath me. If I were to stand up, sir, you would see a river of pus run across these flags' (*SC* 69). On hearing this, 'the soldier's lip twitch[es]' (*SC* 69) with nausea at the mere imagination of what her clothes hid.

According to Lacan, the male child, during the pre-Oedipal period, is in the 'imaginary', where he feels at one with the mother and has no sense of his own difference from her.[88] In order to mature, he has to enter the 'symbolic' order, which is the order of signs and social and cultural life brought about by the acquisition of language. For Lacan, therefore, the mother's natural realm is the imaginary, while the symbolic is ruled by the 'Law of the father', whose symbol of power is the 'phallus'. From this perspective, the fact that the Dog Woman and Jordan live on the bank of the Thames, in a muddy watery world inhabited only by hounds and a derelict witch, may be read as evidence that they live in the 'imaginary', well away from Puritan London/the symbolic order. As she herself explains, the only reason why she bit off the exhibitionist's member was simply that she agreed to follow his instructions literally: 'I like to broaden my mind when I can and I did as he suggested' (*SC* 41). Likewise, her decision to pluck out the teeth and eyes of every Puritan she came across was exclusively motivated by her desire to fulfil literally the instructions she had been given in a fiery sermon on 'the Law of Moses: "an eye for an eye and a tooth for a tooth"' (*SC* 84). From Lacan's perspective, the Dog Woman's colossal inability to under-stand the metaphors of patriarchy further enhances her position in the unsymbolised realm of the imaginary and confirms the epi-graph's assertion that language is the decisive battle ground for the transformation of the symbolic order. Added to her grotesque monstrosity, the Dog Woman's literalmindedness situates her in a strategic position to reshape patriarchy's false picture of the world, since it is only by transforming the metaphors of patriarchy that she can aspire to create a new symbolic order capable of responding to her own, more feminine and authentic picture of the world. In Mikhail Bakhtin's programmatic terms:

> It is necessary to destroy and rebuild the entire false picture of the world, to sunder the false hierarchical links between objects and ideas, to abolish the divisive ideational strata. It is necessary to liberate all these objects and permit them to enter into the free unions that are organic to them, no matter how monstrous these unions might seem from the point of view of ordinary, traditional associations.[89]

If from Lacan and Campbell's point of view the Dog Woman is a phallic mother, the deadly usurper of the male phallus, and from Bakhtin's perspective she is the carnivalesque, subversive agent of social transformation and renewal, from the perspective of Julia Kristeva's reading of Lacan, she becomes a figure of 'abjection'.[90] According to Kristeva, 'abjection' is the horror-provoking mechanism used in patriarchal societies as a means of separating the human from the non-human and the fully constituted subject from the partially formed subject. Consequently, one of the key figures of abjection in patriarchy is the mother, who becomes a figure of abjection during the Oedipal phase, at that moment when the child, struggling to become a separate subject, rejects her for the father who represents the symbolic order. In order to prevent the child from succumbing to the temptation of remaining locked in the blissful relationship with its mother, patriarchal religions have developed complex rituals of defilement that belong to two basic types: excremental (or external) and menstrual (or internal).[91] From this perspective, the mother's teaching of the child to control its body and to distinguish the clean and unclean areas of it – what Kristeva calls the 'primal mapping of the body' – represents the child's first experience of 'maternal authority', which is prior to and different from the 'paternal law' characteristic of the symbolic.

As Barbara Creed has pointed out, while the acquisition of 'paternal law' involves immersion in a 'totally different universe of socially signifying performances where embarrassment, shame, guilt, desire, etc. come into play', the earlier phase of 'maternal authority' is characterised by the 'exercise of "authority" without guilt, at a time when there is a "fusion between mother and nature"'.[92] Therefore, images of blood, vomit, pus, faeces, etc., which are central to our culturally or socially constructed notions of the horrific, provoke a double reaction that reflects the split between the two orders: the maternal authority and the law of the father.

> On the one hand, these images of bodily wastes threaten a subject that is already constituted, in relation to the symbolic, as 'whole and proper.' Consequently, they fill the subject – both the protagonist in the text and the spectator in the cinema – with disgust and loathing. On the other hand, they also point back to a time when a 'fusion between mother and nature' existed; when bodily wastes, while set apart from the body, were not seen as objects of embarrassment and shame.[93]

With this distinction in mind it is easy to see why Jordan, Tradescant and the Dog Woman's female friends are not at all revolted or fright-ened by her and even yearn to be like her, as happens to Jordan, who, conscious of his bodily limitations, imagines the possibility of using the new technique of grafting for himself in order to 'become some-one else in time, grafted on to something better and stronger' (*SC* 87). Indeed, as we have seen, only the men who feel their phallogocentric symbolic order threatened find the Dog Woman monstrous, like the parson, the Dog Woman's father, who wanted to sell her as a freak in a travelling fair (*SC* 107), or Puritans like Preacher Scroggs and Neighbour Firebrace (*SC* 63), who are seized not only by disgust and loathing but by sheer horror at the sight of her.

Still, as Julia Kristeva further notes, the relationship between mother and son in the natural realm of the 'maternal feminine' is problematic because, while the child tries to break free from her, the mother feels the contrary urge to retain him as a way to authenticate her existence. Their separation, therefore, 'is a violent, clumsy break-ing away, with the constant risk of falling back under the sway of a power as securing as it is stifling. The difficulty the mother has in acknowledging (or being acknowledged by) the symbolic realm – in other words, the problem she has with the phallus that her father or husband stands for – is not such as to help the future subject leave the natural mansion.'[94] However, the Dog Woman's relationship with Jordan lacks the possessiveness of Kristeva's abject mother, as she makes clear when she observes that she had decided to call the foundling baby 'Jordan' because she wanted him to have 'a river name, a name not bound to anything, just as the waters aren't bound to anything' (SC 11). Further, when he grows old enough to undertake long journeys to remote lands, she never complains about his frequent absences, although she sorely misses him. Jordan, who is still very fond of his mother, resents the freedom she grants him, significantly mistaking it for indifference: 'We never discussed whether or not I would go; she took it for granted, almost as though she had expected it. I wanted her to ask me to stay' (SC 101).

After Tradescant takes Jordan under his protection, the young man is given the opportunity to undertake many a transatlantic voyage in search of exotic plants and fruits. However, he is not satisfied, as he is in fact painfully aware of his own shortcomings and incompleteness by comparison to his mother: 'I want to be like my rip-roaring mother who cares nothing for how she looks, only for what she does. She has never been in love, no, and never wanted to be either. She is self-sufficient and without self-doubt' (SC 101). While for the Puritans the Dog Woman is the monstrous embodiment of the phallic mother, Jordan's admiring remark points to her symbolic role of Lacanian *je-idéal*, the substitute father figure with whom Jordan identifies during his 'mirror stage' phase. In keeping with this reading, Jordan presents himself as a purblind hero at the beginning of his self-quest.

As Jordan points out, during his sea voyages to remote lands he meticulously kept 'the log book'. But side by side with it, he has also 'written down my own journey and drawn my own map' (SC 102). This private book was not meant to record 'the truth as you will find it in diaries and maps and log-books' but rather the things 'I might have made, or perhaps did make in some other place or time'. It is a book dealing with 'the hidden life' and written 'with invisible ink' between the lines of Jordan's ordinary travel book (SC 10). The distinction between 'factual' and 'hidden' books and journeys echoes the difference between Henri's war journal and the therapeutic writing of his 'secret story' in the madhouse, while Jordan's contention that the book of his secret life requires invisible ink brings to mind Virginia Woolf's comment in *A Room of One's Own* that the reader of a good novel can always detect if the writer is telling the truth, by holding

every phrase, every scene to the light as one reads – for Nature seems very oddly, to have provided us with an inner light by which to judge of the novelists' integrity or disintegrity. Or perhaps it is rather that Nature, in her most irrational mood, has traced in invisible ink on the walls of the mind a premonition which these great artists confirm; a

sketch which only needs to be held to the fire of genius to become
visible. When one so exposes it and sees it come to life one exclaims in
rapture, But this is what I have always felt and known and desired![95]

In the light of Virginia Woolf's contention that the writer's integrity is
invisibly imprinted in the work, Jordan's apparently irrelevant remark
becomes a paradoxical assertion of the truthtelling capacity of his
imaginary journey, comparable to Henri's refrain, 'I'm telling you
stories. Trust me.' Once this is realised, it is easy to see that, at the
beginning of the novel, Jordan finds himself in the situation Henri
was in in *The Passion* when he decided to tell the reader the 'secret
story' of his life as the therapeutic activity that would allow him to
round off his maturation process.

Comparing his secret book to the invisible letters written by the
ancient Greeks, Jordan says that they were 'written in milk' (*SC* 10).
This remark adds crucial insight into the type of individuation
process he is initiating, since it points to Jordan's invisible book as an
example of *écriture féminine*, the type of writing written with *langue-
lait*, the 'white ink' of 'mother's milk' that Hélène Cixous proposes as
an alternative to the 'phallogocentric' writing of patriarchy, carried
out, as she contends, with a pen/penis.[96] As becomes evident at the
end of the novel, Jordan's individuation process involves his understanding of the constructedness of binary oppositions like father/
mother; man/woman; culture/nature; head/heart and the eventual
revelation of his bisexuality.[97]

Unlike Henri, who devotes a lot of space to narrating the physical
stages of his quest, Jordan is mainly concerned with its 'invisible' side
– that is, with Jung's '*Innenwelt* phase' of the quest. In this sense,
Jordan is, literally, a 'Mental Traveller' in Blake's understanding of
the term. With loving accuracy, the Dog Woman records the first time
her son undertook a mental journey. He was only three years old
when she took him to see the first banana that had arrived in London.
Suddenly, she saw Jordan standing stock still and staring at it. Putting
her head next to his, the Dog Woman looked where he looked and saw
'deep blue waters against a pale shore and trees whose branches sang
with green and birds in fairground colours and an old man in a loin-
cloth' (*SC* 13). Describing his decision to record his hidden life, Jordan
says that he had 'resolved to set a watch on myself like a jealous father,
trying to catch myself disappearing through a door just noticed in the
wall' (*SC* 10). By lowering her head to the level of Jordan's head and
following the child's ecstatic gaze, the Dog Woman manages to share

with Jordan the precise moment when the door in the wall of Jordan's mind opens, granting him access to the beautiful (and imaginary) world behind it.

The way in which the Dog Woman manages to share the child's vision is strikingly reminiscent of the way in which the narrator found 'the aleph' in the corner of a dark cellar by gazing at a precise point in Jorge Luis Borges' tale.[98] At the same time, Jordan's description of his visionary experience as a door opening in the wall echoes Bernard's description of a similar occurrence in *The Waves*, when the beauty of a phrase in a poem he had just created makes him feel that 'a hole had been knocked in my mind, one of those sudden transparencies through which one sees everything'.[99] Rhoda, another character in *The Waves*, describes similar experiences in the same terms. For example, after reaching a state of harmony with her friends, she is filled by the 'still mood, the disembodied mood' and experiences a 'momentary alleviation [. . . .] when the walls of the mind become transparent' and 'nothing is unabsorbed'.[100] Of the seven characters in *The Waves*, Rhoda is by far the 'lightest' in both the physical and the spiritual sense of the word. When she goes to bed, she stretches her 'toes so that they touch the rail at the end of the bed' to assure herself of 'something hard'.[101] And when, for all this stretching and touching of hard matter, she finds herself suspended above her bed, she is no longer afraid of being 'knocked against and damaged', for it is at these moments that she can set sail to her imaginary ships: 'Out of me now my mind can pour. I can think of my Armadas sailing on the high waves. I am relieved of hard contacts and collisions. I sail on alone under white cliffs.'[102] Sailing imaginary Armadas is precisely what Jordan used to do as a little boy when he played with his toy boat (*SC* 23) and what he continues to do in his imaginary journeys as a young man. In contrast to Rhoda's 'lightness', Louis, the banker, is charac- terised by an extraordinary 'heaviness', an unflinching dedication to carrying 'the weight of the world [on his] shoulders'.[103] Thus, his aim in life is to 'drop heavy as a hatchet and cut the oak with my sheer weight'.[104]

Louis's 'heaviness' prefigures that of the Dog Woman, just as Rhoda's 'lightness' prefigures that of Jordan. But the theoretical con- text for this opposition is provided by Milan Kundera in *The Unbear- able Lightness of Being*. As Kundera explains in Part One, entitled 'Lightness and Weight', this opposition goes back to Parmenides's division of the world into pairs of opposites of the type 'light/darkness, fineness/coarseness, warmth/cold, being/non-being'.[105] For Parmenides lightness was positive, weight negative. As Kundera further explains, Nietzsche, who also had a negative outlook on weight, considered 'the idea of eternal return the heaviest of burdens (*das schwerste Gewicht*)'. Therefore, from Nietzsche's perspective, '[i]f every second of our lives recurs an infinite number of times, we are nailed to eternity as Jesus Christ was nailed to the cross. It is a terrible prospect. In the world of eternal return the weight of unbearable responsibility lies heavy on every move we make'.[106] However, Kundera himself is not at all sure that lightness is preferable to weight, since:

> the myth of eternal return states that a life which disappears once and for all, which does not return, is like a shadow, without weight, dead in advance, and whether it was horrible, beautiful, or sublime, its horror, sublimity, and beauty mean nothing [. . .]. There is an infinite difference between a Robespierre who occurs only once in history and a Robespierre who eternally returns, chopping off French heads.[107]

Thus, while for Virginia Woolf lightness and weight simply symbolise utterly opposed attitudes to life, for Milan Kundera these attitudes are seen as an effect of the individual's historical or mythical outlook on it. As in *The Waves*, in *Sexing the Cherry* the characters' lightness or heaviness symbolises their particular attitude to life, with the difference that in Winterson's novel this attitude is specifically associated with desire or its lack.[108] At the same time, Kundera's definition of lightness as the unbearable consciousness of the futility of human life deprived of the possibility of transcendence may be said to provide the ideological justification for Winterson's advocacy of myth in her work in general.

Jordan learns the difference between lightness and heaviness in one of the unreal cities he visits. This is the city where Zillah lives. Zillah is a 'young girl caught incestuously with her sister [who had been] condemned to build her own death tower' (*SC* 38). Zillah's dreadful story parodies the fairytale of Rapunzel, the golden-haired girl kept in a tower by an evil witch, who was rescued by a valiant prince. Unlike the prince, Jordan abandons Zillah to her fate, leaping out of the tower in panic when he realises that she is a living corpse. It is then that he learns that Zillah's story of impossible lesbian love had divided the inhabitants of the city into two 'schools' of thought. 'The school of heaviness, who would tie down love, [contended] that those driven by desire, the lightest of things, suffer under weights they cannot bear'.

By contrast, the school of lightness 'believed that only passion freed the soul from its mud-hut' (SC 38–9, 38). A similar difference exists between the Dog Woman's and Jordan's attitudes to love. Although the Dog Woman says that in 'the dark and in the water I weigh nothing at all' and admits that she 'would enjoy the consolation of a lover's face' (SC 40), she rejects a job as prostitute for fear of falling in love: 'Surely such to-ing and fro-ing as must go on night and day weakens the heart and inclines it to love?' (SC 40). Indeed, her only fear is not that Jordan might be bodily injured in the course of his journeys, but that he might lose 'his heart. His heart' (SC 41), knowing as she does that 'he has not my common sense and will no doubt follow his dreams to the end of the world and then fall straight off' (SC 40). If Jordan is to mature, then, he will have to overcome his feeling of incompleteness, symbolised by his obsessive search for Fortunata, and acquire his mother's self-sufficiency and wholeness.

At the beginning of his narration, Jordan says that, although he has seen the 'shining water and the size of the world' again and again, in his imagination he always returns to the same place: 'To escape the weight of the world, I leave my body where it is, in conversation or at dinner, and walk through a series of winding streets to a house standing back from the road' (SC 17). These labyrinthine streets and house are in 'the city of words' (SC 20), an uncanny city where, once uttered, 'words resist erasure' (SC 17) and have to be brushed away by a host of cleaners, lest they go on for ever producing the effect for which they were uttered. The transformation of verbal utterances into solid artefacts may be read as a parodic literalisation of the Sapir-Whorf hypothesis that language determines reality, while the winding structure of the streets points to 'the city of words' as a projection of Jordan's unconscious – or rather, as the materialisation of the words suggests, of the specific area in Jordan's mind where the unconscious becomes conscious.[109] The house that Jordan recurrently visits in the city of words is an ancient house inhabited by a family 'dedicated to a strange custom. Not one of them would allow their feet to touch the floor' (SC 20). Consequently, the house has 'not floors, but bottomless pits' and the furniture 'is suspended on racks from the ceiling' (SC 20). In the course of time, the inhabitants added more and more storeys to the original house, making the ceiling of one room into the floor of another, so that 'their house never ends and they must travel by winch or rope from room to room, calling to one another as they go' (SC 21). It is in this ethereal Babel Tower-like house that Jordan has a first glimpse of Fortunata, the youngest and 'lightest' of the Twelve Dancing Princesses in the Grimm brothers' fairytale, as she is 'climbing down her window on a thin rope which she cut and re-knotted a number of times during the descent' (SC 21).[110] Astonished and delighted by her indifference to the laws of gravity, Jordan is consumed from this day on by the desire to find her. In his determination to 'comb the city for the dancer', Jordan visits all types of public places until he finds a 'pen of prostitutes kept by a rich man for his friends' (SC 30). The women allow Jordan to stay with them, provided that he assumes a female disguise so as to pass undetected. In this privileged position, the young man learns that, although each of their doors have 'thirteen locks', the prostitutes come and go as they please and are in fact constantly changing places with the nuns in the nearby Convent of the Holy Mother (SC 30). Thus, what Jordan thought to be an unendurable situation, comparable to that of Bluebeard's wives locked in the castle, gives way to the exhilarated realisation that the women are giving their owner the slip and living their own lives. He also discovers that they communicate 'without words' (SC 30), or in their own 'private language. A language not dependent on the construction of men' (SC 31). In the light of Lacan's tenet that entrance into the symbolic order is negotiated through the acquisition of language, there is no doubt that this language without words is what he calls *lalangue*, the feminine language or 'mothertongue' used by women in the unsymbolised realm of the imaginary (Kristeva's 'semiotic'), which Jordan has to master if he is to write his invisible book with white ink.

The development of Jordan's female facet comes to a climax when he is given a copy of the 'rule book' with the instructions on how to deal with men. After reading it Jordan admits that what the women say about men, although ludicrously essentialist, is true. This revelation so depresses him that 'my heaviness was at its limit and I could not raise myself up from where I was sitting' (SC 33). He finds that the way to recover his lightness is to wave a red mullet over his head in order to draw the attention of some sea birds, who, eagerly seizing at the bait, succeed in carrying him 'over the city and out to sea' (SC 33). This scene is intertextually indebted both to the episode that closes Gulliver's voyage to Brobdingnag, when an eagle seizes the box he is locked in and lets it fall into the sea,[111] and to the episode in which, after falling asleep, Chaucer is carried by an eagle to the House of Fame.[112] In the hypotexts as well as in the hypertext, the

birds' intervention is meant to help the protagonists cross the boundary between two different worlds. In Jordan's case, the birds take
him from Zillah's city to the dwelling place of eleven of the Twelve
Dancing Princesses. As he later learns from Fortunata, the princesses
used to fly through the window every night to dance in a silver city,
which, 'being freed from the laws of gravity' circled above the earth at
leisure (*SC* 97), so that 'the city itself danced' (*SC* 95).[113] Their angry
father put an end to this practice by forcing them to marry the eleven
brothers of the prince who had discovered the well-kept secret of
their worn-out dancing shoes. Like the story of Zillah, the princesses'
stories are parodic versions of well-known literary texts. Thus, as
Elizabeth Langland has pointed out, the narration of the second
princess begins with the words, '"That's my last husband painted on
the wall . . . looking as though he were alive," explicitly evoking
Browning's Duke, the speaker of "My Last Duchess"'. Likewise, the
narration of the third princess, beginning 'He walked in beauty', parodies Byron.[114] In keeping with Winterson's revisionary intent, the
princesses' married lives are utterly unsuccessful, frustrating or
dreadful, with the sole exception of the princesses whose husbands
turned out to be, respectively, a mermaid (*SC* 47) and a woman (*SC*
54).[115]

Jordan leaves the gruesome literary world of the Dancing
Princesses when he is told that Fortunata, the only one who did not
marry, is not with them. At this stage, the young man has already
intuited that the eerie dancer he is looking for might not be a different person, but his own anima, the projection of his soul or spirit:
'Was I searching for a dancer whose name I did not know or was I
searching for the dancing part of myself?' (*SC* 40). When he eventually finds her in her intangible and atemporal dancing school, Fortunata is teaching her pupils to conquer time and space, literally
transforming their material bodies into 'empty space and points of
light' by making them spin around in a dance that strikingly resembles the Celtic ritual dances in honour of the White Goddess, or the
round dance of Sufi dervishes, in which the dancers spin ever faster
and faster with their arms upraised and their long, white skirts
spiralling around their waists like the rings of a planet, until they look
like a perfectly attuned and immobile constellation of stars:

> She asks them to meditate on a five-pointed star in the belly and to watch the
> points push outwards, the fifth point into the head. She spins them, impaled
> with light, arms upraised [. . .] until all features are blurred, until the human

*being most resembles a freed spirit from a darkened jar. [. . .] And at a single
moment, when all are spinning in harmony down the long hall, she hears
music escaping from their heads and backs and livers and spleens. Each has
a tone like cut glass. The noise is deafening. And it is then that the spinning
seems to stop, that the wild gyration of the dancers passes from movement into
infinity.* (SC 72, original italics)

Jordan's later description of his first impression of Fortunata as 'a
young woman, darting in a figure of eight' (SC 93) leaves no doubt
that she is performing a cosmic dance, capable of arresting time and
transforming herself and her pupils into a constellation of 'star men'
or *Anthropoi*, attuned to the music of the spheres. Thus Fortunata
situates herself in the position of the dancer in W. B. Yeats's poem
'The Double Vision of Michael Robartes'. This young girl 'had danced
her life away [. . . .] So she had outdanced thought. / Body perfection
brought, / [until] Mind moved yet seemed to stop / As 'twere a spinning top'.[116] Situated between 'A Sphinx' and 'A Buddha' (II. ll. 2, 3) –
that is, between chaos and cosmos, hell and heaven – the dancer's
wild gyrations open a chink in the door separating the physical from
the metaphysical world:

> In contemplation had those three so wrought
> Upon a moment, and so stretched it out
> That they, time overthrown,
> Were dead yet flesh and bone. (II. ll. 29–32)

In other words, through their dance Yeats's dancer and Fortunata
have reached what T. S. Eliot called in 'Burnt Norton' 'the still point':

> At the still point of the turning world. Neither flesh nor fleshless;
> Neither from nor towards; at the still point, there the dance is,
> But neither arrest nor movement. And do not call it fixity,
> Where past and present are gathered.[117]

Reaching the still point brings about 'release from action and suffering, release from the inner / And the outer compulsion, yet surrounded / By a grace of sense, a white light still and moving [. . . .]
both a new world / And the old made explicit, understood / In the
completion of its partial ecstasy, / The resolution of its partial
horror'.[118] It is a moment of illumination and wholeness, when the
barriers between self and world collapse and the human being is
absorbed into the divine. In this sense, the dancers' state is comparable to the alchemical process of 'exaltation' that culminates the

making of the Philosopher's Stone. As Richard Cavendish has
pointed out, this 'is achieved through an emotional and spiritual
frenzy, which rises to a peak of ecstasy when the magician is flung out
beyond the bounds of his own being into communion with all
things'.[119]

After this tantalising experience, Jordan 'stayed with Fortunata for
one month, learning more about her ways and something about my
own' (SC 99). During his stay, he realises for the first time that the
numerous affairs with women he had entangled himself in in the past
'had nothing to recommend them' and that what he believed to be
love was self-infatuation, 'seeing only that I loved myself through
them' (SC 73, 74). Fortunata tells Jordan that, like him, she had lived
for years 'in hope of being rescued; of belonging to someone else, of
dancing together. And then she had learned to dance alone, for its
own sake and for hers' (SC 99). This lesson in self-esteem and autonomy is the same lesson the Dog Woman had tried to teach Jordan but
failed because, as he now realises, he was then lost 'in the gap
between my ideal of myself and my pounding heart' (SC 101). Only
when his dream of Fortunata becomes an actuality Jordan comprehends that 'very rarely is the beloved more than a shaping spirit for
the lover's dreams. And perhaps such a thing is enough. To be a muse
may be enough' (SC 75).

Jordan's yearning for lightness materialised in his finding 'the city
of words'. Now his understanding of the dangers of passion brings
about his finding of the city where love was a plague that had wiped
out the whole population 'three times in a row' (SC 75). Escaping
from this world of uncontrollable passion, Jordan eventually rejoins
Tradescant's ship and they continue the journey to the Bermudas in
search of exotic seeds and fruits, before returning to England (SC 78).
Their hope is to make a success with the technique of grafting and
sexing fruit trees, recently made fashionable by the French. As Jordan
explains, '[g]rafting is the means whereby a plant, perhaps tender or
uncertain, is fused into a hardier member of its strain, and so the two
take advantage of each other and produce a third kind, without seed
or parent' (SC 78).

According to Elizabeth Langland, Sexing the Cherry is 'a parodic
rewriting of Andrew Marvell's "The Mower, Against Gardens" in
particular and the heroic tradition in general'.[120] As she explains,
'[t]he subtitle of Marvell's poem expresses his speaker's opposition to
altering what is most "plain and pure" in nature',[121] first, through

enclosing natural spaces; secondly, by importing new species and varieties of plants; and thirdly, through the creation of 'Forbidden mixtures', which produce 'uncertain and adulterate fruit'.[122] Thus, the gardener's

> green seraglio has its eunuchs too,
> Lest any tyrant him outdo;
> And in the cherry he does Nature vex,
> To procreate without a sex.[123]

Langland's conclusion is that, in the light of Marvell's poem, grafting provides Winterson as well as Jordan with 'one of the central means to escape the tired binarism of reproduction'.[124] However, the fruit symbolism in the novel is more complex than this, since it involves not only cherries but also bananas and pineapples. The first banana was imported from the island of Bermuda when Jordan was a little child (*SC* 12). The Dog Woman makes its symbolic meaning explicit when she says that it 'resembled nothing more than the private parts of an Oriental' (*SC* 12). Thus, in keeping with her condition of phallic mother, the chapters narrated by the Dog Woman are preceded by the drawing of a banana. As we have seen, Jordan describes his quest for individuation as a process of feminisation. However, his chapters are preceded by the drawing not of a cherry (a common euphemism for clitoris), but of a pineapple. Like the banana, the pineapple is an exotic fruit, which, significantly, was brought to England by Jordan himself from the island of Barbados (*SC* 104). As I have pointed out elsewhere, this journey echoes another poem by Andrew Marvell, 'Bermudas' (1624).[125] In it, a providential God leads a group of disoriented seafarers to an exotic island, where besides oranges, pomegranates and melons, they find 'apple plants [i.e. pineapples] of such a price / No tree could ever bear them twice'.[126] These lines, expressing the belief that the pineapple can only grow once, effectively undermines Marvell's moral scruple about grafting, for if the pineapple can only grow once, it exists in nature independently of the laws of reproduction. Thus, as a fruit growing 'in Paradise' (*SC* 12), the pineapple justifies the existence of the Dog Woman, who is a mother as well as a virgin and possesses the male/female duality of the phallic mother. In other words, the existence of the pineapple proves the artificiality of the binary opposition male/female, exposing it as a linguistic construction. In *Le Corps lesbien*, Monique Wittig contended that the only way in which women

can undo this opposition is by doing violence to the language of patriarchy. Hence, she italicised and slashed the first-person pronoun (j/e)
to indicate the disruptive force of women's entry into language.[127]
From this perspective, the fact that the chapters narrated by the ecologist and Nicolas Jordan are, respectively, a banana and a pineapple
sliced into two halves acquires a similar symbolic meaning, suggesting a breach in the late twentieth-century discourse of patriarchy that
was absent from seventeenth-century Puritan discourse.

During his stay with her, Fortunata tells Jordan the mythical story
of Artemis and Orion.[128] Artemis was a Greek goddess who 'didn't
want to get married, she didn't want to have children. She wanted to
hunt' even though 'she knew about the heroes and the home-makers.
The great division that made life possible' (SC 131). When Orion
invaded her territory, ate her goat and raped her, Artemis killed him
with a scorpion (SC 132). Clearly, Artemis is a mythical counterpart of
the Dog Woman, since they are both females who refuse to accept the
role prescribed for them by patriarchy and defend the liberty to
choose their way of life to the point of murder. However, there is a
crucial difference between them. The Dog Woman (like Villanelle,
with her webbed feet) is a hybrid whose entity combines diverse and
contradictory essences, like werewolves (dog-woman) or sirens and
bearded ladies (phallic mother). By contrast, Artemis has a perfectly
normal female figure and, like Jordan, is immersed in her individuation process. Describing her eventual understanding of her own true
self, Fortunata compares it to the alchemists' finding of the Philosopher's Stone: 'The alchemists have a saying, "*Tertium non data*
[*sic*]": the third is not given. That is, the transformation from one element to another, from waste matter into best gold, is a process that
cannot be documented' (SC 131). Jeffrey Roessner interprets these
words as evidence of 'the novel's celebration of irrationality' in opposition to the binary logic of science.[129] However, it should not be forgotten that the search for the Philosopher's Stone is both a physical
and a spiritual activity and that the alchemists' dictum points both to
a mysterious element in the physical refinement of base metal into
gold, as Roessner seems to imply, and to the fact that the spiritual
absorption of man into the divine, which is the ultimate aim of
alchemical research, involves a metamorphosis – that is, an essential
transformation 'from an entity that is one thing to an entity that is
another'.[130] As Bynum explains, although hybrids 'shake our assumptions about the boundaries between the sexes and between species

[. . . . n]onetheless hybrid and metamorphosis reveal or violate cate-gories in different ways. Hybrid reveals a world of difference, a world that *is* and is multiple [. . .]. Metamorphosis breaks down categories by *breaching* them'.[131] Thus, the sense of identity gained by Artemis at the end of her quest offers Jordan an example not so much of the type of sexual hybridity or androgyny represented by his mother, but of Hélène Cixous's more fluid and nuanced concept of bisexuality, understood not principally as a form of sexuality, but as an embodied recognition of plurality and the coexistence of masculinity and femi-ninity within individual subjects.[132]

Jordan alludes to this when, imagining the possibility of becoming 'someone else in time, grafted on to something better and stronger' (*SC* 87), he unwittily echoes Ariel's description of Alonso's 'sea change / Into something rich and strange' in *The Tempest*.[133] Like Alonso's sea change, Artemis's essential transformation is more mys-terious and complex than the hybrid mixing (or grafting) of male and female components and, as Fortunata explains to Jordan, can only be achieved by honest confrontation with the true self: 'What would it matter if she [Artemis] crossed the world and hunted down every living creature so long as her separate selves eluded her? In the end when no one was left she would have to confront herself' (*SC* 131). A similar revelation situates Jordan at the end of his hero's quest:

> When I left England I thought I was running away from uncertainty and confusion but most of all running away from myself. I thought I might become someone else in time, grafted on to something better and stronger. *And then I saw that the running away was a running towards.* An effort to catch up with *my fleet-footed self*, living another life in a different way. (*SC* 80, emphasis added)

Jordan's climactic realisation that in order to mature he cannot simply 'graft' himself on to 'something better and stronger' signals the end of his mirror-stage infatuation with his mother. After this, he is able to distinguish between himself and his ideal I: 'I'm not look-ing for God, only for myself' (*SC* 102); as well as between his spirit or anima (Fortunata), and 'the ego [. . .], the hollow, screaming cadaver that has no spirit within it' (*SC* 103). As he further reflects: 'I think that cadaver is only the ideal self run mad, and if the other life, the secret life, could be found and brought home, then a person might live in peace and have no need of God. After all, He has no need for us being complete' (*SC* 103). As his identification with 'fleet-footed'

Achilles suggests, Jordan's true self has the sexual ambiguity of the mythical hero signalled by Hélène Cixous as a pointed example of the 'other bisexuality' she postulates.[134] At this point, Jordan may be said to have reached the position of the quester at the end of *Four Quartets*:

> We shall not cease from exploration
> And the end of all our exploring
> Will be to arrive where we started
> And know the place for the first time.[135]

In clear allusion to these words, Jordan's narration begins: 'MY NAME IS Jordan. This is the first thing I saw' (*SC* 9).[136] Then he tells an episode in which he found himself walking in heavy fog, feeling bitterly cold and disoriented and trying 'to find the path' he had lost: 'I began to walk with my hands stretched out in front of me, as do those troubled in sleep, and in this way for the first time, I traced the lineaments of my own face opposite me' (*SC* 9). The Dog Woman recounts the same episode in the last chapter of her narration, situating it on 2 September 1666, the day of the outbreak of the Great Fire of London. She explains how she was waiting for Jordan to go on board ship with her and how, when he was coming through London Fields at midnight, he was covered by the fog: 'he had fallen and banged his head. He came to, and feeling his way, arms outstretched he had suddenly touched another face and screamed out. For a second the fog cleared and he saw that the stranger was himself' (*SC* 143). Jordan's thought at this climactic moment – 'Perhaps I am to die [. . . .] Or perhaps I am to live, to be complete as [Fortunata] said I would be' (*SC* 143) – , with its symbolism of death and rebirth, leaves no doubt that he has finally brought about the metamorphic unification of his fragmented self. This interpretation is enhanced by the fact that the episode both opens and closes the novel, thus suggesting a circularity that is in keeping with the mythical structure both of Jordan's quest and of the novel as a whole.

Yeats believed that the human mind, whether expressed in history or in the individual life, has a precise movement, which can be quickened or slackened but cannot be fundamentally altered. As he explained in *A Vision*, this movement can be expressed by a mathematical form, the gyre.[137] The gyre starts at its origin and moves progressively wider in a spiral, while time adds another dimension, creating the form of a vortex or funnel. Once the gyre reaches its point of maximum expansion it then begins to narrow until it reaches its endpoint, which is also the origin of the new gyre. Another way of seeing the same thing, if time is not taken as being fixed in one direction, is that once the maximum is reached, the gyre begins to retrace its path in the opposite direction. The spiralling figure cast by Fortunata and the dancer in 'The Double Vision of Michael Robartes' symbolises this movement, which is compared by Jordan to the number eight, the symbol of the infinite. Jordan's 'secret' journey also takes this form, since it is both circular and intertwined with his physical journeys to remote lands. As he himself puts it, '[t]he journey is not linear, it is always back and forth' (SC 80). The alternation and merging of the seventeenth- and twentieth-century narrative voices in the last section suggests a similar spiralling structure for the historical events that frame Jordan's and the other characters' stories. Likewise, the fact that Jordan's individuation process ends on the day of the outbreak of the Great Fire of London suggests a complementarity between the individual and the historical facts that is wholly in keeping with the mythical conception of human beings as microscopic replicas of the macrocosm.

As Mircea Eliade points out in *The Myth of the Eternal Return*, in order to avoid the irreversibility of history – what Milan Kundera calls the unbearable lightness of being – archaic humanity conceived the passing of time as the cyclical repetition of God's original act of creation of the cosmos. Thus, the New Year, signalling the beginning of a new cosmogony, permitted the return of the dead to life and maintained the hope of the faithful in the resurrection of the body, while the end of the year amounted to a veritable end of the world.[138] Therefore, from a mythical perspective, the Great Fire of London becomes an apocalyptic fire signalling the end of the historical cycle initiated by the Puritan revolution. Similarly, the end of the next historical cycle is marked by the apocalyptic burning of the factory by Nicolas Jordan and the ecologist in the late twentieth century (SC 142). The two characters' active participation in this event, like the Dog Woman's 'act of pouring a vat of oil on to the flames' to 'encourage' the Great Fire of 1666 (SC 143), enhances the complementarity and reversibility of the individual lives and the historical events, caught as they are in a similarly recurrent pattern of reincarnations and cyclical repetition. As Jordan points out in his closing remarks, the only way out of this predetermined and cyclical life in time lies in the comprehension that the 'future and the present and the past exist only in our minds' and that 'even the most solid of things and the most real, the best-loved and the well-known, are only hand-shadows on the wall. Empty space and points of light' (*SC* 144). Thus, like the narrators in the earlier fictions, Jordan points to the individual imagination as the alchemical laboratory where he may transcend the limitations of human life and achieve his essential transmutation from man to (specifically bisexual) *Anthropos*.

Notes

1 'The Jeanette Winterson Column', *Guardian* (9 June 2003). www.jeanettewinterson.com/pages/content/index.asp?PageID=121. Consulted on 15 August 2003.

2 Anne Duchêne, 'After Marengo: Jeanette Winterson's *The Passion*', *Times Literary Supplement* (26 June 1987): 697.

3 Lodge, 'Outrageous Things', 26.

4 Mercedes Monmany, 'Pasión y muerte de Napoleón', *Insula* 511 (July 1989): 19–20; 20.

5 Matthew Gilbert, 'Illuminating the Human Condition', *Boston Globe* (15 June 1988): 79.

6 Tamás Bényei, 'Risking the Text: Stories of Love in Jeanette Winterson's *The Passion*', *Hungarian Journal of English and American Studies* 3.2 (1997): 199–209; 199.

7 *Ibid.*, 199.

8 *Ibid.*, 199.

9 See Scott Wilson, 'Passion at the End of History,' in Grice and Woods (eds), *'I'm telling you stories,'* 61–74.

10 Hayden White, *Metahistory: The Historical Imagination in Nineteenth-Century Europe*. Baltimore and London: Johns Hopkins University Press, (1985) [1973]: 1.

11 Hutcheon, *A Poetics of Postmodernism*.

12 The identification of Henri with Jason is made explicit when, after murdering the cook, he returns to Villanelle's family home distraught and soaked and is wrapped 'in a fleece and put [. . .] to sleep by the stove' (*P* 136).

13 As Jean-Michel Ganteau suggests, this refrain reworks Virginia Woolf's comment that *Orlando* is 'truthful, but fantastic'. Jean-Michel Ganteau, 'Fantastic, but Truthful: The Ethics of Romance', *Cambridge Quarterly* 32.3 (2003): 225–38; 238. In the introduction to the script of *Oranges*, Jeanette Winterson explains its meaning with reference to the 'Deuteronomy' chapter of *Oranges*, as pointing to 'at least two definitions of reality', the reality of history and that of storytelling (*OS* viii).

14 'We went to his room and he was a man who liked his women face down, arms outstretched like the crucified Christ' (*P* 70). However,

unlike Christ, Villanelle endured no pain, and the episode ended in a parodic re-enactment of Moll Flanders' picaresque habit of robbing her sleeping customers: 'He was able and easy and soon fell asleep. He was also about my height. I left him his shirt and boots and took the rest' (*P* 70).

15 See Northrop Frye's description of this poem's spiralling structure, quoted in Chapter 1.
16 Eliot, 'The Love Song of Alfred Prufrock', *Prufrock* (1947), in *Collected Poems*: 13–17; 17, 13.
17 *Ibid.*, 17.
18 'Patrick says the Channel is full of mermaids. He says it's the mermaids lonely for a man that pull so many of us down' (*P* 24).
19 Carl G. Jung, 'A Psychological Approach to the Dogma of the Trinity' (1948), trans. R. F. C. Hull, in Sir Herbert Read *et al.* (eds), *Psychology and Religion: East and West. The Collected Works* XI. London and Henley: Routledge and Kegan Paul (1981): 107–200; 175–8.
20 Their archetypal complementarity is similar to that of Mr B., Rebecca Lee and Dick Thurlow in John Fowles's *A Maggot*. See Susana Onega, *Form and Meaning in the Novels of John Fowles*. Ann Arbor and London: U. M. I. Research Press (1989): 137–63. It also brings to mind Orlando's successive male/female reincarnations in Virginia Woolf's novel and, as Reynier suggests, 'the different facets of being' embodied by the six characters in *The Waves*. Christine Reynier, 'Venise dans *The Passion* de Jeanette Winterson', *Études britanniques contemporaines* 4 (1994): 25–37; 33.
21 Sigmund Freud, *'Más allá del principio del placer' y otros ensayos* (1940–52), trans. Luis López Ballesteros y de Torres, in Virgilio Ortega (ed.), *Obras completas* XIII. Barcelona: Ediciones Orbis S. A. (1988): 2507–41.
22 Malcolm Bowie, *Freud, Proust and Lacan: Theory as Fiction*. Cambridge: Cambridge University Press (1988) [1987].
23 I first broached this subject in '"Self" and "Other" in Jeanette Winterson's The Passion', *Revista Canaria de Estudios Ingleses* 18 (April 1994): 177–93.
24 Wilson, 'Passion at the End of History,' 59.
25 Paulina Palmer, '*The Passion*: Story-telling, Fantasy, Desire', in Grice and Woods (eds), *'I'm telling you stories'*: 104–16; 107.
26 Jean-Michel Ganteau, 'Heart Objects', in Onega and Gutleben (eds), *Refracting the Canon*: 165–85; 176.
27 Reynier, 'Venise dans *The Passion*', 30.
28 Palmer, '*The Passion*: Story-telling, Fantasy, Desire', 111.
29 *Ibid.*, 11–12.
30 *Ibid.*, 112.

31 Bowie, *Freud, Proust and Lacan*, 105.

32 Eliot, 'A Game of Chess', *The Waste Land* (1922), in *Collected Poems*: 66–9; 66.

33 Villanelle gives up hope of breaking up their matrimony the only time she sees them together: 'I watched them together and saw more in a moment than I could have pondered in another year. They did not live in the fiery furnace she and I inhabited, but they had a calm and a way that put a knife to my heart' (*P* 75).

34 This association is in keeping with the general belief of foreigners that Venice is 'the city of Satan' (*P* 104).

35 The lady's collection of insects and her attempt to pin down Villanelle in her tapestry like a butterfly are reminiscent of the collecting activities of Frederick Clegg in John Fowles's *The Collector* (1963). Besides insects, the lady collects all kinds of curios, including a 'few Chinese ornaments that she liked to collect when the ships came through' (*P* 66), an allusion to the commercial route opened by Marco Polo that brings to mind his description of Venice in Italo Calvino's *Le città invisibile* (1972), one of Winterson's favourite novels.

36 In 'Holy Matrimony' (*WOP* 1977–85), the narrator, who, like Villanelle, is going to marry somebody she does not love, repeats these lines and varies them as: 'What you sell reveals what you value' (*WOP* 185, 179).

37 Borges, 'La lotería en Babilonia', *Ficciones*, in *Obras completas* I, 456–60.

38 Alexander Pushkin, 'La dama de espadas', in *La ventisca y otros cuentos*, trans. Odile Gommes. Madrid: Biblioteca Edaf (1967) [1834]: 153–202; 186, 189.

39 Smith, *Rape and Revelation*.

40 Eliot, 'The Burial of the Dead', *The Waste Land*: 63–5; 65.

41 Eliot, 'Burnt Norton' (1935), *Four Quartets*: 189–95; 189.

42 Eliot, 'The Burial of the Dead', 64.

43 Douglas, *The Tarot*, 56–68.

44 *Ibid.*, 142.

45 *Ibid.*, 34–5.

46 Eliot, 'Little Gidding', 214. Christine Reynier interprets this title differently, as an allusion to the episode of the Great Frost in *Orlando*. Reynier, 'Venise dans *The Passion*', 25.

47 Eliot, 'Little Gidding', 215.

48 *Ibid.*, 214.

49 *Ibid.*, 215.

50 Eliot, 'The Burial of the Dead', 63.

51 Eliot, 'What the Thunder Said', *The Waste Land*: 76–9; 76–7.

52 Seaboyer identifies an important intertext of *The Passion* when she points to San Servolo as 'the island Shelley's protagonists travel to in his *Julian and Maddalo* in order to visit a French madman who bears some

resemblance to Henri and who would have been an inmate at the same time'. Judith Seaboyer, 'Second Death in Venice: Romanticism and the Compulsion to Repeat in Jeanette Winterson's *The Passion*', *Contemporary Literature* 38.3 (Fall 1997): 483–509; 491n.

53 J. Sharman-Burke and L. Greene, *El tarot mítico: Una nueva aproximación a las cartas del tarot*, trans. Felicitas di Fidio. Madrid: Editorial EDAF (1988) [1986]: 136–8.

54 Seaboyer, 'Second Death in Venice', 497.

55 The birth of her daughter may be read as evidence that Villanelle has rounded off her own individuation process, since the child is a common symbol of the completed self. Significantly, although she is born without webbed feet, Villanelle's daughter will in due time master the male art of boat steering, thus naturalising her mother's 'monstrous' androgyny.

56 Bényei, 'Risking the Text', 207.

57 Eliot, 'Little Gidding', 223; 'Notes on the *Waste Land*', in *Collected Poems*: 80–6; 86.

58 Carl G. Jung, *Memories, Dreams, Reflections*. New York: G. P. Putnam's Sons (1965): 117, emphasis added.

59 Gabriel Josipovici, *The World and the Book: A Study of Modern Fiction*. Stanford, CA: Stanford University Press (1971): 306.

60 See Susana Onega, '*The Passion:* Jeanette Winterson's Uncanny Mirror of Ink', *Miscelánea: A Journal of English and American Studies* 14 (1993): 112–29.

61 Bényei, 'Risking the Text', 204.

62 James Joyce, *A Portrait of the Artist as a Young Man*. Introduction and notes by J. S. Atherton. London: Heinemann Educational Books (1969) [1916]: 201–2.

63 Charlotte Innes, 'Rich Imaginings: *Sexing the Cherry*, by Jeanette Winterson', *Nation* (9 July 1990): 64–5; 64.

64 *Ibid.*, 64.

65 Lewis Buzbee, 'Hidden Journeys, Mythical History', *San Francisco Chronicle* (15 April 1990): 9.

66 Hutcheon, *A Poetics of Postmodernism*, x, xi.

67 Besides these four narrative voices intertwining with each other at the first narrative level, there are also several second-level narrator-characters within Jordan's narration. These are overtly fantastic, fairytale characters, who tell Jordan the often bleak 'true' stories of their lives. This multiplication of narrative voices and levels may be said to take the baroque principle of repetition and excess to a point of saturation.

68 Eliot, 'Burnt Norton', 189.

69 Edward Sapir, 'The Status of Linguistics as a Science', *Language* 5 (1929): 207–14. Reprinted in D. G. Mandelbaum (ed.), *The Selected*

Writings of Edward Sapir in Language, Culture and Personality. Berkeley: University of California Press (1949): 160–6.

70 Benjamin Lee Whorf, 'Science and Linguistics', *Technology Review* 42 (1940): 227–31, 247–8.

71 Maureen Duffy, *The Microcosm.* London: Virago (1989) [1966]: 23–4.

72 Anira Rowanchild, 'The State of the Heart', in Hutton (ed.), *Beyond Sex and Romance?*: 29–45; 29. *The Microcosm* shares striking features with *Sexing the Cherry.* It has a cyclical structure. It combines elements from myth, saga, romance and fairytale. Each character's story slides into the next, and the historical time of the narrative (the mid-1960s) is undercut by the account of the adventures of an eighteenth-century cross-dressing lesbian (*Ibid.*, 30). Other novels by Maureen Duffy also prefigure important formal and thematic features in Winterson's fiction, so that her work as a whole may be seen as a (specifically lesbian) key 'missing link' between Virginia Woolf and Jeanette Winterson.

73 Paul Davies and John Gribbin, *The Matter Myth: Beyond Chaos and Complexity.* London: Penguin (1992) [1991]: 229.

74 See Paul Davies, *The Cosmic Blueprint.* London: William Heinemann (1989).

75 Jeanette Winterson *et al.*, 'Revolting Bodies', *New Statesman and Society* 2.8 (1989): 22–9; 32.

76 Eugene Wildman, '*Sexing the Cherry*, by Jeanette Winterson', *Chicago Tribune* (5 June 1990): Section 5, 3; Buzbee, 'Hidden Journeys, Mythical History', 9; Michael Dirda, 'A Cornucopia of Earthy Delights', *Washington Post* (13 May 1990): X09.

77 Dirda, 'A Cornucopia of Earthy Delights', X09.

78 Patricia Waugh, '*Harvest of the Sixties': English Literature and its Background 1960 to 1990.* Oxford and New York: Oxford University Press (1995): 194.

79 Susana Onega, 'Jeanette Winterson's Politics of Uncertainty in *Sexing the Cherry*', in Chantal Cornut-Gentille and José Ángel García Landa (eds), *Gender I-deology: Essays on Theory, Literature and Film.* Amsterdam and Atlanta, GA: Rodopi (1996): 297–369; 303.

80 Swift, *Gulliver's Travels*, 117.

81 *Ibid.*, 143.

82 *Ibid.*, 158.

83 Mikhail Bakhtin, *Rabelais and His World*, trans. Helen Iswolsky. Bloomington: Indiana University Press (1984) [1965]: 21.

84 Waugh, '*Harvest of the Sixties*,' 194.

85 Sandra M. Gilbert and Susan Gubar, *The Madwoman in the Attic: The Woman Writer and the Nineteenth-century Literary Imagination.* New Haven and London: Yale University Press (1984): 3–44.

86 John Milton, *Paradise Lost* (1654): Book II, ll. 650–4.

87 Joseph Campbell, *The Masks of God: Primitive Mythology*. New York: Penguin (1969): 73.

88 Jacques Lacan, 'Le stade du miroir comme formateur de la fonction du Je telle qu'elle nous est révélée dans l'éxpérience psychanalytique', (Communication faite au XVIè congrés international de psychanalyse à Zurich, le 17 juillet 1949) in *Écrits I*. Paris: Seuil (1966): 89–97; 93–5.

89 Mikhail Bakhtin, *The Dialogic Imagination: Four Essays*, trans. Caryl Emerson and Michael Holquist. Austin: University of Texas Press (1981) [1934–5]: 169.

90 I first broached this subject in 'Postmodernist Re-writings of the Puritan Commonwealth: Winterson, Mukherjee, Ackroyd', in Heinz Antor and Kevin L. Cope (eds), *Intercultural Encounters. Studies in English Literatures*. Heidelberg: Universitätsverlag Carl Winter (1999): 439–66.

91 Julia Kristeva, *Powers of Horror: An Essay on Abjection*. New York: Columbia University Press (1982): 7.

92 Barbara Creed, 'Horror and the Monstrous-Feminine: An Imaginary Abjection', *Screen* 27.1 (1986): 63–89; 69.

93 *Ibid.*, 70.

94 Kristeva, *Powers of Horror*, 13.

95 Woolf, *A Room of One's Own*, 61–2.

96 Hélène Cixous, *'Coming to Writing' and Other Essays*, ed. and trans. Deborah Jenson, trans. Sarah Cornell, Ann Liddle, Susan Sellers, Susan Rubin Suleiman. Cambridge, MA: Harvard University Press (1991): 49.

97 Hélène Cixous, 'Sorties', in Hélène Cixous and Catherine Clément, *The Newly Born Woman*, ed. and trans. Sandra M. Gilbert London: I. B. Tauris (1996) [1975]: 63–132; 90–8.

98 Borges, 'El Aleph', *El Aleph* (1949), in *Obras Completas* I (1989): 617–28; 623. Jordan has a similar experience when, following Zillah's gaze, he is astonished to discover that they were 'at the top of a sheer-built tower' (*SC* 36).

99 Virginia Woolf, *The Waves*. London: Vintage (1992) [1931]: 161.

100 *Ibid.*, 152, 149.

101 *Ibid.*, 15.

102 *Ibid.*, 15.

103 *Ibid.*, 111.

104 *Ibid.*, 110.

105 Milan Kundera, *The Unbearable Lightness of Being*, trans. Milan Kundera. London and Boston: Faber and Faber (1990) [1984]: 5.

106 *Ibid.*, 5.

107 *Ibid.*, 3–4.

108 This subject is further developed in Winterson's film script, 'Great Moments in Aviation' (*GMA* 1–67), published in 1990, only one year after *Sexing the Cherry*. A shorter version of the same story, entitled

'Atlantic Crossing', appears in Winterson's collection of short stories, *The World and Other Places* (*WOP* 15–28). The title story in this collection also tackles the related questions of lightness/weight and mental flight into imaginary worlds (*WOP* 87–100), as does her novella, *Weight* (2005, forthcoming at time of writing), which is a rewriting of the myth of Atlas and Heracles.

109 In this sense, 'the city of words' is comparable to Villanelle's Venice in *The Passion*, while Jordan's journeys to various imaginary cities follow the pattern of Marco Polo's journeys in Italo Calvino's *Le città invisibile* (1972).

110 This episode echoes Munchausen's descent from the moon sliding down a rope of twisted straw. Rudolph Erich Raspe, *The Surprising Adventures of Baron Munchausen*. Oxford: Project Gutenberg Literary Archive (1895) (1793): Ch. VI. www.ibiblio.org/gutenberg/etext02. Consulted on 7 April 2004.

111 Swift, *Gulliver's Travels*, 182. Jordan's flight also echoes the Baron Munchausen's extraordinary flight on the back of an eagle over France to Gibraltar, South and North America, the polar regions, and back to England, narrated in the 'Supplement' to the first chapter in the fifth edition of Raspe's *The Surprising Adventures of Baron Munchausen* (1895). This edition, derived from the seventh edition of 1793, had a new subtitle acknowledging the influence of *Gulliver's Travels*: 'Gulliver reviv'd, or the Vice of Lying properly exposed'.

112 Geoffrey Chaucer, *The House of Fame* (1374–85?): Book I, ll. 529–56. After their first love-making with Louise, the narrator of *Written on the Body* describes their room as 'our House of Fame. Perhaps we were in the roof of the world, where Chaucer had been with an eagle' (*WB* 52).

113 This dancing city brings to mind both the cloud where the Unpronounceable lives with the angels in *Boating for Beginners* (*BB* 85) and their common hypotext, Laputa, the floating island in *Gulliver's Travels*.

114 Elizabeth Langland, '"Sexing the Text": Narrative Drag as Feminist Poetics and Politics in *Sexing the Cherry*,' *Narrative* 5.1 (January 1997): 99–107; 101.

115 Winterson's lesbian rewriting of 'The Twelve Dancing Princesses' follows the lead of Angela Carter and other feminists' subversive rewritings of classical fairytales. Heterosexual marriage is also depicted in similarly negative terms in Winterson's short story, 'Holy Matrimony' (*WOP* 179–85).

116 W. B. Yeats, 'The Double Vision of Michael Robartes', *The Wild Swans at Coole* (1919), in *Poems of W. B. Yeats*. Introduction and Notes by A. Norman Jeffares. Basingstoke and London: Macmillan Education (1985) [1962]: 681–3.

117 Eliot, 'Burnt Norton', 191.

118 *Ibid.*, 191.
119 Richard Cavendish, *The Magical Arts: Western Occultism and Occultists.*
      London: Arkana (1984) [1967]: 110.
120 Langland, 'Sexing the Text', 99.
121 *Ibid.*, 100.
122 Andrew Marvell, 'The Mower, Against Gardens,' in *The Complete Poems.*
      Elizabeth Story Donno (ed.), Harmondsworth: Penguin (1976) [1972]:
      105, l. 22, l. 25.
123 *Ibid.*, ll. 27–30.
124 Langland, 'Sexing the Text', 100.
125 Onega, 'Jeanette Winterson's Politics of Uncertainty', 452.
126 Marvell, 'Bermudas', in *The Complete Poems*, 116, ll. 23–4
127 Monique Wittig, *Le Corps lesbien*. Paris: Éditions du Minuit (1973).
128 A similar version of this story, entitled 'Orion', appears in *The World
      and Other Places* (*WOP* 53–63).
129 Jeffrey Roessner, 'Writing a History of Difference: Jeanette Winterson's
      Sexing the Cherry and Angela Carter's *Wise Children*', *College Literature*
      29.1 (Winter 2002): 102–12; 106.
130 Caroline Walker Bynum, *Metamorphosis and Identity*. New York: Zone
      Books (2001): 30.
131 *Ibid.*, 31, emphasis added.
132 Cixous, 'Sorties', 84–5.
133 William Shakespeare, *The Tempest* (1611) I.2. 400–1.
134 Cixous, 'Sorties', 73.
135 Eliot, 'Little Gidding', 222.
136 Fortunata also begins the narration of her life story with these words
      (*SC* 93), thus enhancing her anima complementarity to Jordan.
137 W. B. Yeats, *A Vision*. New York: Collier Books (1965) [1937].
138 Mircea Eliade, *The Myth of the Eternal Return: Cosmos and History*, trans.
      William R. Trask. London: Arkana (1989) [1954].

3

The art of love

The publication of *Written on the Body* in 1992 marked a change from the structural complexity of *Sexing the Cherry*, with its duplications and intertwining of narrative voices and historical periods, by turning back to the simplicity of the single narrative voice of *Oranges Are Not the Only Fruit*. However, as in Winterson's first novel, this simplicity is more apparent than real; in the case of *Written on the Body* because the gender and physical aspect of the autodiegetic narrator are never made explicit, thus suggesting that s/he enjoys the type of bisexuality Jordan achieved in *Sexing the Cherry* at the end of his quest for individuation.

Winterson is not the first lesbian writer who has problematised the identity of her narrators. The representation of lesbian characters has always been a central issue of lesbian fiction. According to Clare Hemmings, Radclyffe Hall's *The Well of Loneliness* and Virginia Woolf's *Orlando: A Biography*, both published in 1928, are key texts in the representation of 'a friendship and an invert model of lesbianism, where Woolf's legacy is identified with the former, and Hall's with the latter'.[1] As she further explains, the invert model represented by Hall's martyred masculine protagonist, Stephen Gordon, materialises the 'myth of the lesbian as a pseudo-male'. Gordon's masculinity is that of 'the invert who desires women because she has the gender traits of a man'.[2] Defended by 'old style lesbianism' and queer criticism, this model consolidates gendered same-sex eroticism and celebrates female-bodied masculinity 'as peculiarly transgressive of heteronormative gender relations', to the detriment of 'femininity (or femme)' which thus remains 'unable to signify lesbianism in its own right'. Consequently, only 'dissonantly gendered bodies (drag in males; butch in female) can be seen to signal queer desire'.[3] By contrast, the 'friendship model' represented by Virginia Woolf's *Orlando* proposes romantic friendship and androgyny as an alternative to the butch/femme dichotomy of the invert model. Endorsed by second-wave lesbian/feminist criticism in the 1970s, 'Woolf/Orlando's androgyny becomes an extremely useful vehicle to allow lesbian critics to reject masculinity as the a priori sign of same-sex desire, without having to embrace an equally politically dubious femininity in its stead'.[4]

The increasing influence of the friendship model becomes apparent in the representation of lesbian fictional characters from the 1970s onwards. For instance, in her 1966 novel, *The Microcosm*, Maureen Duffy used the male pronoun for Matt, the 'shadowy female Prospero' presiding over a 'microcosmic' lesbian community, thus observing, as Anira Rowanchild notes, 'a tradition among lesbians who see themselves as butch'.[5] However, in the following decade, the identity of Duffy's narrators becomes more diffuse and unstable, as they move from inversion to bisexuality. Thus, the gender and sexual identity of Kit, the autodiegetic narrator of *Love Child* (1977) is never revealed, and neither is that of Al, the narrator of *Londoners* (1983), who, like the nameless narrator of *Written on the Body*, is a translator.[6] M. Daphne Kutzer has pointed to other examples of this kind of ambiguity. As she explains, Marge Piercy's *Woman on the Edge of Time* (1975) is set in 'a utopian, androgynous world, where gendered pronouns have ceased to exist in favour of "per" as both nominative and genitive. For example, "Per picked up per shoes from the floor"'. June Arnold's *The Cook and the Carpenter* (1973) 'plays similar linguistic games, but has a more complicated linguistic system in which "Na picked up nan's shoes from the floor"'.[7] At the same time, as the binarism of the invert model is replaced by the fluidity of the friendship model, the utopic and romantic vision of Woolf's *Orlando* replaces the tragic vision of lesbianism provided by Radclyffe Hall's *The Well of Loneliness*, a novel that makes lesbianism visible but only at the cost of associating it with sickness or unhappiness.

In *Art Objects*, Jeanette Winterson explicitly dissociates herself from Radclyffe Hall – 'Our work has nothing in common' (*AO* 103) – and signals *Orlando* as her model (*AO* 61–77). In keeping with this, the characterisation of Winterson's protagonists shows a steady progression in the refinement of the friendship model, with its definition of identity as fluid and relational rather than fixed and oppositional. Thus, in *Oranges*, Jeanette's sense of identity is directly related to her position in her mother's religious community of female friends. In *Boating for Beginners*, the protagonist's female friends decisively help Gloria in her maturation process and in the dismantling of Noah's version of the Flood. In *The Passion*, the fluidity of Villanelle's identity is symbolised in her transvestism: she dresses as a woman during the day and wears male drag during the night. In *Sexing the Cherry*, the Dog Woman enjoys the friendship of prostitutes and nuns, and so does Jordan after he learns to crossdress. Villanelle and Henri's baby daughter, who has a normal female body and the inborn ability to row boats of Venetian boatmen, may be said to possess the type of bisexuality that Jordan achieves at the end of his self-quest. But the novel ends soon after she is born, so her story remains untold. In this sense, *Written on the Body*, with its nameless and genderless narrator, may be said to begin at the point where both *The Passion* and *Sexing the Cherry* end.

Despite all these antecedents, the programmatic nature of the narrator's bisexuality in *Written on the Body* has not always been taken into consideration by the critics. Thus, Rachel Wingfield considers the narrator's 'androgyny' as simply an example of formal experimentation, the result of the author's 'postmodernist preoccupation with writing about writing', and she thoroughly resents the fact that Winterson's intended audience is not 'feminists, lesbians or even the general public: it is the (male) mainstream literati itself'. Wingfield's conclusion is that 'the narrator's lack of gender simply becomes an irritating ploy by which the author seems to be playing games with us'.[8] Another lesbian critic, Cath Stowers, extends this type of criticism to Jeanette Winterson's work as a whole when she quotes Lynne Pearce (1994) to exemplify the view that 'many feminist readers and critics have felt cheated by Winterson's handling of gender, while Winterson herself has further problematised the issue with her reluctance to be cast as a "feminist" or "radical lesbian"'.[9] Significantly, Stowers's own article, which is meant to dismantle this view, evinces a great anxiety about her own position being misread as some form of authoritarian and exclusivist critical position: 'this essay aims to [. . .] trace the possibilities for a lesbian reading. But this is not to claim this is the one "correct" reading. As I will suggest in my conclusion, this novel is also open to a *bisexual* reading.'[10]

Although interesting in many respects, Stowers's reading of *Written on the Body* stems from the wrong premise that the novel allows for *two different* readings, a 'lesbian' and a 'bisexual' one. Ironically enough, this distinction plunges Stowers into the same kind of binary logic that second-wave feminist critics and lesbian writers defending the friendship model of lesbianism have been trying to deconstruct since the 1970s. Her blunder constitutes a telling example of the difficulty in *imagining* an alternative to binarism even for a lesbian critic who values *Written on the Body* highly. Characteristically, critics like Stowers tend to ignore the ideological questions posed by the narrator's bisexuality, insisting on referring to the nameless author-narrator as a woman – Sutherland,[11] Sheehan,[12] Stuart[13] – or, as Ute Kauer does, devoting the whole article to gathering textual evidence that the 'point of view is a female one' even though the narrator 'does not want to be identified by some of the categories that are usually believed to form an identity, namely gender and age'.[14] Other critics have even tried to justify the same assumption by providing extratextual evidence that the narrator is a persona for Jeanette Winterson and that the novel's plot is based on her love affairs in real life. Thus, Heather Nunn cites several journals as the source of her reading: 'In the *Evening Standard* article Winterson herself is quoted invoking old and new loves: "There are many loves in *Written on the Body*, and not all of them are Pat"[15] [. . .]. All the parts of the book that are about love and the fear of losing someone concern Peggy'.[16] By contrast, a male critic, Walter Kendrick, is convinced that the narrator is male because of the way in which 'he broadcasts his current affairs without hesitation, even to near-strangers; it's difficult to imagine that such love is not heterosexual'.[17]

The contradictory evidence found by different critics points to the incontestable fact that, as Gregory J. Rubinson notes, 'there is no information about the narrator's body that can lead us to determine whether the narrator is male, female, transsexual, intersexed, or XXY, [. . .]. Any attempt to determine the narrator's sex is necessarily dependent on essentialized or stereotypical readings of gender or both'.[18] In other words, the critics' attempts at disambiguating the identity of the narrator miss the very point Winterson is at pains to make – namely, that identity is not a natural given, but a fluid, ever-changing and complex ideological process, determined by the individual's relationship with other individuals. We cannot refer to the narrator as a 'she' ignoring the text's insistence that we use the slashed forms 's/he' and 'her/his' even if having to use the slashes is irritating, precisely because it is this irritation that will challenge and set into question the objectivity of our patriarchal assumptions about identity.

As we saw in Chapter 2, at the end of *Sexing the Cherry*, Jordan achieved his metamorphic 'change' from heterosexuality to bisexuality by writing the 'secret story' of his life with the 'white ink' Hélène Cixous prescribes for *écriture feminine*, a type of writing specifically meant to deconstruct binary oppositions such as man/woman; self/other; active/passive, etc., on which patriarchal ideology is based.[19] Jordan's bisexuality, then, is wholly ideological, the product of his conscious act of writing himself into existence. The same description would be applicable to the bisexuality of the nameless author-narrator in *Written on the Body*. Unlike those of other feminists, Cixous's attempt to deconstruct the binary logic of patriarchy involves a reinvention, or rather a rewriting, of the self both for women and men. Consequently, she distinguishes between, on the one hand, the terms 'masculine' and 'feminine' as referring to traits that have been socially constructed through language and manifested in everyday experience to reinforce the binary of the couple, and hence of gender; and, on the other hand, the terms 'male' and 'female', which refer to the sexual reproductive role (the body parts) of men and women.[20] This distinction between gender and sex allows her to state that human beings are not 'essentially' women and men but living structures caught up or frozen within historiocultural structures to such a degree that it has long been impossible and is still difficult to imagine anything else. From this, she concludes that all human beings have the capacity to be bisexual in that we all have the qualities and capacities of socially constructed 'masculine' and 'feminine' traits: we can all be emotional, reasonable, passive, active, etc. Thus, although she privileges women in achieving what she calls the 'other bisexuality' because historically and culturally they are more open or accustomed to accepting different forms of subjectivity than men, nonetheless, Cixous has no qualms in signalling Jean Genet as one of her favourite examples of a writer of *écriture feminine*, an assertion that has infuriated many of her critics.

The fury of these critics, like the hostility of the reviewers of *Written on the Body* mentioned above, may be said to stem from the same imaginative deficiency that was evinced by Aristophanes – who, it should not be forgotten, is the author of some of the funniest comedies in antiquity – when he described the androgynes in Plato's *Symposium* as cylindrical creatures with two faces, four ears, arms and legs and male and female organs (189E–190A). Whether Plato intended Aristophanes to speak in jest or not, the fact remains that his preposterous description of androgyny as a duplication of male and female physical traits entails an impoverishment of the *pure myth* of androgyny or Hermaphroditism, which, as Marie Delcourt has pointed out, is a divine attribute enjoyed by many a Greek deity, both male and female. Originally devoid of erotic connotations, the pure myth of androgyny designated an *idea* of perfection rather than a physical condition.[21] Cixous's concept of bisexuality is to be similarly understood as an idea of perfection and wholeness meant to do away with Freud's definition of woman as 'lack'.

Both Freud and Lacan believed that there is no libido other than the masculine. Therefore, they assumed that the subject is necessarily masculine. In keeping with this, Lacan privileged the phallus as the organising point of sexual identity and desire. Cixous rejects this on the reflection that, for all his attempts to differentiate between phallus (the symbol) and penis (the male organ), Lacan's theory inescapably relies on the physical – that is, on the presence or absence of the penis. Her contention is that sexual difference is unrelated to any physical trait and that it is in fact most apparent in how women and men experience sexual pleasure (*jouissance*).[22] While Lacan situates the phallus in the symbolic order, which is the order of signs and social and cultural life brought about by the acquisition of language, *jouissance* operates in the feminine realm of the imaginary (Kristeva's 'semiotic'). As Morag Shiach has pointed out, this is clearly a strategic move on the part of the French writer: it removes any possibility of identifying femininity and masculinity with the certainties of anatomical difference, allowing her to place sexual difference at the level of the libido – that is, in the realm of the unknowable.[23]

Following a similar argument, Julia Kristeva stresses the revolutionary nature of female pleasure in 'About Chinese Women', where she explains that, in order to gain admittance into the symbolic, women must choose between virginity or motherhood, thus being forced to 'atone for their carnal *jouissance* with their martyrdom'.[24] If they are to avoid the prescribed roles of virgin or mother, then, women must call into question everything that they have been taught to think and must learn to avoid submitting to the laws of habit and cultural objectification. According to Cixous, the way to do this is through the practice of *écriture féminine*, a type of writing that stems from the admittance of bodily *jouissance*. Thus, against the Lacanian phallus/penis/pen, Cixous sets up the female body, with its multierogenous potential for sexual pleasure, as the basic metaphor or primary signifier of the new 'feminine writing'. As she contends:

> By writing her self, woman will return to the body which has been more than confiscated from her, which has been turned into the uncanny stranger on display – the ailing or dead figure, which so often turns out to be the nasty companion, the cause and location of inhibitions. Censor the body and you censor breath and speech at the same time.[25]

As the title suggests, *Written on the Body* is a self-conscious experiment in *écriture féminine*, carried out by an autodiegetic author-narrator, whose aim, as Ute Kauer has succinctly put it, 'is no longer self-discovery, but rather self-construction'.[26] In this sense, it is important to realise that, like earlier Winterson autodiegetic narrators at the beginning of their narration, the nameless narrator of *Written on the Body* is a purblind hero/ine engaged in a quest for self-individuation.

The novel begins with the narrator presenting her/himself as a reckless Lothario (*WB* 20) involved in numberless love affairs with partners of both sexes that only last for a brief span of time, either because of the partners' various oddities; because of sheer characteriological incompatibility; or, more often, because the narrator's sexual partner is a married woman who tries to assuage the unhappiness and barrenness of her married life by indulging in a secret and passionate sexual affair, without ever, however, contemplating the possibility of setting her marriage at risk. This is a source of endless suffering for the narrator, who hopes for a more stable and affective relationship and invariably ends up heartbroken, feeling misused, objectified and forced to find refuge in her/his own private 'island' (*WB* 27).[27] The narrator's rakish behaviour unexpectedly comes to an end when s/he meets Louise Fox, a beautiful Australian woman who, like Winterson's earlier heroines, has splendid red hair. Unlike the narrator's earlier partners, Louise falls in love with her/him, sees no reason to hide their relationship and is ready to divorce her husband, Elgin Rosenthal, a well-to-do cancer specialist, whose orthodox Jewish background is made to symbolise his uncompromising patriarchal ideology. After several months of shared bliss, the narrator learns that Louise is suffering from leukaemia and makes the unilateral decision to leave her in the hands of her husband so that she can undergo specialist treatment in his private Swiss clinic.

The narrator's rakish behaviour and self-indulgence have infuriated many a reviewer of the novel. Thus, Valerie Miner describes her/him as 'this strangely disembodied, decontextualized character, [who] is such a shallow sophomoric egoist that it's hard to keep reading'.[28] Likewise, Anna Vaux detects 'something odd and self-indulgent about a sensibility that can dwell so much on its own high passions while portraying the feelings of other characters in the book as one-dimensional or comic and easy to dismiss'.[29] This kind of reaction takes the narrator's account of her/his past life at face value, overlooking the possibility that it might be meant to shock the reader into realising both the narrator's unreliability and her/his inadequacy as a lover. A pointed example of a preposterous and ludicrous story begging for an ironic reading is that of the narrator's love affair with Dutch Inge, 'a committed romantic and anarcha-feminist' (*WB* 21), who thought that men's urinals were 'a symbol of patriarchy and must be destroyed' (*WB* 22), and who tried to use pigeons to communicate with the narrator from Holland (*WB* 23). After telling this story, the narrator raises the question of her/his own reliability, addressing the reader in a self-conscious frame-break: 'I can tell by now that you are wondering whether I can be trusted as a narrator. Why didn't I dump Inge and head for a Singles Bar? The answer is her breasts' (*WB* 24). The narrator repeatedly addresses the reader with this type of rhetorical questions, so that, as Kauer has noted, s/he 'ironises his/her own role constantly as well as the role of the reader [and] plays with the moral objections the implied reader might raise by anticipating them'.[30]

Near the end of the novel, the narrator, who is now living alone in a remote cottage in the Yorkshire countryside and is feeling quite sick with yearning for Louise, overtly acknowledges the fictionality of her/his account, when s/he admits that s/he is 'making up my own memories of good times' (*WB* 161). This remark confers a circular structure on the novel and situates the author-narrator in the position of earlier Winterson protagonists like Jordan and Henri, who also wrote the stories of their lives in retrospect and warned their addressees that they were telling stories or reporting imaginary voyages, not facts. The question that triggered off the narrator's desire to write the memoirs is 'Had I been true to her?' (*WB* 161) coupled with her/his growing conviction that, unlike the 'wandering bark' in Shakespeare's Sonnet CXVI, that 'looks on tempests and is never shaken' (*WB* 162), s/he has not been up to her/his promises. This adds a confessional element to the memoirs that contradicts its humoristic tone and its self-reflexivity, paradoxically affirming their

capacity to establish the truth about the narrator's and Louise's relationship. Following a characteristic baroque tendency to accumulate
intertextual allusions, the narrator subsequently mentions Dylan
Thomas's *Portrait of the Artist as a Young Dog* (*WB* 162). A parody of
Joyce's *Portrait of the Artist as a Young Man*, Thomas's *Portrait* is primarily concerned with explaining the development of the poet's sexuality. Therefore, this reference acutely points to the narrator's
memoirs as a *Künstlerroman* that specifically takes sexuality as the
focal element in her/his creative process of self-construction.

Once the fictionality of the memoirs is taken into account, it is easy
to see that the one-dimensionality of the narrator's lovers is that of
well-worn literary types. Inge, for example, is a butch in the invert tradition of the butch/femme couple of early lesbian fiction. By contrast,
Jacqueline, the narrator's latest partner, is a clear example of lesbian
'femme'. She is described as a 'sort of household pet' (*WB* 25), and we
learn that she installed herself in the narrator's house and assumed
the role of housewife without asking first. When the narrator tells her
that she must leave the flat because s/he has fallen out of love with
her, Jacqueline removes all the furniture, vandalises the flat and
smears the walls with excrement (*WB* 70). Her fit of hysteria points
to Jacqueline as a parodic example of Cixous's 'excessive woman' as
defined in 'The Laugh of the Medusa'. In this essay, the French poet
and critic rereads Freud's famous 1905 'Fragment of an Analysis of a
Case of Hysteria', the case study on 'Dora', the girl who so obsessed
Freud in the months before his writing of *The Interpretation of Dreams*
that she called forth his most extreme (counter)transference, thereby
enticing Lacan, Sartre and others to retell her story. In Cixous's
retelling, Dora becomes a model of the excessive ('monstrous',
according to patriarchy) woman who threatens patriarchy because
she speaks her body. She is the human equivalent of Medusa, the
Serpent-Goddess worshipped by the Lybian Amazons, the sight of
whose face was sure death for men. With neat symmetry, the narrator responds to Jacqueline's hysteria as 'a cheap thug' would have
done, 'slap[ping] her across the face' (*WB* 86).

Other lovers mentioned by the narrator are equally one-dimensional and parodic. Amy, who has installed 'the head of a yellow and
green serpent [. . .] poking out of the letter-box just at crotch level [. . .]
with a rat-trap in the jaw' especially meant 'for the postman'
(*WB* 42, 42), is a ludicrous version of the *vagina dentata*, the castrating woman of men's archetypal fears. By contrast, Crazy Frank, a

boyfriend the narrator met for the first time 'at a Toulouse-Lautrec exhibition in Paris' and who had been brought up by midgets, is a Rabelaisian giant 'with the body of a bull' (*WB* 92–3). As the narrator ironically comments, he had tried to intensify this image 'by wearing great gold hoops through his nipples [. . . .] with a chain of heavy gold links. The effect should have been deeply butch but in fact it looked rather like the handle of a Chanel shopping bag' (*WB* 93). Like the narrator, Crazy Frank is a bisexual rake, whose only ambition is 'to find a hole in every port. He wasn't fussy about the precise location' (*WB* 93).

The novel opens with the question: 'Why is the measure of love loss?' (*WB* 9). This question reflects the narrator's state of mind at the time of writing, which is of utter despair and misery after having lost Louise. This is the question the narrator tries to answer by writing her/his fictional 'memories' and the sentence that, according to Jeanette Winterson, concentrates the 'single image' around which the whole novel develops (*AO* 169–70). Once posed, the question triggers off what can be described as the narrator's 'remembrances of things past'. Structured chronologically in the form of diary entries, the evolution of the narrator and Louise's relationship follows the natural rhythm of the seasons through the year, thus suggesting that it has the wholeness of a cosmogonic cycle: it begins with the happy memory of 'a certain September' (*WB* 9) when Louise declared her love; reaches a climax of passion in a torrid August (*WB* 98); is interrupted by the chilling news of Louise's leukaemia on 'Christmas Eve' (*WB* 100); and concludes in October with the lovers' reunion (*WB* 180).

In the first entry we find the narrator struggling for the right words to write about love. As s/he reflects, '[l]ove demands expression' but it is difficult to express love adequately, since '"I love you" is always a quotation' (*WB* 9) and there are too many clichés surrounding the question of love:

> Love makes the world go round. Love is blind. All you need is love. Nobody ever died of a broken heart. You'll get over it. It'll be different when we're married. Think of the children. Time's a great healer. Still waiting for Mr Right? Miss Right? And maybe all the little Rights?
> It's the clichés that cause the trouble. (*WB* 10)

The narrator's words bring to mind Umberto Eco's definition of postmodernist irony by reference to love in the Postscript to *The Name of the Rose*:

I think of the postmodern attitude as that of a man who loves a very cultivated woman and knows he cannot say to her 'I love you madly' because he knows that she knows (and that she knows that he knows) that these words have already been written by Barbara Cartland. Still, there is a solution. He can say, 'As Barbara Cartland would put it, I love you madly'. At this point having avoided false innocence, having said clearly that it is no longer possible to speak innocently, he will nevertheless have said what he wanted to say to the woman: that he loves her, but he loves her in an age of lost innocence.[31]

According to Eco, then, the only way in which we can still use the well-worn words of love with the purity and intensity of their pristine meaning is by having recourse to irony. From this perspective, the jokes made by the narrator of *Written on the Body* in the recounting of her/his preposterous sexual feats and her/his acknowledgement of the fictional nature of the events narrated acquire the double irony of Swift's satire at its best, for, although s/he makes constant use of literary clichés to describe her/his sexual feats, the narrator seems to be candidly unaware that s/he is behaving according to these clichés. The lack of self-directed irony in the narrator's report surely is what produces a distancing effect in the readers, undermining their willing suspension of disbelief and revealing the narrator's moral bluntness. This is made evident, for example, when, surprised by the realisation that Louise is not reacting like her/his previous married partners, the narrator says that she is not following the prescribed directions: 'This is the wrong script. This is the moment where I'm supposed to be self-righteous and angry. This is the moment when you're supposed to flood with tears and tell me how hard it is to say these things' (*WB* 18). What the narrator means to be a joke is only a thin cover for her/his deep fear of change and her/his incapacity to respond to Louise's love adequately. If s/he is to grow morally and spiritually, then, s/he will have to become aware of the seriousness of Louise's proposal and of the artificiality and wrongness of her/his sexual behaviour.

Before falling in love with Louise the narrator was bisexual in the sense that s/he had sexual intercourse both with women and men, but the relations with her/his partners followed traditional patriarchal patterns of binary opposition and inequality. Her/his bisexuality simply meant that s/he could switch sexual roles: s/he could be the victimiser and the victim, the butch and the femme, the rakish Don Juan/Lothario/Casanova and the masochistic sexual toy of middle-aged married women. Thus, in her/his role of rake, the narrator admits that, while Louise 'was careful not to say those words that soon became our private altar', so as not to wear them out, s/he had 'given them as forget-me-nots to girls who should have known better' (*WB* 11). And s/he also avows that s/he 'used to think of marriage as a plate-glass window just begging for a brick' (*WB* 13). By contrast, in her/his relationships with numberless married women, the narrator invariably assumed the role of pleasure-giver and victim. Significantly stressing the artificiality of these relations, s/he summarises them in the form of a dialogue between '*A naked woman of a certain age [lying] on the bed looking at the ceiling*' and '*Her lover*' (*WB* 14, original italics). Just as the narrator's remark that s/he is writing her/his 'memories' reminds the reader of the birth of the memoir as a genre in seventeenth-century France, so this scene points to an intertextual connection between the narrator's sexual exploits with married women and the characteristic triangle of Restoration 'sex comedy': the rake, the pretty wife and the doting and jealous husband. From this perspective, the fact that the narrator wrongly believes at one point that one of her/his married lovers, Bathsheba the dentist, 'had given me the clap' (*WB* 25) points to Horner, the witty and unfaithful rake in William Wycherley's *The Country Wife* (1675), as an unexpected literary predecessor. Indeed, the woman in the narrator's scene treats her lover with the crudity and egotism of the adulterous wives in Restoration comedies: 'If I hadn't met you I *would* be looking for something. I might have done a degree at the Open University' (*WB* 14). And she plainly admits to being exclusively interested in her lover's body, to the point of anthropophagy: 'When I try to read it is you I am reading. When I sit down to eat it's you I'm eating. When he touches me I think about you. I am a middle-aged happily married woman and all I can see is your face. What have you done to me?' (*WB* 15).

The married woman's desire to eat the narrator's body echoes Hélène Cixous's illustrating an individual's relationship with pleasure by means of the Biblical story of Eve and the apple. Cixous equates getting 'inside' with the acquisition of knowledge and says that Eve was punished for disobeying the law which prohibited her from eating the fruit because to eat the fruit is to get to the 'inside' of the fruit and let the fruit get inside you. Thus, referring to Monet, who refused to eat an apple because it was too beautiful, she concludes: 'I would have eaten it [. . .] in my need to touch the apple. To know it in the dark. With my fingers, with my lips, with my tongue.'[32] In

Cixous's reading, then, Eve shared the apple with Adam and paid for her acquisition of knowledge of the 'inside' of pleasure with expulsion from Paradise. Unlike Eve, the married woman in the play simply tries to feed her sexual appetite (in Cixous's terms, to fill her Freudian 'lack'), without ever, however, putting at risk the comfort of her (pseudo-Edenic) married life, although at the cost of transforming her lover into a sheer object of consumption. This type of unequal relationship reinforces the patriarchal pattern, since, as Cixous further explains, it is only by realising that the desire for the other is born out of love and not lack, that you can 'listen to what your body hadn't dared let surface'.[33]

When the narrator realises that Louise is not behaving like other married women, that she is in fact offering her/him a relationship built on terms of equality and love, s/he is panicstricken about living an experience that does not respond to the habitual scheme: 'Yes you do frighten me. You act as though we will be together for ever. You act as though there is infinite pleasure and time without end. How can I know that? My experience is that time always ends' (*WB* 18). It is this fear of 'infinite pleasure' (*jouissance*), then, that the narrator must overcome if s/he is to acquire the wholeness and maturity of Cixous's 'other bisexuality'.

In keeping with this, the narrator's fear progressively yields to a growing passion that, significantly, is also expressed as a desire to eat each other. However, while the married woman's anthropophagic drive was based on her unilateral desire to fill her Freudian 'lack', the narrator and Louise's mutual desire to eat and to be eaten by each other is prompted by a need to know 'the inside' of the beloved.[34] With neat accuracy, the narrator draws this distinction when, answering her/his own question 'Is food sexy?', s/he retorts, assuming the flippant tone of her/his rakish persona:

> *Playboy* regularly features stories about asparagus and bananas and leeks and courgettes or being smeared with honey or chocolate chip ice-cream. I once bought some erotic body oil, authentic Pina Colada flavour, and poured it over myself but it made my lover's tongue come out in a rash. (*WB* 36)

But then s/he adds: 'Context is all, or so I thought, until I started eating with Louise' (*WB* 36). The description that follows shows Louise eating soup and the narrator wishing to trade 'the blood in my body for half a pint of vegetable stock [. . . .] just so that you will take me in your mouth' (*WB* 36). Together with this yearning to get 'inside' Louise, the narrator simultaneously wishes to get her into her/himself: 'I knew that she spat in the frying pan to determine the readiness of the oil. [. . .] I will taste you if only through your cooking' (*WB* 37). Further echoing Cixous's reading of Eve sharing the forbidden apple with Adam, the narrator pictures Louise splitting 'one of her own pears' from her Edenic garden: 'Where she lived had been an orchard once and her particular tree was two hundred and twenty years old' (*WB* 37). Needless to say, the narrator had already compared her/himself to Adam (*WB* 18).

In 'Theorizing Lesbian: Writing – A Love Letter', Elizabeth Meese plays an elaborate Derridean game on 'The Letter of the Law', 'The Law of the Letter' and the letter to 'Dear L', where L stands for 'lesbian', in an attempt to foreground the 'shadowy' nature of lesbian identity and the intrinsic difficulty in 'de-ciphering' the thing from its reflection.[35] Echoing this, the narrator suggests Louise's uniqueness by comparing the initial letter of her name, the capital L, with the beautifully decorated capital L of an illuminated manuscript, whose first word is 'Love'. And, following a well established tradition in lesbian writing, s/he equates finding Louise to creating a new symbolic space: 'I don't want to lose this happy space where I have found someone who is smart and easy and who doesn't bother to check her diary when we arrange to meet' (*WB* 38). Though still 'microcosmic' in Maureen Duffy's sense of the word, this private and enclosed (lesbian) space is much happier than the solitary 'island' (*WB* 27), where the narrator used to find refuge from the frustrations of her/his love affairs with married women. After Louise abandons Elgin, they live 'together in great happiness for nearly five months' (*WB* 99) in this space, enjoying a relationship of mutual love and perfect bliss, where the self/other patriarchal pattern of inequality is substituted for a new feminine pattern of equality and mutual knowledge of the 'inside' of the beloved, a pattern the lesbian writer Nicole Brossard has defined as the equation 'desiring subject/subject of desire'.[36] In the narrator's own words: 'Neither of us had the upper hand, we wore matching wounds. She was my twin and I lost her' (*WB* 163). Indeed, the two partners are so identical that the narrator feels a shock of recognition whenever s/he looks at her/his face in the mirror: 'When I look in the mirror it's not my own face I see. Your body is twice. Once you once me. Can I be sure which is which?' (*WB* 99).

The comparison to identical twins brings to mind the split androgynes in Plato's *Symposium*, desperately searching for their identical half.[37] When they encounter their twin, they fall into a tight embrace until, incapable of separating themselves, they die of hunger and inaction (191A–B). The narrator uses a similar image to describe her/his relationship with Louise when s/he says that Louise 'would have bound me to her with ropes and had us lie face to face unable to move but move on each other, unable to feel but feel each other. She would have deprived us of all senses bar the sense of touch and smell. In a blind, deaf and dumb world we could conclude our passion infinitely' (*WB* 162). The narrator uses the same image again, when, after saying that 'Louise and I were held by a single loop of love', s/he tells about a fourteenth and fifteenth-century Italian sport, in which the fighters were fastened 'together with a strong rope and let them tear each other to death. Often it was death because the loser couldn't back off and the victor rarely spared him' (*WB* 88). In contrast to the lacerating ropes fastening the Italian fighters, the 'cord passing round our [the narrator and Louise's] bodies had no sharp twists or sinister turns' (*WB* 88).[38] Further, their 'loop of love' is a mystical loop, overtly compared to 'Solomon's knot, said to embody the essence of all knowledge' (*WB* 87). Associated with truth and perfection, Solomon's knot consists of the interlacing of two identical and reversible loops, suggesting both the infinitude of a double Möbius strip and the chthonic transcendence symbolised by the motif of the two entwined serpents such as the Naga serpents of India or, in Greek mythology, the snakes intertwined on a staff belonging to the god Hermes.

Before mentioning Solomon's knot, the narrator had said that '[e]ven the simplest pedigree knot, the threefoil, with its three roughly symmetrical lobes, has mathematical as well as artistic beauty' (*WB* 87). The threefoil or Borromean knot, consisting of three interlaced

rings, is a mathematical symbol frequently used by Lacan to symbolise the interdependence of the imaginary, the symbolic and the real.
As Diana Fuss has pointed out, the reversibility of Lacan's Borromean
knot 'demonstrates how the unconscious itself has neither an inside
nor an outside'.[39] Drawing on this idea, Fuss proposes a new mathematical figure she calls the 'figure-eight or four knot' as an intentional
twist or variation on Lacan's threefoil knot to suggest the reversibility
of gay and lesbian relationships: 'Like the Borromean knot, the four
knot, when pulled inside out, appears as its own mirror image; it is
what mathematicians call an "invertible" knot, and so might be
glossed in the context of this book as a figure for (sexual) inversion'.[40]
Like Fuss's 'invertible knot', the narrator and Louise's 'loop of love'
with the shape of Solomon's knot may be read as a similar intentional
twist on Lacan's Borromean knot, suggesting the perfection,
reversibility and atemporality of their love relationship.

The passion of the split androgynes in Plato's *Symposium* is infinite. However, as Aristophanes makes clear, their relationship is
not merely sexual. When they encounter their true half, they feel a
marvellous impact of friendship, affinity and love. Therefore, their
everlasting union is both a physical and a spiritual communion, a perfect understanding of each other's soul without the need of words
(Plato, 192D, 192B–C). As the comparison to Solomon's knot suggests, the narrator and Louise's loop of love is a similarly perfect
union both physically and spiritually: 'Sleeping beside Louise had
been a pleasure that often led to sex but which was separate from it'
(*WB* 110). However, unlike that of the androgynes, their experience of
jouissance is specifically brought about by the mutual writing/trans-
lating of the body of the beloved:

> You tap a message on to my skin, tap meaning into my body. Your
> morse code interferes with my heart beat. [. . .] Written on the body is a
> secret code only visible in certain lights: the accumulations of a lifetime
> gather there. In places the palimpsest is so heavily worked that the let-
> ters feel like Braille. [. . .] I didn't know that Louise would have reading
> hands. She has translated me into her own book. (*WB* 89)

Drawing on Saussurean linguistics, Derrida famously postulated
the existence of a 'supplement', a metonymic remainder of meaning
left out in the shift from signifier to signified, whose existence only
becomes apparent in translation. This 'surplus' or 'excess' of
meaning that endlessly shifts from signifier to signifier without ever

entering the signified is explicitly identified by Cixous with the feminine. As Sinclair Timothy Ang notes, this means that the feminine:

> is necessary in articulation, but in itself cannot be articulated because the Symbolic Order functions on the grounds of the *propre* (signifier to signified), and this excess belongs to the realm of the non-*propre* (signifier to signifier in an endless chain) [. . .]. Thus, feminine desire can only be demonstrated through unveiling of the *propre* through play and translation.[41]

In this light, the narrator's words quoted above as well as the fact that s/he works as a translator from Russian into English (*WB* 94) acquire symbolic meaning, suggesting that they are both capable of undertaking the practice of *écriture feminine* and, by so doing, of giving expression to and making real their unrealisable desires and dreams. In this sense, their activity of writing/translating each other's body has revolutionary intent, since as Nicole Brossard has pointed out, 'the skin of a woman which slides on to the skin of another woman provokes a sliding of meaning creating the possibility of a new version of reality and of fiction, which I would call a tridimensional vision'.[42] It is this 'sliding of meaning' brought about by the mutual writing/translating of the narrator's and Louise's bodies that creates *le corps/texte* or 'cortex', the new feminine space in the symbolic order within which they can give expression to their perfect love as desiring subjects/subjects of desire.

This experience of *jouissance* is brought to an abrupt end by the intervention of Louise's jealous husband, who, incapable of accepting the social stigma associated with the loss of his wife, informs the narrator that Louise is suffering from leukaemia and that 'The prognosis was about 100 months' (*WB* 104). This communication initiates a battle for possession over Louise in sheer patriarchal terms. While Elgin behaves as the *senex iratus* of Plautinian comedy, the narrator assumes the role of all-enduring and romantic lover, a melancholy Werther, ready to sacrifice himself for the good of his beloved. The assumption of these roles by husband and lover forces Louise into the role of sickly and inert damsel awaiting the prince charming who will 'win' her hand. The narrator's 'heroic' decision to leave Louise in the hands of her husband against her will shows that s/he has unreflectively assumed the role of protective male, without realising that by so doing s/he is objectivising her. The farewell letter s/he writes to Louise is full of clichés about love of the type associated with Mills and

Boon novelettes: 'I love you more than life itself. I have not known a happier time than with you. I did not know this much happiness was possible. [. . .] I'm going away tonight. I don't know where, all I know is I won't come back. [. . .] Our love was not meant to cost you your life. I can't bear that. If it could be my life I would gladly give it' (*WB* 105). From a lesbian perspective, Louise's cancer would be in keeping with the tragic view represented by Radclyffe Hall's *The Well of Loneliness*, where lesbianism is symbolically fused with sickness or unhappiness. This symbolic association is enhanced by the fact that Louise does not trust Elgin's diagnosis. She has asked for 'a second opinion;' she thinks that her condition 'is not serious' (*WB* 103); and she refuses to undergo treatment (*WB* 173). Likewise, the narrator's behaviour would be comparable to that of Hall's self-sacrificing protagonist, Stephen Gordon, who chivalrously relinquishes her lover, Mary, so that she can lead a 'happy' and 'healthy' married life.

The decision to separate her/himself from Louise brings about the narrator's fragmentation of the self, accompanied by shivering and fever: 'I ran a schizophrenic dialogue with myself through the hours of darkness and into the small hours' (*WB* 95). In keeping with the equation body/text = symbolic space, the disintegration of Louise's body by cancer, 'bone by bone, fractured from who you are, you are drifting now, the centre cannot hold' (*WB* 100–1), is described in apocalyptic terms as a blowing up of their Solomon's knot that projects the narrator out of 'gravity' into a 'slow-motion space', where s/he cannot find anything solid to brace her/himself against (*WB* 101).

As her/his self and world disintegrate, the narrator realises that s/he cannot continue her/his work as a translator (*WB* 94). Therefore, instead of the Russian section in the library, s/he starts frequenting the medical sections, led by a growing obsession with anatomy. As s/he reflects, '[i]f I could not put Louise out of my mind I would drown myself in her. Within the clinical language, through the dispassionate view of the sucking, sweating, greedy, defecating self, I found a love-poem to Louise. I would go on knowing her, more intimately than the skin, hair and voice that I craved' (*WB* 111). The narrator's desire to 'know' Louise 'intimately' shows that s/he is attempting to recover the *jouissance* they had previously enjoyed. However, s/he seems to be mistaken in thinking that the language of science will provide her/him with this intimate knowledge of Louise's body, just as s/he was tragically mistaken in assuming that Elgin had the key to her recovery. As

Rubinson has noted, the fact that 'Winterson portrays Elgin [. . .]
playing computer games that enable him to simulate surgery and
gene-splicing free from any "real" consequences [. . .] highlights
Winterson's negative view of the technological treatment of the body
as a mere machine that reckless, boyish scientists deconstruct and
reconstruct heedless of the humanity they circumscribe'.[43] The narrator ponders on this: 'In doctor-think the body is a series of bits to be
isolated and treated as necessary, that the body in its very disease may
act as a whole is an upsetting concept. Holistic medicine is for faith
healers and crackpots, isn't it?' (WB 175). But s/he seems to be
unaware of the lethal element in the scientific splitting of the human
body, since s/he divides her/his love-poem into four sections, respectively devoted to 'The cells, tissues, systems and cavities of the body'
(WB 113–20); 'The skin' (WB 121–5); 'The skeleton' (WB 127–32) and
'The special senses' (WB 133–9). Each section begins with an epigraph
containing a medical description of some bodily part or function,
which is subsequently elaborated on by the narrator in overtly literary
terms. Thus, for example, to the objectifying and authoritative voice of
medical discourse describing 'THE MULTIPLICATON OF CELLS BY
MITOSIS', the narrator opposes a highly metaphorical counterdiscourse. Comparing Louise's laeukemia to a political uprising, s/he
says that Louise's 'white T-cells have turned bandit;' that they 'are
swelling with pride;' that the 'security forces have rebelled;' and that
'Louise is the victim of a coup' (WB 115). Commenting on these
metaphors, Rubinson has noted how 'Susan Sontag demonstrates in
Illness as Metaphor [. . .] that disease metaphors have often been crassly
employed to describe political and historical events. Winterson inverts
that model, using political metaphors to describe Louise's diseased
body'.[44] Although there is no denying that there is a long metaphoric
tradition in Western culture associating the human body with politics,
the narrator's metaphors are no less outworn than the model they
'invert', since they in fact repeat, in words that amount to quasi-literal
pastiche, a conceit used by John Dryden in his elegy, 'Upon the Death
of The Lord Hastings', to describe the untimely death of Henry, the
eldest son of the sixth Earl of Huntingdon.[45]

The narrator's counternarrative, then, is as overtly literary and
derivative as the earlier sections of her/his memoirs. As another
example, the narrator's description of Louise's body as 'a voyage of
discovery' evokes, as Antje Lindenmeyer has pointed out, 'the trite
metaphor of Woman's body as a dark continent, passively waiting for

the male conqueror to penetrate, explore and exploit it'.[46] According to Lindenmeyer, the narrator's attempt at mapping Louise's body gives way to 'a necrophiliac obsession of exploring and mapping the body's insides',[47] and to a perception of it as 'an inner space or grave-like cavity, as "womb-tomb-home"' that is disturbingly similar to that of a (male) pathologist.[48]

By contrast, M. Daphne Kutzer sees the narrator's repetition of the Freudian metaphor of woman as 'a dark continent' as an attempt at recreating/remapping the scientific discourse on the female body. As she acutely notes, '[t]his section of the novel clearly owes a debt to Wittig's Le Corps Lesbien: both women attempt to rescue and recreate, re-map, the masculinist scientific language of the body'.[49] Kutzer's justification for this assertion is that although 'Louise is the undiscovered country and the genderless narrator the explorer [. . . .] S/he is] an explorer who can discover only that which Louise allows [and] Louise is also a map-maker'.[50]

The fact that different critics have responded to the narrator's 'love poem' to Louise in such contradictory ways points to the striking fact that her/his literary counterdiscourse is built on the accumulation of metaphors as dead and patriarchal as the metaphors of science, coined, as Heather Nunn has noted, by 'Shakespeare, Piranesi, Donne, Renoir and Henry Miller, males who write or paint "with their pricks"'.[51]

In a fragment of A Lover's Discourse entitled 'The Other's Body', Roland Barthes says that to scrutinise the inert lover's body is like 'fetishizing a corpse'. The alternative to this is to see the loved one 'doing something', that is, to allow the loved one to act.[52] In this light, the narrator's necrophiliac obsession with disintegrating Louise's body seems to deny the validity of her/his attempt to 'translate' Louise from a cancer-ridden married woman – i.e. from a passive and dead object of desire – into an active amorous subject. Gregory J. Rubinson suggests as much when he remarks that, 'although invoking Louise complexly, the narrator never construes her as a subject in her own right. Despite, or because of, all the transcendent images she inspires, she is an object for worship, and the narrator inscribes her in such a multitude of discourses and metaphors that Louise seems almost imprisoned in them'.[53] According to this reading, Louise, deprived of her right to speak for herself and impossibly placed between two equally possessive lovers, would be reduced to 'an object to be fought over [in a] power struggle between the narrator and Elgin [played out] through opposed [scientific and literary] discourses of the body'.[54]

In contrast to this reading, Heather Nunn interestingly suggests that the narrator's counternarrative constitutes an attempt to subvert the rituals of defilement that associate woman with the abject, by redefining 'the impure as the desired self'.[55] From this feminist perspective, the narrator's apparent failure to represent Louise, like the narrator's lack of name and gender, may be read as evidence of the unrepresentability of woman. In the light of Cixous's equation of the feminine with Derrida's 'supplement', the interplay of scientific and literary metaphors in the narrator's 'love poem' to Louise acquires an unsuspected symbolic dimension, pointing to Louise as the unrepresentable 'surplus' or 'excess' of meaning issuing out of the clash between the two patriarchal discourses. This reading is supported by the progressive transformation of the narrator's love poem into a fully poetic text which, as Nunn notes, is 'suffused with biblical references and biblical rhythms and intonation [that] recalls the Old Testament *Song of Songs* in which the amorous incants, an amatory voice celebrated by Kristeva as the poetic account of the dispersed identity'.[56] Considered to be the product of Solomon's pen, the *Song of Songs* is the noblest of songs – 'das Hohelied', as Luther called it – an allegorical poem setting forth the mutual love of Christ and the Church, under the emblem of bridegroom and bride. Therefore, the narrator's progressive assumption of the rhythm, intonation and vocabulary of the *Song of Songs*, in what Nicci Gerrard has described as an 'increasingly rhapsodic prose',[57] suggests a symbolic equivalent between the protagonists' human passion and Christ's holy passion for His Church, which reinforces the symbology of Solomon's knot discussed above. At the same time, the narrator's incantatory tone brings to mind the magician in Jorge Luis Borges' tale 'The Circular Ruins', who eventually succeeds in creating a beloved son by dreaming into existence one vital organ and physical trait after another, beginning with his beating heart.[58]

After completing her/his 'love poem' to Louise, the narrator resumes the retrospective account of her/his memoirs, to recount a conversation with her drunk patron, Gail Right, an appositely named middle-aged *deus ex machina*-cum-orange demon, who bluntly tells the narrator that s/he has made a mistake (*WB* 158).[59] This remark is enough to set 'the worm of doubt' (*WB* 159) gnawing at the narrator's patriarchal self-assumptions: 'Who do I think I am? Sir Launcelot?

Louise is a Pre-Raphaelite beauty but that doesn't make me a medieval knight. Nevertheless I desperately wanted to be right' (*WB* 159). With preternatural exactness, Gail tells the narrator where the origin of her/his mistake lay: 'The trouble with you [. . .] is that you want to live in a novel [. . ..] This isn't War and Peace honey, it's Yorkshire' (*WB* 160). On hearing this, the narrator decides to go back to London, only to discover that Elgin has got a new lover and has completely lost track of Louise. Her disappearance sets the narrator off on a frenzied search that increases her/his self-fragmentation, expressed in a series of good and bad dreams about what might have happened to her: 'In the night, the blackest part of the night, when the moon is low and the sun hasn't risen, I woke up convinced that Louise had gone away alone to die. I didn't want that. I preferred my other reality; Louise safe somewhere, forgetting about Elgin and about me' (*WB* 174). Fully aware that her/his 'equilibrium, such as it was, depended on her happiness', the narrator concentrates on imagining variations on the good dream: 'I built different houses for her, planted out her garden. She was in the sun abroad. She was in Italy eating mussels by the sea. She had a white villa that reflected in the lake. She wasn't sick and deserted in some rented room with thin curtains. She was well. Louise was well' (*WB* 174). The narrator's new role of 'Cassandra plagued by dreams' (*WB* 179) neatly echoes Roland Barthes's description of the amorous subject's 'hallucinatory manipulation of the possible outcomes of the amorous crises':

> By *imagining* an extreme solution (i.e. a definitive one) I produce a fiction, I become an artist, I set a scene, I paint my exit; the Idea is *seen*, like the pregnant moment (pregnant = endowed with a strong, chosen meaning) of bourgeois drama: sometimes this is a farewell scene, sometimes a formal letter, sometimes, for much later on, a dignified reencounter. The art of the catastrophe calms me down.[60]

Calmed down, then, by consoling fictions of her/his own making, the narrator decides to abandon the search for Louise and return to Yorkshire. At the end of *A Lover's Discourse*, Barthes says that the only alternative to the amorous subject's 'ceaseless desire to appropriate the loved being in one way or another' is the decision to abandon all 'will-to-possess': 'Not to kill oneself (for love) means: to take this decision, not to possess the other. It is the same moment when Werther kills himself and when he could have renounced possessing Charlotte: it is either that or death.'[61] On the train to Yorkshire, the narrator finds her/himself in Werther's position: 'I want to accept what I've done and let go. I can't let go because Louise might still be on the other end of the rope' (*WB* 184). Thus holding on to this tiny hope, the narrator rejects the possibility of committing suicide. And, as s/he definitively renounces the will-to-possess Louise, s/he is granted access to the true nature of love: 'There's freedom. We can be kites and hold each other's string. No need to worry the wind will be too strong' (*WB* 181). As the image suggests, in this new version of Solomon's knot, the ropes that form the narrator and Louise's 'loop of love' are loosely held, allowing the twin kites the freedom they need to intertwine their cords while soaring ever upwards into infinite space.[62]

The novel ends with an illustration of this image, in an episode situated in the novel's present when, opening the door of her/his Yorkshire cottage, the narrator is amazed to find Louise coming from the kitchen, in an uncanny scene that wavers between the spectral and the real: 'From the kitchen door Louise's face. Paler, thinner, but her hair still mane-wide and the colour of blood. I put out my hand and felt her fingers, she took my fingers and put them to her mouth. The scar under the lip burned me. Am I stark mad? She's warm' (*WB* 190). Her materialisation is comparable to that of the young man dreamt by the magician in 'The Circular Ruins'. The effect of her phantasmal figure entering the 'threadbare room' is expressed in an apocalyptic language that suggests the end of the old world and the beginning of a new one:

> The walls are exploding. The windows have turned into telescopes. Moon and stars are magnified in this room. The sun hangs over the mantelpiece. I stretch out my hand and reach the corners of the world. The world is bundled up in this room. Beyond the door, where the river is, where the roads are, we shall be. We can take the world with us when we go and sling the sun under your arm. (*WB* 190)

As the allusion to John Donne's poem 'The Good Morrow' (1633) suggests, the narrator and Louise's reunion has the cataclysmic force to transform 'one little roome [into] an every where' (l. 11). Thus, the private and enclosed 'microscosmic' space of the two lovers stretches to cover the entire universe, providing definitive evidence that the narrator's experiment in *écriture féminine* has succeeded in translating the patriarchal into a new feminine self/text/world. Still, in keeping with the multivocality of *écriture féminine*, the narrator's closing remark – 'Hurry now, it's getting late. I don't know if this is a happy ending but here we are let loose in open fields' (*WB* 190) – undermines the expectations of an unproblematic 'happy ending' for the narrator and Louise, with an ironic counterallusion to the lady's refrain in 'A Game of Chess': 'HURRY UP PLEASE ITS TIME',[63] thus pointing to the danger of triteness and boredom that threatens all long-term love relationships and further enhancing the openness of the novel's ending. In her next novel, *Art & Lies: A Piece for Three Voices and a Bawd* (1994), Winterson will attempt a similar imaginative 'revival of the dead', but with important structural and thematic differences.

Art & Lies is arguably Winterson's most experimental novel so far and also the one that has received the harshest criticism. Generally considered to be too pretentious and arty, it sparked a heated debate between reviewers and author that did Winterson's public image a lot of damage.[64] One of the reasons why the novel fails to engage the reader is its lack of a plot in the traditional sense of the word. Thus, Nicci Gerrard complained that 'in *Art and Lies*, Jeanette Winterson has unfettered herself from any story. Her soaring writing is *about* writing. Bodies are texts, deaths are closed books, other authors are like ghosts in the margins.'[65] According to this critic, Winterson's increasing lack of interest in 'the world' results in a dangerous loss of solidity as well as in solipsistic meaninglessness: 'Where once her writing was light as a soufflé, now it's light as a balloon, gorgeous, streaming colours, buoyed with clear light, and bobbing on its way into solipsistic, meaningless stratosphere'.[66] A similar charge of meaninglessness was made by Phillip Hensher, who contended that 'for quite large parts of *Art & Lies*, what she has written makes absolutely no sense on any level whatsoever'.[67] For Hensher, this was due to an unforgivable carelessness both in the writing of the book and in the transcription of the music score that appears at the end of the novel, evincing that the book was 'simply the result of putting the first thing that came into [Winterson's] head down on paper'.[68] Yet another general complaint was the book's lack of originality, what Peter Kemp described as Winterson's unwise insistence on 'parroting routine modernist opinions', to the effect that 'the book's beliefs and bigotries are unadventurously second-hand'.[69] D. S. fittingly summarised the reviewers' general reaction when he said in 'Nota Bene' that '[a]lmost the only favourable publicity Winterson has enjoyed recently was a long "Face to Face" interview with Jeremy Isaacs on

BBC2 (June 28) [. . .]. That indulgence apart, her new book *Art and Lies* has received one of the great critical roastings of modern times'.[70]

As the quasi-homophony between the novel's and the essay's titles suggests, *Art & Lies* may be regarded as the fictional counterpart of *Art Objects* (1995), the non-fictional book in which Jeanette Winterson formulates her definition of art and literature and sets out to explain the ideological grounds for her anti-realist, visionary stance and her whole-hearted allegiance to Modernism. In *Art & Lies*, Winterson already makes this allegiance explicit in the epigraph, which is taken from one of the Oxford lectures on poetry delivered by F. H. Bradley in 1901. In it, the philosophy professor rejects the definition of art as 'A COPY OF THE REAL WORLD' and defines the work of art as 'A WORLD IN ITSELF, INDEPENDENT, COMPLETE, AUTONOMOUS'. The epigraph, then, situates *Art & Lies* alongside the anti-mimetic position endorsed by turn-of-the-century and early twentieth-century literary movements such as aestheticism, imagism, French symbolism and Modernism.[71]

As is well known, the mimetic definition of art as a copy of the real world is derived from Plato's remark in *The Republic* that art is an imitation of nature which in its turn imitates the original Forms or Ideas. As an imitation of an imitation, Plato concludes, art is a twice devalued form. In *Poetics*, Aristotle refutes this conclusion with the counterargument that art improves on nature, which continues to be the model, in the sense that art highlights nature's elements by imposing a pattern on them. Further, in *Metaphysics*, Aristotle differentiates between, on the one hand, the practical knowledge that ensures the survival of animals and, on the other, the knowledge procured by art, which is a knowledge of 'universals' untainted by any utilitarian function. According to Aristotle, it is this superior knowledge of 'being *qua* being' that constitutes the *telos* or goal towards which human beings naturally tend (I.1–2). As the materialisation of this specifically human form of knowledge, the work of art is unbound by natural laws, such as time, space or gravity. Further, unlike history, which can only deal with what has been, art is solely concerned with what might have been according to the rules of possibility, not truth (*Poetics*, XXIV). The Romantic definition of art as a superior form of knowledge is based on these ideas, as is Professor Bradley's definition of a work of art as a complete world in itself. Consequently, as the epigraph recommends, 'TO POSSESS IT FULLY YOU MUST ENTER THAT WORLD, CONFORM TO ITS LAWS,

AND IGNORE FOR THE TIME THE BELIEFS, AIMS, AND PAR-
TICULAR CONDITIONS WHICH BELONG TO YOU IN THE
OTHER WORLD OF REALITY'. In the light of this epigraph, the
reviewers' complaints that *Art & Lies* is not about 'the world' are accurate since what the novel offers the reader is entrance into an
autonomous world ruled by artistic laws that have nothing to do with
the physical laws governing the material world.

In Winterson's earlier novels, as we have seen, the protagonists'
quests for maturation were simultaneously developed physically and
spiritually. Thus, for example, in *Sexing the Cherry* Jordan distinguished between his 'real' journey to remote lands recorded in his
logbook and the 'imaginary' journey written between its lines with
invisible ink. Winterson denied the protagonists of *Art & Lies* the
physical side of their quests when she described the novel as 'a journey into deep inner space, [a journey that] is not one of the clock: it's
an interior one, and in it you travel though time, through space,
through place'. Consequently, as the author further remarked, the
protagonists, Handel, Picasso and Sappho, 'are not characters in the
physical sense that we know them on the street or perhaps even in our
own lives. They are consciousnesses.'[72] This description of the characters as sheer 'consciousnesses' existing only in an 'interior' world
situates *Art & Lies* on a par with Modernist experiments in stream-of-
consciousness fiction such as the 'Penelope' chapter of *Ulysses*, which
is narrated in direct interior monologue. This association, supported
by the novel's subtitle, *A Piece for Three Voices and a Bawd*, was ratified
by Peter Kemp when he wrote that *Art & Lies* essentially 'consists
of three interior monologues, each emanating from a character associated with an art-form: music, painting, poetry. [. . .] their main
importance is as aesthetic exemplars or avatars'.[73]

Although there is no denying that the readers are granted direct
access to the minds of the three protagonists and that they have a representative character, to describe the novel as essentially three interior
monologues would do little justice to the narrative complexity of
Art & Lies. In direct interior monologue the reader has access to the
workings of the character's mind as s/he is musing to her/himself,
without the intervention of a narrative instance. By contrast, in *Art &
Lies*, the narration constantly alternates between the first and the third
person, indicating the fragmentation of the characters' selves (rather
than the intervention of an external narrative instance).[74] Further,
besides the 'Three Voices' of Handel, Picasso and Sappho, we also

hear the voices of an external narrator and of Doll Sneerpiece, 'The Bawd' in the mirror text alluded to in the novel's subtitle, entitled 'The Entire and Honest Recollections of a Bawd' (*AL* 29, 165). This pornographic and comic eighteenth-century text is contained, together with numberless other texts, in a book Handel, Picasso and Sappho read on a train that is taking them from London to the Aegean sea in the year 2000 AD – that is, in the novel's future at the time of publication.

The multiplication of narrative voices and perspectives is echoed structurally by the novel's division into eight chapters entitled after the three main protagonists in a sequence of repetitions and inversions (Handel, Picasso, Sappho; Picasso, Handel, Sappho; Picasso, Handel) that suggests both temporal circularity and the complementarity of the characters' life stories. Similarly, the characters' narrations are not linear and univocal, but rather fragmentary, repetitive and even sometimes contradictory, above all in the cases of Handel and Picasso, as if they are making a titanic effort to remember and their streams of thought are constantly spinning around the same crucial events in their lives, each time yielding more revealing information as the characters progressively bring to the surface memories that lay deeply repressed in their unconscious. In keeping with this, the narrative structure of the novel as a whole may be said to move in ever-closer spirals from dispersion to unification, reaching a climax at the end of the novel. This spiralling structure is mirrored by the train's movement, described by Handel as 'the still train spinning' (*AL* 171).

The first chapter begins with a third-person description of a 'stretching train' and the marvellous effect of yellow light flashing on the various objects and people on it, including a busy man with a book, who 'hasn't time to see the light that burns his clothes and illuminates his face' (*AL* 3). After a blank line, indicating a change of narrative perspective, this man, who turns out to be Handel, contradicts the third-person narration, telling the reader how he had noticed the strange effect of light on the book, on his own clothes and hands and how he had explained what seemed a miracle as 'a trick, of course, a fluke of the weak sun magnified through the thick glass' (*AL* 4). Perusing the book, Handel remarks that he 'was not the first one to find [it]', and he describes it paradoxically as both much used – an old, coverless volume with 'notes in the margins, stains on the pages, a rose pressed between leaves 186 and 187' – and unfinished: '[t]he cut pages had tattered edges but not all of the pages had been cut. In spite of its past, this book had not been finished' (*AL* 3). Opening it at the pages marked by the desiccated rose, Handel finds 'a map of The Vatican' (*AL* 3) and is reminded of the aroma of roses of 'La Mortola' – that is, the famous Botanical Gardens in Cape Mortola, near Vintimiglia in the Côte d'Azur, that Handel had visited long ago. Handel, who is a defrocked Catholic priest and cancer specialist, had been a seminarian and choir boy at the Vatican, where he had been seduced by the powerful and ancient Cardinal Rosso at the age of ten (*AL* 188 ff.). The seventy-year-old cardinal had himself been the lover, also from the age of ten, of the 'last castrato to sing in St Peter's' (*AL* 190), a legendary soprano singer of unparalleled voice who died in 1924, and who had been all his life 'consumed with a passion to sing the role of Marie Theres', the sophisticated and wealthy Marschallin who helps her young lover to love someone else' in Richard Strauss's *Der Rosenkavalier* (*AL* 196). In an attempt to transform the child, whose real name is Frederick (*AL* 200), into a replica of his former lover, Cardinal Rosso nicknamed him Handel and taught him every-thing he knew about opera and the arts. Convinced as he was of the superiority of art over nature, the cardinal felt no moral scruples in persuading the child to be gelded, with the argument that a castrato is the perfect man, the original androgyne of Genesis: 'The operation, he said, did not in any way interfere with manhood. Woman had been taken out of man. Why not put her back into man? Return to a man his femininity and the problem of Woman disappears. The perfect man. Male and Female He created him' (*AL* 195–6). The relation, which the child saw as positive – 'I cannot recall being happier, safe in the invented city [Venice], purposeful in our pleasure' (*AL* 199) – , came to an abrupt end two years later, when it was discovered by Handel's horrified parents, who immediately separated them and sent Handel to England.

The white rose Handel finds pressed between the pages of the book, then, is both the external stimulus that triggers off his process of reminiscence and the symbol of his wasted life, his 'punishable sin [which] is not lust, not even adultery [. . .] is not to do with sex at all. It is a failure of feeling. Not an excess of passion but a lack of passion' (*AL* 120). In this sense, the dry rose would be comparable to the 'bowl of [dusty] rose-leaves' disturbed by the narrator's attempt to open 'the door we never opened / Into the rose-garden', at the beginning of 'Burnt Norton'.[75] However, where for Eliot's narrator, entrance into this primeval rose garden symbolises a spiritual retracing of the path leading to 'our first world',[76] for Handel it literally involves entering the book, which, among many other texts, contains Handel's own life story precisely on the pages marked by the rose. More surprising still, when the reader of *Art & Lies* reaches pages 186–7 of Winterson's novel s/he will find that the rose found by Handel between pages 186 and 187 of the book on the train is the same white rose young Handel had put between the pages of a book belonging to Cardinal Rosso and which he had later inherited, during a trip to La Mortola: 'holidays, that day with you, the white rose, La Mortola, I keep pressed between the pages of a book' (*AL* 187).[77] This coincidence in the pagination points to the book as a *mise en abyme* of *Art & Lies*. As such, it is also the work of art Professor Bradley invited the reader to enter in the novel's epigraph.

Cardinal Rosso's book is described as a 'fabulous' compendium of rare, miscellaneous texts, whose 'manuscript leaves had been saved from the sacking of the great Library at Alexandria in AD 642' (*AL* 202). After opening the book on the train, Handel's narration is interrupted by a description of the Library of Alexandria, the greatest library of antiquity, founded by the Ptolomies in 300 BC (*AL* 4). This description, strikingly reminiscent of Jorge Luis Borges' Library of Babel, presents the library as a fabulously large and autonomous world in itself, a labyrinthine structure of infinite shelves soaring up to the sky, populated by numberless slave boys, who are racked 'at various levels around the library, so that they could form a human chain, and pass down any volume within a day or two' (*AL* 5). As a volume made up of the manuscripts that had survived the destruction of the Library of Alexandria, the cardinal's book may be said to constitute the unique materialisation of that fabulous text/world. But the book contains many other texts as well, including the Bible, scattered stanzas of the *Odyssey*, drawings of Pythagoras, Bede's *A History of the English Church and People*, Ovid's drama *Psappho and Phaeon the Ferryman*, the poetry of the Pleiad and *The Romance of the Rose* (*AL* 203); and, as Handel remarks, it still has unused, blank pages. In other words, like Borges' 'The Book of Sand' (1975), the cardinal's book is infinite, atemporal and unfixed, not just a palimpsest of literary texts but a compendium of Western culture at large.[78] Handel himself suggests as much in a reflection that would be perfectly applicable to *Art & Lies* as well:

The Book was his but not his. [. . .] The leaves had been cut and bound and new pages had been added to the book as it made its strange way down stranger centuries.

The work had not been arranged chronologically; those who had owned it, and through whose hands it had passed, had each left their contribution, as writer, scholar, critic, eccentric, collector, and each according to temperament and passion. The book owed nothing to the clock. (*AL* 202–3)

Once it is realised that the book is a *mise en abyme* of *Art & Lies*, it is easy to see a similar specular relation between the three characters reading/entering the book and us readers reading/entering Winterson's novel. Thus, *Art & Lies* reveals itself both as a Babel Tower of self-multiplying mirrors made up of nothing less than the sum total of Western culture, and a linguistic prison-house, trapping characters and readers alike. In keeping with this, towards the end of the novel, Handel asks himself whether what he thought to be a process of recollection of his lived experiences is only in fact invention: 'What makes up a life; events or the recollections of events? / How much of recollection is invention? / Whose invention?' (*AL* 183). At this point Handel is seized by a bout of existentialist angst as he entertains the troubling thought that, like the narrator in Borges' 'The Circular Ruins' (1944), he might be a character existing only within somebody else's dream: 'Look deeper: How much of your thinking has been thought for you by someone else? / Speak Parrot!' (*AL* 184).[79] Handel answers his self-addressed question with the reflection that although all human beings are artificial – 'I know I am made up of other people's say so, veins of tradition, a particular kind of education, borrowed methods that have disguised themselves as individual habits' (*AL* 184) – , yet we still have the freedom to choose the master and to imitate the best: 'Parrot may not learn to sing but he will know what singing is. That is why I have tried to hide myself among the best: music, pictures, books, philosophy, theology' (*AL* 185). This consideration (itself a reflection of Winterson's own ideas on art) motivates Handel's decision to reject the Church's dogmas and choose instead the discipline of art: 'In order to escape the arbitrary nature of existence I do what the artists do, and impose the most rigorous rules on myself, even if, inevitably, those rules are in turn arbitrary' (*AL* 186). Thus, paradoxically, Handel finds 'inexhaustible freedom' in the very artificiality and arbitrariness of artistic rules: 'What liberties they [the arts] take are for the sake of freedom. Of course rules are made to be

broken but when they have been broken they must be made again'
(*AL* 186). Handel's choice of art over dogma aligns him with earlier
visionary characters, like the Jeanette of *Oranges*, who consider art as
a superior form of knowledge. It also evinces the influence of
Handel's tutor, Cardinal Rosso, the book's owner and, as the reader
eventually learns, also the author of some of the manuscripts contained in it.

The description of the Library of Alexandria mentioned above
includes a transcription of what appears to be a historical (i.e. truthful
and original) report on the library, written in Latin by '[a] contemporary of Pliny the Younger', the first-century AD historian (*AL* 5).
However, this Latin text is spurious (i.e. fictional and derivative), a fact
that adds an ironic touch to the description and throws overboard
the Aristotelian distinction between history and literature so dear to
realism. Sandwiched as it is between Handel's narration and the
beginning of 'The Entire and Honest Recollections of a Bawd', this
description has a problematic narrative status: it can be read as an
associative leap of Handel's mind after perusing the book, since, as a
Catholic priest, he is supposed to be fluent in Latin and to know
the classics well; or, more significantly, as forming part of Doll and
Ruggiero's story, which Handel has just started to read. This interpretation is supported by the fact that Ruggiero is a scholar whose
formidable life's work is 'to reconstruct an index of those manuscripts
likely to have been stored in the Great Library at Alexandria' (*AL* 29).
Given the symbolic identification of the library with the cardinal's
book, this is tantamount to saying that Ruggiero's (impossible) task is
to reconstruct the book's index, which, as we know, contains the manuscripts that survived the sacking of the library. Once this connection
is made, it is easy to conclude that the author of the spurious description of the Library of Alexandria and, by extension, of the bawdy story
within which it is contained, can only be Cardinal Rosso, who used to
entertain his beloved child inventing stories and adding them to the
fabulous book: 'the Cardinal and his boy had worked their own inventions [. . . .] Handel remembered the long, dark Vatican afternoons,
and his old friend chucking over some Latin of his own devising' (*AL*
202). This interpretation is reinforced by the fact that Doll and Ruggiero's story is nothing but a pornographic and comic parody of the
relationship between the cardinal and Handel.

When, in her turn, Sappho reads this bawdy story, she writes on the
margin of the book, 'CLUE (Handel, German 1685–1759 Occupation:

Composer), "Di, cor mio, quanto t'amai"' (*AL* 168), thus associating the text with Italian opera and Ruggiero with the eighteenth-century musician. This association works to diffuse Handel's identity, setting on a par the fictional Handel/Frederick (the character in *Art & Lies*) and Georg Friedrich Händel, the flesh-and-blood composer. Similarly, the striking coincidence in the pagination of the cardinal's book and *Art & Lies* mentioned above suggests a shared identity between Cardinal Rosso and Jeanette Winterson. This type of association effectively erases the difference between recollection and invention and blurs the theoretical boundary between fiction and autobiography, as Handel pointedly remarks with reference to Doll's story: 'A fiction? Certainly, although I see from the extravagant and torn frontispiece that it parades itself as autobiography' (*AL* 29). Doll's 'fictional autobiography', then, may be said to materialise the central idea conveyed by the novel's title, itself a rewriting of the real Sappho's remark: 'There's no such thing as autobiography, there's only art and lies' (*AL* 141).

The complementarity of the bawdy story of Doll Sneerpiece and Ruggiero and the dramatic stories of Handel, Picasso and Sappho, comparable to that existing between *opera buffa* and *opera seria*,[80] is enhanced by the characteriological traits shared by Ruggiero and Handel, on the one hand, and by Cardinal Rosso, Doll Sneerpiece and Sappho, on the other. Described by Doll as 'a Gentleman of the Back Door' (*AL* 80), Ruggiero, like Handel, 'was high-minded, chaste [. . .] and loved opera' (*AL* 28). He was also probably castrated, as is hinted at by his unresponsiveness to Doll's charms and her discovery, on seeing him naked, of 'a very curious fact about her lover's mezzo parts' (*AL* 168). As a young man, Handel had panicked away from the woman he loved (*AL* 110), condemning himself to a solitary life of sexual repression, self-denial and guilt over his medical malpractice. Ruggiero, likewise, infuriates Doll with his unresponsiveness and with his priestly summons to repent: 'when he smells the passing of my perfumed body, what does he say? He says, "Madam, Madam, do you not repent?"' (*AL* 7). The cardinal possessed vast and sophisticated sexual expertise, and he used it to seduce Handel, but the most important weapon in his seduction scheme was to expose the child's feelings to the beauty of opera and the arts. Similarly, Doll succeeds in seducing Ruggiero by a combination of sexual deftness and the reading of Sappho's love poems, which, implausibly for a prostitute, but not for a classics scholar like the cardinal, she can read in the original Greek out of her own copy, a book as rare as Cardinal Rosso's book and with the same fabulous origin: 'Her own copy, in its original Greek, had come from a one-eyed trader in antiquities, who claimed to have stolen it from the Medici themselves. It had come to them by way of Alexandria' (AL 29).

At the same time, Doll Sneerpiece, the prostitute-cum-scholar, shares key traits with Sappho, the Greek poet whose love poems were condemned as indecent and pornographic by the Inquisition. In The Sappho Companion, Margaret Reynolds explains how '[j]ust about the beginning of the Dark Ages, about the ninth century AD, Sappho's poetry disappeared. [. . .] Sappho, the tribade, Sappho the outspoken woman, had her works destroyed, publicly burned, by the fanatical hands of the early Christians' while the poet herself was condemned as 'the heretic who speaks of carnal love'.[81] Still, as the fictional Sappho remarks, the ensuing scarcity and fragmentariness of records about herself and her work have not deterred men of all kinds ever since from 'poking through the history books, telling you all about me' (AL 52). The result, as Reynolds convincingly argues, has been a proliferation of strikingly bizarre and contradictory legends about Sappho, leading to 'the theory of the two Sapphos', a wise lyre player and lyric poet, and a sexually promiscuous courtesan and a suicide.[82] Echoing this, Sappho describes her journey across time and space to meet Picasso and Handel as 'a Fantasy Cruise from Mitylene to Merry England by way of Rome and passing through La Belle France', a journey taking '[n]ot much more than two and a half thousand years of dirty fun and all at my own expense' (AL 51). As her subsequent allusion to 'semolina' (Noah's favourite food in Boating for Beginners) suggests, Sappho's journey is meant to expose the falsity of the views on herself and her work passed on as historically accurate and truthful by '[f]amous Men', from Plato and Ovid, through Alexander Pope and Dr Johnson, to Baudelaire: 'I am no gourmet but I know a bucket of semolina when I've got my head in it. You can lead a whorse [sic] to water but you can't make her drink. My advice? Don't swallow it' (AL 51–2). In Ovid's version, Sappho, the sexually promiscuous courtesan, put an end to her life by leaping from the cliffs of Lesbos into the Aegean sea, devastated by her unrequited love for Phaeon the Ferryman (AL 72). The story of Doll's sexual obsession for Ruggiero is a clear parody of this version. However, Sappho herself rejects it as spurious when she says that her suicide was motivated not by being spurned by Phaeon, but by her loss of Sophia, the ninth muse, her real love and source of inspiration (*AL* 72).

Sappho's suicidal leap for love of Sophia is re-enacted by Picasso, the unloved daughter of Sir Jack Montgolfier, whose real name is Sophia (*AL* 157). In the morning of Christmas Day, 1997 (*AL* 132), Picasso, at the age of twenty-one, climbed on to the roof of the house and, Icaruslike (*AL* 79), found her freedom by throwing herself off the parapet (*AL* 85). Sappho, who is witnessing her fall from outside the mansion, sees, instead of Picasso's broken body on the snow, 'a cliff bent over the sea, she was looking at her body bent over the cliff' (*AL* 72). After this, the Greek poet follows Picasso to the station, where she is due to take the morning train (*AL* 35). Running 'to where the sun was just beginning the sky', she arrives just in time to leap into the crowded train and join her (*AL* 76).

Before meeting on the train, the three characters had led separate lives. Sappho lived in 'Mitylene 600 B. C.', while the other two characters lived in London in the twentieth century. Handel was born in Rome in 1949 (*AL* 192). Therefore, he is fifty-one when he catches the train. He is the Catholic doctor who refused to allow Picasso's mother, a young Spanish maid who had been raped by her master (*AL* 205), to have a legal abortion (*AL* 178–9, 205); and he is also the doctor who later assisted Picasso's mother at the time of her delivery (*AL* 181–3). Abandoned in the big hall of Sir Jack's mansion shortly after her birth (*AL* 205), Picasso grew into a sensitive young woman with flashing red hair and a frustrated passion for painting. Although, ironically, her wealthy father 'had a right to call himself a patron of the arts. He had commissioned fifty-five pictures over the years, all of them self-portraits' (*AL* 38), he had always prevented Picasso from developing her talent, since, like Charles Tansley in Virginia Woolf's *To the Lighthouse*,[83] he was convinced that '[a] woman who paints is like a man who weeps. Both do it badly' (*AL* 38). Rendered utterly miserable by her father's lovelessness, her depressive foster mother's neglect and the repeated sexual assaults of her big half-brother Matthew (*AL* 42, 46), Picasso, on the morning of Christmas 1997, after once more having been raped, smeared her father's Queen Ann mansion with bright coloured paint (green for the drawing-room, orange for the kitchen, blood red for the study), poured whitewash on Matthew's hair and clothes and covered her own naked body 'in camouflage colours. Orange against the sodium lights, purple against the livid sky, gold against the lure of money, silver-dabbed for luck' (*AL* 71).

After this, Handel, the family doctor, is asked by Sir Jack to declare her insane and send her to a mental asylum (*AL* 154–5). However, when Matthew breaks into her locked bedroom to seize her, the room is empty (*AL* 176). The official version was that she had climbed on to the roof of the house and thrown herself off the parapet. Although the fall should have killed her, Picasso believes that 'she had been saved from death by a deep bank of snow' (*AL* 85). Sitting on the train, Picasso will eventually force herself to admit: 'I did not fall on my own. As I stood slightly swaying, completely unafraid, my father pushed me off the roof' (*AL* 158).

After interning her in the psychiatric asylum, Handel 'never saw any of them [the Montgolfiers] again for twenty-three years' (*AL* 183) until the day when Handel and Picasso meet on the train (*AL* 81). After travelling for a while in the same carriage, Handel faints (*AL* 125, 153) and Picasso starts perusing his book. Then, after a lapse of time Sappho cannot properly assess,[84] Handel is abruptly brought to his senses by the terrifying impression that the train is falling down in a vertiginous spin: 'Twisted faces lurched at him as he was caught in a kaleidoscope of arms. Round and round, the sick of his stomach, and the rouletting train. He fell' (*AL* 171). At this moment, when he is experiencing what he wrongly takes for a train accident, Handel recalls in the third person a car crash he had suffered '[y]ears ago' (*AL* 172). He had been driving steadily along a smooth road, listening to an opera and 'then, as he tried to turn the wheel, the car disobeyed' (*AL* 172). After the accident, Handel tells the police that he was perfectly all right, although he was in fact badly wounded and he wonders 'what the grace was for and why he had never acknowledged it. A second life' (*AL* 172). That day Handel had been driving 'to the station, hoping to meet the morning train' (*AL* 177). Like Picasso, then, Handel takes the train after surviving a mortal accident.

Driving to the station the day of the car crash, Handel saw 'a young woman walking lightly and with a quick spirit' and he offered her a lift. Although he didn't see her face, the reader knows the woman is Sappho because 'her voice [. . .] had yellow in it' (*AL* 176); that is, it has the colour of the sunlight that floods the train, the same 'strange vital yellows' of Van Gogh's sunflowers that saved Picasso from madness (*AL* 155). What is more, the woman can only be Sappho because she is there to accompany Handel, just as she has done with Picasso, in an after-death journey that, according to Sappho, takes place in the year '2000 After Death' (*AL* 67, 150).

The qualification 'after death', then, should be read both metaphorically and literally. Metaphorically, it signifies that the twentieth-century characters are living in an Eliotean waste land populated by hollow men. This is Picasso's intended meaning when she describes her family as living dead,[85] or 'the box houses in yellow brick' of the London suburb she sees from the train as 'the cemeteries of the Dead' (AL 83). Sappho extends this metaphoric meaning to twentieth-century people in general when she describes them as 'zombies' and says that '[t]he world is a charnel house racked with the dead' (AL 64). Echoing Eliot's description of the crowd swarming to work in 'The Burial of the Dead', Sappho also says that '[e]ach man and woman goes to their particular scaffold, kneels, and is killed day after day. Each collects their severed head and catches the train home. Some say that they enjoy their work' (AL 65). This remark may also be read metaphorically. However, the fact that, as Eliot himself explained, his lines 'A crowd flowed over London Bridge, so many, / I had not thought death had undone so many', are based on Dante's 'Inferno' (III, ll. 55–7) begs for a literal (as well as a mythical) interpretation.[86]

Similarly, the qualification 'After Death' should be read literally (and mythically) when it comes to analysing what happens to Handel and Picasso after their accidents. Although they think that they are still alive, in fact the train they take after their accidents is not the usual morning train taking them from the suburbs to the 'old and patched' city that 'thrives on fear' (AL 68) for work, but a 'dead train' (AL 153) taking them to the 'invisible city' where Sappho lives: 'There is another city too, but we don't like to mention it, because officially it doesn't exist. People vanish everyday. That's where I live' (AL 68).

In Virginia Woolf's *The Waves* the main narrative is constituted by the soliloquies of six characters, rendered simultaneously, as they are formed in the characters' minds around a shared perception or situation, arranged sequentially through the main stages of their lives, from childhood, through youth and maturity to old age and death. These soliloquies are undercut by ten italicised sections or 'interludes' in which an external narrative instance describes the effects of sunlight on the earth and the sea progressing in the course of a single day from dawn to dusk. In these interludes, sunlight is associated with life and the breaking of the waves on the shore with death. Thus, the beginning of life is symbolised by the progressive revelation of the line of the horizon separating the sky from the sea.[87] The interludes, then, symbolise the span of human life from childhood to death and provide the spatiotemporal frame that the soliloquies themselves lack. The train in *Art & Lies* travelling east from London to the Aegean sea and following the course of the sun from dawn to sunset may be said to fulfil a similar structural function, providing the referential frame for the fragmentary and repetitive reminiscences of the characters. However, whereas time in the interludes is linear, equating the chronological progression of a day with the span of human life, the train is both whirling around at the speed of light and standing still (*AL* 171).

This puzzling behaviour brings to mind the train Stephen Hawking uses in *A Brief History of Time* to explain Newton's theory of gravity and how it led Einstein to postulate the inseparability of space and time on which the Theory of Relativity is based.[88] As Hawking explains, where Aristotle believed that the earth was at rest, Newton observed that all movement is relative, so that 'one could say that the earth was at rest and that a train on it was travelling north at ninety miles per hour or that the train was at rest and the earth was moving south at a ninety miles per hour'.[89] The train in *Art & Lies* displays a similarly relative behaviour: while for external observers like us readers the journey lasts for the whole span of the characters' recollections, for those sitting on the train the journey lasts for 'an infinitesimal space' (*AL* 31), the millisecond that it would take a dying person's mind to recreate in a flash his or her whole life, what Handel appositely describes as a 'div[ing] down through layers of light to his shipwrecked past' (*AL* 31). As this watery image suggests, Handel and Picasso's train journey may be interpreted psychologically, as a plunge into the unconscious comparable to the inward-looking phase in the maturation processes of earlier Wintersonian characters. From this perspective, Handel and Picasso may be said to be involved in a process of remembering/healing the wounds of their respective pasts as a way to reconstructing their fragmented selves. While Handel's process of unification involves his imagining/writing his life story on the remaining blank pages of the book he inherited from the cardinal, the tool Picasso uses in her healing process is painting, a therapy (like writing), much used by Carl G. Jung with schizophrenics.

Still, the psychological interpretation cannot adequately explain Sappho's presence on the train, not only because she has been dead for centuries, but because she does not suffer from self-fragmentation. It is her public figure, not herself, that has been distorted and fragmented by historians. Indeed, if Sappho appears at Picasso's door at the moment of her fatal leap and accepts Handel's lift after his car crash it is with the only purpose of leading the way for them in their afterlife journey to the underworld, where she herself lives.

As we saw in Chapter 2, the descent to the underworld is a current motif in visionary and utopian fiction, whose origins go back to the descent to Hades. In its function as crypt, the underworld is the dwelling place of all dead writers and artists whose works have contributed to shaping a given culture. Or, in Winterson's aestheticist terms, the sublime and unitary World of Art Professor Bradley invited the reader to enter, the mythical Library of Alexandria of which the cardinal's book is its fictional and *Art & Lies* its real counterpart.

In the *Divine Comedy* Dante equated the task of Virgil, the poet in search of *eidola* (archetypes or universals), with that of Hermes, the guide of souls to the underworld. Similarly, in the Modernist adaptation of the myth, the artist is defined as a Hermetic quester, or 'mediator' – Jung's shaman; Blake's poet/prophet; Yeats's *daimon* – someone capable of shaping and giving overall significance (a complete Idea) to the anarchy and futility of particular phenomena by the use of myth. Accordingly, the artist's role is the healing of the split between soul and world through the sacrificial rituals of the imagination, what Thomas Mann called his 'mediating task, his Hermetic and magical role as broker between the upper and the lower world'.[90] This is the task allotted to Tiresias, placed by Eliot at the centre of *The Waste Land* as the unifying figure directing the search for self-knowledge.[91] As we saw in the Introduction, Ezra Pound gives a similar task to the poet as wandering Odysseus or mythical quester travelling across time zones and ontological boundaries in *A Draft of XXX Cantos*. In *Art & Lies*, the poet Sappho performs a similarly unifying role, as Winterson pointed out in an interview: 'She holds the book together through her commentary and her reasoning and also her emotional power, which is eventually what brings the book to a proper close, finishes it'.[92] In keeping with this, Sappho (echoing the Jeanette of *Oranges*) describes herself as a prophet crying in the wilderness (*AL* 54–5). Her task as Hermetic mediator between the two worlds is made explicit by the 'correspondence' established between Apollo's dragging of the stars and Sappho's picking up white rose petals and throwing them again into the sea:[93]

She carried white roses never red.

As Apollo dragged the stars through his wheels she picked up the petals at her feet. Above her, the full moon like a clear coin, and in the water her reflection [. . .].

She wore the moon behind her head as a saint wears a halo.

She threw the petals in the water and stirred the stars. (AL 55)

For Renaissance magi following the Hermetic tradition like Marsilio Ficino the force that drives magic, unites human beings with the cosmos and allows them to participate in the Totality is their capacity to love. This view of love is itself based on the Greek myth of Eros as the primal force of love springing forth from primordial Chaos along with Gaea (Earth) and Tartarus (the Greek concept of the underworld as hell). Therefore, as the foremother of love poetry, Sappho is the quintessential mediator. This role is enhanced by her association with the moon, 'often believed to be the abode of the dead'.[94] The poet herself suggests this reading when she attributes the extinction of the prophetic Word ('the Word was gone') in the contemporary 'dead land' to ignorance of the true goal of alchemy (i.e. the search for spiritual illumination, not the transformation of base metal into gold): 'Ignorant of alchemy they put their faith in technology and turned the whole world into gold. The dead sand shone' (AL 57).

In Western culture, from Dante to Yeats and Eliot, the multifoliate rose (like the lotus in the east) has always symbolised transcendental unity.[95] In The Waves, Virginia Woolf varies this motif using a carnation instead of a rose to symbolise the protagonists' attempt to grant overall significance to their fragmentary perceptions of reality. Thus, to the fragmentariness symbolised by the seven chairs surrounding the characters' dinner table at Hampton Court, she opposes the vase containing a red carnation at the centre, as a symbol of their sought-for unity. As Bernard reflects:

We have come together [. . .] to make one thing, not enduring – for what endures? – but seen by many eyes simultaneously. There is a red carnation in that vase. A single flower as we sat here waiting, but now a seven-sided flower, many-petalled, red, puce, purple-shaded, stiff with silver-tinted leaves – a whole flower to which every eye brings its own contribution.[96]

A similar transcendental unity, symbolised by the white rose in Richard Strauss's Der Rosenkavalier, is achieved by the characters at the end of Art & Lies. After the train whirls them down into the cliffs of Lesbos, and they get out of the train, Handel realises that his life is now starting to acquire definitive shape: 'His past, his life, not fragments nor fragmented now, but a long curve of movement that he began to recognise' (AL 206). At this point, in a scene that has all the artificiality and excess of an opera's *grand finale*, Handel starts singing *Der Rosenkavalier* with a soprano voice he has surely inherited from Cardinal Rosso's earlier lover and, as he takes his place in the chain of dead sopranos who have contributed to the shaping of opera and his voice joins theirs, he becomes like them a mediator between the two worlds, as is suggested by the magical 'rod and staff' that budded at his hand (AL 206).

The novel ends with Handel and 'the two women standing together' at the cliffhead, sharing a vision of the World of Art they have just entered: 'Held in the frame of light, was not the world, not its likeness but a strange equivalence, where what was thought to be known was re-cast, and where what was unknown began to be revealed, and where what could not be known, kept its mystery but lost its terror' (AL 206). In Eliot's terms, they may be said to have reached 'The point of intersection of the timeless / With time', where 'the impossible union / Of spheres of existence is actual'.[97]

Remembering her beloved Sophia's kiss on the seashore of Lesbos, Sappho has suddenly been invaded by the certainty that 'it is possible to resist Time's pull. The body ages, dies, but the mind is free. If the body is personal, the mind is transpersonal, its range is not limited by action or desire. Its range is not limited by identity' (AL 62). Handel and Sappho's participation in this essentially artificial and collective vision of the World of Art is good proof that they have transcended the limitations of individual life and live for ever in their newly acquired transpersonal identity with the writers and artists of the past, in a sublime World of Art they themselves have contributed to imagining into being.[98] In the next two novels, the characters will take for granted the multiplicity and artificiality of their selves and worlds.

Notes

1 Clare Hemmings, 'Lesbian (Anti-)Heroes and Androgynous Aesthetics: Mapping the Critical Histories of Radclyffe Hall and Virginia Woolf', *Revista Brasil de Literatura: Literatures in English Language*. Online journal, Rio de Janeiro, Brazil (2000): 2. http://members.tripod.com/lfilipe/. Consulted on 18 March 2004.

2 *Ibid.*, 3.

3 *Ibid.*, 3.

4 *Ibid.*, 5.

5 Rowanchild, 'The State of the Heart', 31.

6 According to Rowanchild, Duffy's *Love Child* 'has reverberated through many subsequent [lesbian] fictions' including *Gut Symmetries* (*ibid.*, 38). The influence of *The Microcosm* is also evident in *Sexing the Cherry*. Further, the name of its narrator, Al, foreshadows that of Ali/Alix, the genderless narrator of *The.PowerBook*.

7 M. Daphne Kutzer, 'The Cartography of Passion: Cixous, Wittig and Winterson', in Jürgen Kleist and Bruce A. Butterfield (eds), *Re-naming the Landscapes*. New York and Bern-Frankfurt: Peter Lang (1994): 133–45; 134.

8 Rachel Wingfield, 'Lesbian Writers in the Mainstream: Sara Maitland, Jeanette Winterson and Emma Donoghue', in Hutton (ed.), *Beyond Sex and Romance?*: 60–80; 66.

9 Cath Stowers, 'The Erupting Lesbian Body: Reading *Written on the Body* as a Lesbian Text', in Grice and Woods (eds), *'I'm telling you stories'*: 89–101; 89. Lynne Pearce, *Reading Dialogics*. London: Edward Arnold (1994).

10 *Ibid.*, 90.

11 John Sutherland, '"On the Saliery Express": Review of *Written on the Body*, by Jeanette Winterson', *London Review of Books* (24 September 1992): 18–20.

12 Aurelie Jane Sheehan, 'Review of *Written on the Body*, by Jeanette Winterson', *Review of Contemporary Fiction* 13 (Fall 1993): 208–9.

13 Andrea Stuart, '"Terms of Endearment": Review of *Written on the Body*, by Jeanette Winterson', *New Statesman and Society* (18 September 1992): 37–8.

14 Ute Kauer, 'Narration and Gender: The Role of the First-Person Narrator in Jeanette Winterson's *Written on the Body*', in Grice and Woods (eds), *'I'm telling you stories'*: 41–51; 50, 44.

15 Kauer's sources are 'Fruits of a Love Affair', *Evening Standard* (27 August 1992) and 'Affairs of the Literary Heart', *Sunday Times Express* (30 August 1992). Pat Kavanah was Winterson's literary agent and the wife of Julian Barnes at the time of the novel's publication.

16 The allusion is to Peggy Reynolds, the editor and academic who left her marriage and lived with Winterson from 1989 until 2002. Like Louise, she was born in Australia and has flashing red hair. Heather Nunn, '*Written on the Body*: An Anatomy of Horror, Melancholy and Love', *Women: A Cultural Review* 7.1 (1996): 16–27; 16–17. See also Jaggi, 'Redemption Songs'.

17 Walter Kendrick, '"Fiction in Review": Review of *Written on the Body*, by

Jeanette Winterson', *Yale Review* 81 (1993): 131–3; 131.

18 Gregory J. Rubinson, 'Body Languages: Scientific and Aesthetic Discourses in Jeanette Winterson's *Written on the Body*', *Critique* 42.2 (Winter 2001): 218–32; 220.

19 Cixous, 'Sorties', 94, 63–4.

20 *Ibid.*, 81.

21 Marie Delcourt, *Hermafrodita*, trans. Javier Albiñana. Barcelona: Seix Barral (1970) [1958]:10.

22 Hélène Cixous, 'The Laugh of the Medusa' (1976), in Elaine Marks and Isabelle de Courtivron (eds), *New French Feminisms*. Brighton, Sussex: Harvester (1981): 254–64; 233.

23 Morag Shiach, *Hélène Cixous: A Politics of Writing*. London and New York: Routledge (1991): 18.

24 Julia Kristeva, 'About Chinese Women' (1974), trans. Seán Hand, in Toril Moi (ed.), *The Kristeva Reader*. Oxford: Basil Blackwell (1989) [1986]: 138–59; 146.

25 Cixous, 'The Laugh of the Medusa', 250.

26 Kauer, 'Narration and Gender', 41. See also Susana Onega, 'The "Body/Text" as Lesbian Signifier in Jeanette Winterson's *Written on the Body*', in Marita Nadal and María Dolores Herrero (eds), *Margins in British and American Literature, Film, and Culture*. Zaragoza: Servicio de Publicaciones de la Universidad de Zaragoza (1997): 119–29.

27 As pointed out in Chapter 1, the island is a recurrent lesbian image of displacement from Freud's 'dark continent' of femininity. Stowers, 'The Erupting Lesbian Body', 74. In 'The Poetics of Sex' (*WOP* 29–45), Winterson associates it with Lesbos when she has a character named Sappho describe it as a place of freedom – 'my island full of girls carrying a net of words forbidden them' – unknown and unconquerable by the male artist, Salami, living on the heterosexual 'Mainland': 'This delicious unacknowledged island where we are naked with each other. The boat that brings us here will crack beneath your weight. This is territory you cannot invade' (*WOP* 39).

28 Valerie Miner, 'At her Wit's End', *Women's Review of Books* 10.8 (May 1993): 21.

29 Anna Vaux, 'Jeanette Winterson: *Written on the Body*', *Times Literary Supplement* (4 September 1992): 20.

30 Kauer, 'Narration and Gender', 42.

31 Umberto Eco, *Postscript to The Name of the Rose* (1983), trans. William Weaver. New York: HBJ (1994): 67.

32 Hélène Cixous, 'The Last Painting or the Portrait of God', in Jenson (ed. and trans.), *'Coming to Writing' and Other Essays*: 104–31; 130.

33 Hélène Cixous, 'Coming to Writing', in Jenson (ed. and trans.), *'Coming to Writing' and Other Essays*: 1–58; 50.

34 Cath Stowers has pointed out how the narrator's remark that Louise's body is good enough to eat is in keeping with 'that tradition of lesbian writers who equate the female form with the generative brewing qualities of blood and yeast'. Stowers, 'The Erupting Lesbian Body', 91.

35 Elizabeth Meese, 'Theorizing Lesbian: Writing – A Love Letter', in Karla and Joanne Glasgow (eds), *Lesbian Texts and Contexts*. London: Onlywomen Press (1992): 70–87; 87.

36 In Alice Parker, 'Nicole Brossard: A Differential Equation of Lesbian Love', in Jay and Glasgow (eds), *Lesbian Texts and Contexts*: 304–29; 310.

37 In 'The Poetics of Sex', Winterson applies the same image to the lesbian couple formed by Picasso and Sappho: 'We did go, leaving the summer behind, leaving a trail of footprints two by two in identical four. I don't know that anyone behind could have told you which was which' (*WOP* 34).

38 The complementarity of this couple is comparable to the 'twinned royal pair' Winterson describes in 'Turn of the World' (*WOP* 149–60) as 'Male and female, like for like, separate and identical. A man's face in the woman's. A woman's face in the man's, and both faces the face of the traveller [who manages to find them]' (*WOP* 152–3).

39 Diana Fuss (ed.), *Inside/Out: Lesbian Theories, Gay Theories*. New York and London: Routledge (1991): 7.

40 *Ibid.*, 7–8.

41 Sinclair Timothy Ang, '(Giving an Other) Reading (of) Hélène Cixous, *écriture* (and) *feminine*' (1998). www.gradnet.de/papers/pomo2.archives/pomo98.papers/rang98.htm. Consulted on 5 March 2004.

42 In Parker, 'Nicole Brossard', 305.

43 Rubinson, 'Body Languages', 222–3.

44 *Ibid.*, 224.

45 'Blisters with pride swelled, which through's flesh did sprout, / Like rosebuds, stuck I'th' lily skin about. / Each little pimple had a tear in it, / To wail the fault its rising did commit: / Who, rebel-like, with their own lord at strife, / Thus made an insurrection against his life'. John Dryden, 'Upon the Death of The Lord Hastings' (1649): ll. 57–62.

46 Antje Lindenmeyer, 'Postmodern Concepts of the Body in Jeanette Winterson's *Written on the Body*', *Feminist Review* 63 (Autumn 1999): 48–63; 55, 56.

47 'Let me penetrate you. I am the archaeologist of tombs. [. . .] I'll store you in plastic like chicken livers. Womb, gut, brain, neatly labelled and returned' (*PB* 119–20).

48 *Ibid.*, 56.

49 Kutzer, 'The Cartography of Passion', 143.

50 *Ibid.*, 141.

51 Nunn, '*Written on the Body*', 23.

52 Roland Barthes, *A Lover's Discourse: Fragments* (1977), trans. Richard Howard. London: Penguin (1990): 71–2, original emphasis.

53 Rubinson, 'Body Languages', 226.

54 *Ibid.*, 226–7.

55 Nunn, '*Written on the Body*', 25.

56 *Ibid.*, 24.

57 Gerrard, 'The Ultimate Self-Produced Woman', 7.

58 Borges, 'Las ruinas circulares', *Ficciones*: 451–5; 453.

59 Gail herself suggests as much in an ironic and self-conscious comment, before advising the narrator to return to Louise: '"I may not look much like a messenger from the gods but your girl isn't the only one who's got wings. I've got a pair of my own under here." (She patted her armpits.)' (*WB* 160).

60 Barthes, *A Lover's Discourse*, 142–3, original emphasis.

61 *Ibid.*, 232.

62 This image brings to mind the twin souls of the speaker and his beloved, expanding 'Like gold to airy thinness beat' when he must go, in John Donne's 'A Valediction: Forbidding Mourning' (1611): l. 24.

63 Eliot, 'A Game of Chess', 68–9.

64 See, for example, D. S., 'N. B'., *Times Literary Supplement* (14 October 1994): 18; Nicci Gerrard, 'Cold Blast of Winterson at the Door', *Observer* (3 July 1994): 11; Graham Wood, 'Truth or Dare', *Times Magazine* (4 January 1997): 9–10, 13; Tania Unsworth, '*Art & Lies*: Contempt and Condescension'.

65 Gerrard, 'The Ultimate Self-Produced Woman', 7, original emphasis.

66 *Ibid.*, 7.

67 Phillip Hensher, 'Sappho's Mate', *Guardian* (5 July 1994): 13.

68 *Ibid.*, 13.

69 Peter Kemp, 'Writing for a Fall'. Review of *Art & Lies*, *Sunday Times Books* (26 June 1994): VII, 1–2; 1.

70 D. S., 'N. B'., *Times Literary Supplement* (8 July 1994): 14.

71 Professor Bradley's ideas exerted a powerful influence on T. S. Eliot, who wrote his doctoral thesis on him.

72 In Eleanor Wachel, 'Eleanor Wachel with Jeanette Winterson: An Interview', *Malahat Review* III (1997): 61–73; 67.

73 Kemp, 'Writing for a Fall', VII, 1.

74 Winterson uses the same technique in 'The Poetics of Sex', the story of lesbian love between a younger painter called Picasso and a mature poet called Sappho, out of which *Art & Lies* partially stems.

75 Eliot, 'Burnt Norton', 189.

76 *Ibid.*, 190.

77 In 'The Dry Salvages', Eliot describes the future as 'a faded song, a Royal Rose or a lavender spray [. . . .] / Pressed between yellow leaves of a book

that has never been opened'. T. S. Eliot, 'The Dry Salvages' (1941), *Four Quartets*: 205–13; 210.

78 Like the cardinal's book, *Art & Lies* is a patchwork of texts from many a canonical writer, including Sappho, Plato, Dante, Boccaccio, Shakespeare, Byron, Keats, Donne, Dickens, Mallarmé, Baudelaire, Walter Pater, Lawrence, Joyce, Eliot, Woolf and Dylan Thomas.

79 The impression of unfreedom is enhanced by the fact that 'Speak Parrot' is an allusion to John Skelton's scathing satire on the clergy, *Speak Parrot* (1521), thus pointing to the derivative nature of Handel's own words.

80 See Susana Onega, 'Memory, Imagination and the World of Art in Jeanette Winterson's *Art & Lies*', in Constanza del Río and Luis Miguel García Mainar (eds), *Memory, Imagination and Desire in Contemporary Anglo-American Literature and Film* (Anglistische Forschungen Series). Heidelberg: Univesitätsverlag Carl Winter (2004): 69–80.

81 Margaret Reynolds (ed.), *The Sappho Companion*. London: Vintage (2001): 81.

82 *Ibid.*, 7, 74, 359.

83 'Women can't paint, women can't write . . .'. Virginia Woolf, *To the Lighthouse*. London: Vintage (2000) [1927]: 45, *passim*.

84 'How long had they been on the train? Days, Hours? Months? Weeks? Years? Always? Never? The train had died' (*AL* 153).

85 'Jack Hamilton had made sure that his wife was dead before he married her' (*AL* 158); 'Their first child [Matthew] was still born'; 'The dead family and the live baby [Picasso] went to church' (*AL* 159).

86 Eliot, 'Notes on the *Waste Land*', 81.

87 Woolf, *The Waves*, 1.

88 Stephen Hawking, *A Brief History of Time: From the Big Bang to Black Holes*. New York: Bantam (1988): 21–5. Newton appears as a character playing a relevant, though ludicrous, role in the 'Recollections of a Bawd', when Doll asks him to apply his theory of gravity to help Ruggiero out of the sorry condition he finds himself in, after Doll's porcelain codpiece unexpectedly begins to swell inside him (*AL* 129–30).

89 *Ibid.*, 29. Pondering on the truthfulness or falsity of Doll's 'autobiography', Handel reflects: 'No matter how meticulous the scientist, he or she cannot be separated from the experiment itself. Impossible to detach the observer from the observed. [. . . .] When I am alone, and the experience, the emotion, the event, was mine alone, how can I say *for certain* that I have not invented the entire episode, including the faithful memory of it?' (*AL* 30, original emphasis).

90 Quoted in Smith, *Rape and Revelation*, 133.

91 As Eliot explained, 'Tiresias, although a mere spectator and not indeed a "character," is yet the most important personage in the poem, uniting all the rest. [. . .] What Tiresias sees, in fact, is the substance of the poem'.

Eliot, 'Notes on the *Waste Land*', 82.

92 In Wachel, 'Interview', 68.

93 The comparison of white rose petals with stars and of Sappho with Apollo evokes the Hermetic principle of correspondence, synthesised in the dictum 'as below, so above: as above, so below'. This principle, which is the cornerstone of sympathetic magic, expresses the theory that man is the earthly counterpart of God and that events on earth parallel the doings of God in heaven and vice versa, so that the magician capable of manipulating events here 'below' can affect the course of events 'above'. Cavendish, *The Magical Arts*, 13, 17.

94 Douglas, *The Tarot*, 100. In its negative side, the moon is symbolised by Hecate, the guardian of the gates of Hades. *Ibid.*, 100. See Chapter 4 on this.

95 In some Tarot packs, the Fool carries a small white rose in one hand. When this card appears at the beginning of the pack, the rose symbolises the quester's 'soul, the fragment of divinity which he still bears with him through all the trials ahead' (*ibid.*, 44). When the card appears at the end, the white rose symbolises 'the complete psychic integration which is the prize of his past struggle' (*Ibid.*, 111). The first symbolism would be applicable to the dry rose Handel finds in the book at the beginning of his quest for self-knowledge, while Sappho's preference for 'white roses, never red' would be in keeping with the second.

96 Woolf, *The Waves*, 82.

97 Eliot, 'The Dry Salvages', 212, 213.

98 This ending is strongly reminiscent of the ending in virtually every novel by Peter Ackroyd. See Onega, 'The Descent to the Underworld'.

4

Multiple selves and worlds

After *Art & Lies*, Jeanette Winterson published her seventh novel, *Gut Symmetries* (1997), and a collection of short stories, *The World and Other Places* (1998). As the author explains in the Afterword, the seventeen stories contained in this collection were written 'over a period of twelve years, beginning soon after *Oranges Are Not the Only Fruit* was published in 1985' (*WOP* 231). Winterson describes these stories as 'a charting of the ideas that interest me':

> the nature of Time, which I began to grapple with in the Deuteronomy chapter of *Oranges*, and which has occupied every book since. Love, whether between parent and child, (*Oranges*, *Sexing the Cherry*, *Gut Symmetries*) or between women or men and women. The journey or the quest, which is the search after Self that marks the shape of all my work without exception. The Outsider, the Stranger, which in ways obvious and not so obvious my characters are. (*WOP* 233–4)

The short stories, then, may be read as variations on the novels, often containing in inchoate form the same basic *topoi* around which the longer fictions develop. In the earlier chapters we noted in passing the relationship existing, for example, between 'Psalms' (*WOP* 219–30) and *Oranges*; between 'Orion' (*WOP* 53–63) and the story of Orion and Artemis in *The Passion*; between 'Atlantic Crossing' (*WOP* 15–28) and *Sexing the Cherry*; or between 'The Poetics of Sex' (*WOP* 29–45) and *Art & Lies*. In the case of *Gut Symmetries* this relation extends to virtually every short story in the collection, especially 'Atlantic Crossing', 'Lives of Saints' (*WOP* 65–73), 'The World and Other Places' (*WOP* 87–100), 'Newton' (*WOP* 161–75) and 'Adventures of a Lifetime' (*WOP* 205–17), as if in this novel Winterson were attempting to integrate and give definitive shape to ideas she had been grappling with separately for many years.

This richness of accumulated *topoi* produces an intensification of the already characteristic Wintersonian baroque effect of repetition and excess that has baffled realism-biased reviewers and critics of *Gut Symmetries*. Thus, for example, while considering that 'Winterson's descriptions of New York in the 1950s are as vivid and exciting as anything she has done' and while admitting that *Gut Symmetries* tells 'a beautiful, stirring and brilliant story', Katy Emck said that the novel 'does not make sense. It is the song of a romantic outsider; a grand author-as-god attempt to unify a bunch of loosely compatible ideas about the universe'. Emck concluded somewhat incongruously that 'for all its presumptuousness, *Gut Symmetries* has a crazy surreal force and its superstitions are, if nothing else, picturesque'.[1] David Sexton's review was even more negative. Incapable of judging the tale, not the teller, he kept reminding the reader of how, after *Art & Lies*, 'Winterson's writing has itself become steadily more impaired by her self-regard and insularity' and, although he grudgingly admitted that 'strangely enough, this is not a negligible book', he described *Gut Symmetries* as 'conceit[ed], enclosed and repellent', a novel 'extraordinarily difficult to get through', which displays the same disregard for realism and plausibility that makes 'magical realism quickly become [. . .] so dull and then so annoying'.[2] Though positive in other respects, Helena Grice and Tim Woods, in an article significantly entitled 'Grand (Dis)unified Theories? Dislocated Discourses in *Gut Symmetries*', concurred with Emck's and Sexton's opinion that the novel lacks structural coherence and seriousness of purpose, describing it as 'something of a large conceptual linguistic game, [. . .] a novel which sometimes loses itself in the trickeries of its playful parallels, and ultimately produces a narrative which falls apart rather than falls together'.[3] The opinions of these reviewers and critics seem to stem from their refusal to read *Gut Symmetries* in its own terms, as a set of 'symmetries' or harmonically arranged ideas and themes ranging, as the dustcover puts it, 'from the Greeks to the Grand Unified Theories of modern physics (GUTs)'.

Gut Symmetries is the story of three narrator-characters, Alice, Jove and Stella. Alice, really called Alluvia Fairfax (*GS* 203), is a Cambridge postgraduate student of New Physics who has just won 'two years of research funding at Princeton' (*GS* 16). Consequently, at the beginning of the novel we find her on board the *QE2* (*GS* 13), giving a lecture on Paracelsus as a way of paying her passage from Southampton to New York. During the cruise she meets and falls in love with a fellow lecturer, Jove, the middle-aged, second-generation Italian-

American Professor of Superstring Theory at 'the Institute for Advanced Studies, Princeton' (GS 15) where she is also going to work. Jove is at that time married to Stella. This meeting is one of the many coincidences that pins the lives of the three characters to each other and to other characters in the novel, including their ancestors. As we shall see, the whole novel is structured by means of similar random coincidences into a complex web of 'symmetries' comparable to the chaotic arrangement of elements in fractals.

Alice's father, David Fairfax, came from a family of 'Liverpool limeys' (GS 52). As her grandmother explains, theirs was 'the story of a humble family who became a name. My son David whose father grandfather and great-grandfather unto the sixth generation worked the docks. My son David, rich respected, powerful' (GS 67–8). Fittingly named David, then, he seemed, like the biblical king, to be 'able to lay up for himself inexhaustible riches' (GS 54). In order to fulfil his mother's dream, he had dutifully made the difficult leap into the middle class. However, in doing so, he had gone against his nature, since 'He was a man who belonged with an elk, with a moose. A whale man, a bear man' (GS 54). The woman he chose to marry was utterly opposed to him. She was the daughter of an Irish 'nearly well-to-do' partner in the naval firm he worked for. David believed that her refinement and her 'mink and pearls' expressed 'a part of himself' and that she 'completed him' (GS 58). In fact, however, as Alice notes, 'he absorbed her while she failed to absorb him' (GS 59). Thus, she remains nameless in Alice's account, simply described as 'Miss 1950s. The perfect post-war wife. She was pretty, she was charming, she was clever enough but not too, she smiled at the men and gave the women that quizzical bewildered look, as if to say, "What, am I not the only one then?"' (GS 58). Inevitably, when 'I [Alice] was five my father was on pills and my mother was on gin' (GS 60).

Jove's real name is Giovanni Baptista Rossetti (GS 95). He is the son of Signora Rossetti, the owner of 'Rossetti's diner, the most famous little trat in town [New York]' (GS 89), where Stella was accidentally born. Ironically for an atheist, his mother nicknamed him Jove after the 'King of the Gods'. And, as Stella remarks, 'He could not bring himself to disbelieve it quite, nor could he quite forget that his real name was Giovanni, as in *Don Giovanni*, his favourite opera [about one of the] world's most famous seducers' (GS 99). Stella, who is a poet and has worked as a literature teacher (GS 36), is, like Jove, the sibling of New York immigrants. Her mother, Uta, was German.

When she met Ishmael, she was a 'timidly intellectual' girl who had moved to Austria 'to study painting and drawing, supporting herself by selling lightning sketches in cafés' (GS 80). Uta was attracted to Ishmael because he was diametrically opposed to her father, a butcher and 'a lapsed Catholic turned cleaver atheist', who 'had joined the Nazis and had been hung from a hook in his own shop' (GS 80, 90). By contrast, Stella's father, a Jewish dealer in rare second-hand books and an expert Cabbalist, had a wholly visionary outlook on life. During the Nazi regime, Uta saved Ishmael's life at the risk of her own helping him to flee from Austria, and later followed him (GS 75–6). In another example of striking coincidence, Alice and Stella meet for the first time at the Algonquin Hotel (GS 107), the same hotel where, as the reader will eventually learn, Alice's father had had a love affair with Stella's mother many years before.

Although Alice and Jove are both New Physicists, their attitudes to science are diametrically opposed. Jove is a rational materialist and an atheist (GS 27) with 'an organic view of nature' that, he says, 'in no way resembles Newton's Mechanics' (GS 191).[4] He distinguishes 'honest science' from what 'is not science at all. Call it alchemy, astrology, spoon-bending, wishful thinking' (GS 191). By contrast, Alice believes art, magic, religion and science to be equally valid, alternative discourses for explaining the meaning of human life in the universe. Consequently, she describes herself as belonging in 'that band of pilgrims uncenturied, unqualified, who, call it art, call it alchemy, call it science, call it god, are driven by a light that will not stay' (GS 73). Alice's attitude to science situates her in 'the band' of Paracelsus (1493–1541), the early Renaissance Swiss physician described in the Prologue as 'physician, magician, alchemist, urge, demiurge, *deus et omnia*' (GS 1). This description strongly echoes the motto of Agrippa von Nettersheim's book *De incertitudine et vanitate scientiarum* (1527), where this natural philosopher describes himself as '*ipse philosophus, daemon, heros, deus et omnia*'.[5] As Jung points out in his lecture 'Paracelsus', Agrippa's motto, with its emphasis on human potentialities, perfectly characterises the new revolutionary paganism of spirit of the Cinquecento, what Jung describes as 'the explosive, revolutionary, futuristic spirit of the times, which left Protestantism far behind and anticipated the nineteenth century outlook on science'.[6]

In a letter to Marie-Louise von Franz (1947), Wolfgang Pauli, the scientific patron of Jung's Institute, pointed out how, in the Renaissance, medieval natural philosophy was split in two directions:

Neoplatonic and Hermetic (or Hermetico-Cabbalist) alchemy.[7] Those who, like Marsilio Ficino, tried to reconcile Hermeticism with ancient Greek thought, were mainly philosophers. Their goal was 'the spiritualization of matter with its definition of "being" in the Platonic heavens'.[8] As Remo F. Roth points out, this aim is based on a consideration of matter (Mother earth, the female body, the female principle) as negative and evil. By contrast, Hermetic alchemists like Paracelsus, Gerardus Dorneus and Robert Fludd were physicians. Their goal was to find 'symmetry' between the equally valued spirit and matter in an in-between world in the middle. Thus, while the aim of the Neoplatonists was to reach the heavenly sphere (the Platonic *Empyreum*) by means of ascesis, and specifically through *amor coelestis*, or unreproductive spiritual love, by contrast, the aim of Hermeticism was the *hierosgamos* (*coniunctio* or 'chymic wedding') of opposites (light and darkness; spirit and matter; god and goddess), through *amor vulgaris*, procreative sexual love. The product of this love is an androgynous *filius philosophorum*, explicitly identified with the precious *lapis* or stone (in eastern occultism, a diamond) obtained at the end of the alchemical process when the *prima materia* is refined and transmuted into the *anima mundi*, the body-soul hidden in matter.[9] Paracelsus's last and most influential follower was the Rosicrucian magus Robert Fludd (1574–1637). His controversies with Martin Mersenne (1588–1648) and Johannes Kepler (1588–1648) are seen as a conflict between a late revival of the Hermetico–Cabbalist tradition and the seventeenth-century scientific revolution.[10] Therefore, by linking the Cinquecento to the nineteenth century, Jung is suggesting in his lecture that the animistic approach to science constituted a preferable alternative to the deterministic approaches developed in reaction to it by scientists like Kepler, Descartes and Newton in the seventeenth and early eighteenth centuries.

Unlike Newtonian science, Hermeticism is thoroughly holistic. That is, it is based on the absolute certainty of the 'indissoluble, unconscious oneness of man and world'.[11] The central idea lying behind this worldview is that of 'universal harmony, of the harmonious relationships between man, the microcosm, and the greater world of the universe, the macrocosm'.[12] In keeping with this, Paracelsus defined man as a microcosm and the world as the macrocosm existing in a mutual and harmonic relation of 'correspondence': 'The animate world is the larger circle, man is the [. . .] smaller circle. He is the microcosm. Consequently, everything without is within, everything above is below. Between all things in the larger and smaller circles reigns "correspondence" (*correspondentia*)'.[13]

In the novel, Alice alludes to this when she says that 'Paracelsus was a student of Correspondences: "As above, so below." The zodiac in the sky is imprinted in the body. "The galaxa goes through the belly"' (*GS* 2). As Jung remarks in another lecture on him, 'Paracelsus certainly knew the "Tabula smaragdina," the classical authority of medieval alchemy, and the text: "What is below is like what is above. What is above is like what is below. Thus is the miracle of the One accomplished"'.[14] According to Jung, it was from this principle that Paracelsus derived the primordial image of an inner starry heaven in man: 'Not only the stars or the moon etc. constitute the heavens, but also there are stars in us [. . .] the firmament is twofold, that of the heavens and that of the bodies.' Drawing a parallel between the alchemical and the digestive processes, Paracelsus located the 'life-warmth', the source of philosophical cognition, in the belly.[15] Consequently, it was in the belly that he situated man's inner heaven, what he called the 'astrum' or 'Sydus'.[16] Like the spheres, the inner heaven is driven by the *spiritus mundi*, God's creative spark existing in all things. However, each individual's inner 'star' or 'firmament' is unique, 'an endosomatic heaven, whose constellations did not coincide with the astronomical heaven but originated with the individual's nativity, the "ascendant" or horoscope'.[17] The particular astrological circumstances at the time of birth are, therefore, determinant for the future development of the individual.

Echoing these ideas, Paracelsus is described at the beginning of the Prologue, in what amounts to a mandalic image of the totality, as a microcosmic baby or androgynous *filius philosophorum*,[18] inside his mother's belly/Nature/the macrocosm, simultaneously containing inside himself a mountain/Nature/the macrocosm: 'First there is the forest and inside the forest the clearing and inside the clearing the cabin and inside the cabin the mother and inside the mother the child and inside the child the mountain' (*GS* 1). In this light, the pun in the novel's title between 'gut' (the human belly) and 'G.U.Ts'. (the acronym of grand unified theories of modern physics) points to a similarly holistic impulse between Renaissance and contemporary physics, as Alice repeatedly suggests: 'The Miracle of the One that the alchemists sought is not very far from the infant theory of hyperspace, where all the seeming dislocations and separations of the atomic and sub-atomic worlds are unified into a co-operating whole' (*GS* 2).

Two of the main goals of the New Physics are to describe the four fundamental forces in nature (electromagnetism, gravitation and the weak and strong nuclear forces) and to establish the relationships between elementary particles in terms of a single theoretical framework. As Davies and Gribbin have pointed out, this involves fitting together the theory of quantum mechanics and the theory of relativity, a task that has proved impossible in three dimensions: 'Three of these forces can be accurately described in terms of quantum field theory as part of the cosmic network', but gravitation, a force which is closely linked, in the general theory of relativity, with the geometrical structure of space-time, 'has stubbornly resisted the efforts of theorists to cast it in this mould'.[19] Superstring theory was developed as an attempt to overcome this difficulty. Briefly stated, this theory postulates that, instead of point particles or blobs of matter, sub-atomic particles are made up of tiny strings and membranes, which exist in ten or more dimensions, three being the ones we experience, plus other dimensions so tiny that they are imperceptible.[20] Alice alludes to this when, reflecting on our inability to find out the whereabouts of Heaven and Hell, she says that their invisibility may be a simple matter of dimensions: 'As yet nothing. No spacemen, no Heaven, no Hell. But perhaps they have curled up on the Planck scale, in the six-dimension sister universe, smaller than small, bigger than big' (GS 3). For Alice, then, there is an invisible 'sister world' of anti-matter side by side with the material universe:

> In the beginning was a perfect ten-dimensional universe that cleaved into two. While ours, of three spatial dimensions and the oddity of time, expanded to fit our grossness, hers of six dimensions wrapped itself away in tiny solitude.
>
> This sister universe, contemplative, concealed, waits in our future as it has refused our past. It may be the symbol behind all our symbols. It may be the mandala of the East and the Grail of the West. (GS 4)[21]

The postulation of a parallel world of antimatter strikingly recalls the Hermetic alchemists' intermediate psychophysical world, itself the antecedent of the *unus mundus*, Pauli and Jung's 'unified psychophysical reality'.[22] Also striking, as Alice notes, is the similarity between Robert Fludd's description of the 'symmetries' between the constitutive elements of the cosmos with the 'image of the universe as a musical instrument, vibrating divine harmonies' (GS 98) and the superstring theory that 'any particle, sufficiently magnified, will be seen not as a solid fixed point but as a tiny vibrating string. Matter will be composed of these vibrations. The universe itself would be a symphony' (GS 98). Fludd's book, *Utrisque Cosmi Historia* (*The History of the Two Worlds*), is explicitly based upon the macro/micro correspondence of self and world. Echoing this, Alice uses the image of the music of the spheres to describe her own relation with Stella: 'There are vibrations, relationships, possibilities and out of these is formed our real life' (GS 207).

With Alice's words in mind, the word 'symmetries' in the novel's title may be said to point both to the harmonious relationships knitting together every element in Jeanette Winterson's fictional universe and to the 'correspondence' between, on the one hand, the (macrocosmic) development of the novel from initial chaos to overall cohesion and, on the other, the parallel (microcosmic) evolution of the characters from self-fragmentation to unification. Alice suggests as much when she compares the main characters' triangular relationship to the symmetry knitting together the three fundamental forces in nature, according to the standard model in physics:

> The attraction of the Model is that it recognises the symmetries of the three fundamental forces, weak force, strong force, electromagnetic force. Difficulties begin when these three separate forces are arbitrarily welded together.
>
> *His wife, his mistress, met.* (GS 97, original italics)

Hermeticism defined God pantheistically as the One, the totality of everything and the reconciliation of all opposites. The definition of God as the union of three Persons in One (Father, Son and Holy Spirit) in the dogma of the Trinity also points to the complex nature of God's unity. Echoing this, Paracelsus distinguished three 'bodies' in man, roughly equivalent to body, soul and spirit: the 'elemental' (or physical), the 'sidereal' (or astral) and the 'illuminated body' or 'spark of God'.[23] The unification of these three bodies and the integration of man with the cosmos by means of his essential transmutation (Jung's *Wandlung*) is the true aim of the alchemical process, when 'the alchemist is finally carried out beyond the bounds of his own being into a lasting union with the universe. He pervades all space and all time. He enters the impregnable fortress in which the [Philosopher's] Stone lies guarded.'[24]

The dogma of the Trinity and Paracelsus's three bodies of man constitute a telling antecedent of Jung's division of the self into ego, shadow and anima/animus, just as the alchemical search for the Philosopher's Stone foreshadows Jung's individuation process. As we saw in Chapter 2, the individuation process takes place throughout the whole span of the individual's life and is divided into two phases. During the first half of life, the primary task of the psyche is ego development. Consequently, during this (subjective) phase the ego becomes increasingly independent of the archetypal self. The process is reversed in the second (objective) phase, which takes place during the second half of life. During it, the primary task is the ego's acceptance, assimilation and conscious integration with the self.

Originally devised to represent grades or stages in a system of initiation, the arcana of the Tarot constitute powerful visual counterparts of the archetypes or collective symbols that make up the stages in the individuation process. Since the nineteenth century, when the French occultist Eliphas Levi established the esoteric link between the Tarot and the Cabbala, the most important decks in use are founded on Cabbalistic principles. At the same time, the connections between Jewish Cabbala and Hermetic alchemy have been quite close since Pico della Mirandola attempted to supplement *magia naturalis* with Cabbalistic magic at the end of the sixteenth century, and Hermetic alchemists like Paracelsus are often referred to as Hermetico-Cabbalist magi.[25] The Cabbalistic equivalent of the Tarot is the Tree of Life representing the twenty-two 'paths' comprised in the ten *sefirot* (stages or archetypes) through which God has structured both the cosmos and the human mind. Like the stages represented by the Tarot trumps and the alchemical operations in the refinement of base metal into gold, the paths in the Tree of Life represent stages in a process of essential transformation and integration of the material with the spiritual and of self and world. Further, as Sanford L. Drob suggests, the structure of the Tree of Life has interesting analogies to superstring theory: 'Like the "super-string" theorists of contemporary physics, they [the Cabbalists] view the world as being comprised not of four, but of ten dimensions, and they regard each thing in the world, whether spiritual, psychical, or material to be composed of varying combinations of these ten dimensions or structures'.[26] From this perspective, the attempt of MacGregor Mathers, the leader of the Order of the Golden Dawn, to combine the knowledge and practices of these and other occult traditions into one vast all-encompassing system of esoteric thought,[27] like Jung's own attempt to integrate ideas from alchemy, religion, the Tarot and chaos theory in his

depth psychology, are strikingly similar to the attempts of contemporary science to formulate a grand unified theory of modern
physics.[28]

Gut Symmetries responds to a similar attempt to unify the discourses of Hermetico-Cabbalist magic, depth psychology and the
New Physics under the umbrella discourse of literature. As I suggested elsewhere,[29] the division into eleven chapters entitled after
Tarot cards imitates the Celtic Cross Spread (the most popular and
ancient of Tarot spreads, which requires a minimum of ten cards) in
a typical process of fortune telling. According to Joan Bunning, the
usual spread of the Celtic Cross is as follows:[30]

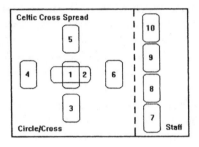

Like the Celtic crosses found everywhere in Ireland, the Circle/
Cross symbolises the joining of spirit and matter and the unity of all
events in time. As the discontinuous line in the scheme suggests, the
ten-card spread can be divided into two sections: the Circle/Cross (the
first six cards) and the Staff (the remaining four cards). According to
Bunning, the combination of the two sections in this spread symbolises the working together of the feminine and the masculine energies,
respectively represented by the Circle/Cross and the Staff. Like the
double-loop structure of the major arcana reproduced in Chapter 2,
this division also symbolises the dual (subjective and objective;
spiritual and physical) nature of the Fool's quest.

In the Celtic Cross spread, cards 1 and 2 represent a central, smaller
cross/circle nesting within the larger cross/circle (cards 3, 4, 5 and 6).
Thus, the choice of this spread to structure *Gut Symmetries* may be
said to mirror Paracelsus's image of the micro/macrocosm as a small
circle within a larger one, used by Alice in her presentation of Paracelsus as a man/mountain (see above). Symbolically, the smaller cross
represents the heart of the matter at the time of the reading. In the

novel, this cross corresponds to the first two chapters – 'The Fool' and 'The Tower', which are respectively narrated by Alice and Stella. As in *The Passion* and *Sexing the Cherry*, the alternation of their narrative voices indicates the complementarity of the two narrator-characters. The fact that the first chapter is entitled 'The Fool' situates Alice as the querent or quester at the beginning of a consultation/initiation process, a position that is wholly in keeping with her symbolic 'ego' role. The archetype of the 'wise Fool' is characterised by his lack of experience in the ways of the world, but this is only an apparent disadvantage, since 'in reality it ensures that his mind is not closed to unusual experiences that are denied to ordinary men. [. . .] The Fool is the seeker after enlightenment chasing the elusive butterfly of intuition in the hope that it will lead to the mysteries.'[31] The Fool is usually represented clothed in rags, with a dog tearing at his leg as he marches along, and carrying slung over his shoulder on the end of a long stick a 'bag containing those elusive memories of what he is leaving behind, memories that will urge him ever onwards in his search to recover what he is about to lose – his primeval innocence'.[32] In the other hand he holds a small flower, usually a white rose: 'this is his soul, the fragment of divinity which he will bear with him through all the trials ahead'.[33]

Alice is well aware of her role, for she describes herself as a fool – 'I know I am a fool' (*GS* 24) – and repeatedly invites an unnamed addressee to accompany her on her journey for self-knowledge: 'Walk with me. Hand in hand through the nightmare of narrative' (*GS* 24). As this quotation suggests, Alice's journey (like those of earlier Wintersonian characters) is textual as well as physical and spiritual, a process of writing into meaning the intangible facts of a 'broken past, named and not' (*GS* 117) through the joint exercise of memory, 'to make connections out of scraps' and project 'coherence' over the 'fragmentariness of life' (*GS* 24), and the imagination, 'puzzling over new joints for words, hoping that this time, one piece will slide smooth against the next' and will reveal the 'vision in broken pieces behind the wall' (*GS* 24). Although at first sight they seem aimed at the reader, Alice's repeated injunctions to accompany her are so concrete that they can only be addressed to Stella, who is also invited to gather her own memories of their common past and to make her own contribution to the final picture: 'Walk with me, memory to memory, the shared path, the mutual view [. . . .] I will not assume you will understand me. It is just as likely that as I invent what I want to say, you will invent what you want to hear. Some story we must have' (*GS* 20, 25). What is more, Alice sometimes imagines Stella's answers in a conversation with her: 'What kind of woman goes to bed with another woman's husband? Answer: a worm?' (*GS* 27). Thus, Alice points to the ego/anima complementarity of herself and Stella (the butterfly she is trying to catch) as well as to her self-fragmentation at the beginning of her quest, expressed in self-addressed remarks, like: 'Undeceive yourself Alice, a great part of you is trash' (*GS* 26).

Structurally, the difficulty in determining her addressee points to a similar indeterminacy in Alice's narrative status: she can be seen as a self-soliloquising, fragmented character; as an internal narrator telling the story of her life to another internal narrator; and as a self-begetting author-character inviting the reader to accompany her in her process of remembering/imagining/writing herself into existence. This third possibility is reinforced by a similar indeterminacy in the authorship of the Prologue, which is divided into two sections. The opening section, heavily indebted to Jung's lectures on Paracelsus, seems to be the beginning of Alice's lecture on him, while the second section, containing a summary of the novel's fabula and a glossary of key words meant to help the reader interpret the novel correctly (*GS* 6–7), can only have been written by Jeanette Winterson. As in *Oranges*, this willed confusion of identities and narrative levels sets the real world of the flesh-and-blood author on a par with the unreal world of the fictional narrator.

In contrast to the teasing indeterminacy of Alice's narrative status, Stella's narration in the second chapter, 'The Tower', clearly is a soliloquy. This Tarot card represents two human figures falling headlong from their stricken refuge as 'the raw power of cosmic energy' strikes down the tower in the form of a lightning flash associated with the bolt of Jupiter/Jove (or Zeus). The destruction of old values symbolised by the power of lightning brings about 'the overpowering light of truth in which all falsehood, and ultimately all duality, is destroyed. It is the flash of inner illumination which brings the freedom of enlightenment.'[34] Closely following this symbolism, the chapter opens with Stella's cataclysmic discovery that her appositely nicknamed husband, Jove, is having an affair with Alice. Her reaction is to go around her apartment, muttering to herself and splitting into two every object they have been sharing so far, including the matrimonial bed. From a Freudian perspective, Stella's state of mind would be comparable to that of 'Dora', the subject of Freud's famous 1905 case study on hysteria,[35] or rather to its historical antecedent, the sorceress, as defined by Cixous and Clément in 'Sorceress and Hysteric'.[36] This reading is enhanced by the ring in Stella's self-addressed instructions as she methodically proceeds in her destructive task, which is strongly reminiscent of the bloodcurdling threats of witches or ogres persecuting a terrified child: 'Ramsack the bedroom [. . . .] Give me a pot and let me turn cannibal [. . . .] Give me a drill [. . . .] Where is the chalk? [. . . .] First sever the headboard. Second, disembowel the mattress. Third, gut the springs. Fourth, amputate the footboard [. . . .] Purge the place, purge it' (GS 29–31).

With clear self-conscious irony, Stella rejects the label of hysterical woman/witch/monster: 'Nervous breakdown? Doctor, pills, rest, shh, shh! The crazy lady who frightens children' (GS 41), while acknowledging her traumatic, newly acquired self-fragmentation: 'Part of you or one of you responds to this [the sun rising]; wakes because the sun wakes' (GS 40). At the same time, Stella's splitting into two of common objects with a force comparable to Jupiter's bolt sets her destructive rage on a par with the splitting of atoms by nuclear fission. Alice suggests as much when she describes Jove as 'unstable as uranium. Stella, a living fission' (GS 198). Their shared association with the King of Gods points to Stella and Jove as Jung's 'syzygy', the divine couple whose marriage symbolises the wholeness and integration of the outer and the inner life.[37] In keeping with the symbolism of the Tarot card, Stella realises that her symbolic 'death by fire' (the common fate of witches at the hands of the Inquisition) is a necessary prerequisite for her spiritual rebirth: 'What is the moment of death? The moment when the heart stops? The rupture of command from brain to body? The soul climbing out of its dark tower?' (GS 44). Like Alice in the earlier chapter, then, Stella presents herself as a fragmented character needing to reconstruct/rewrite herself into a new and better person. Like Alice, she knows that this task of reconstruction involves the recovery of the intangible 'inner life, the other language' (GS 45) by the combined use of memory and the imagination, as well as, in Stella's case, the recuperation of her father's language and visionary wisdom: 'I used to speak Yiddish and Hebrew fluently but I have not spoken either language for thirty years. What else have I lost?' (GS 44). She sees her task of self-reconstruction in alchemical terms, as a godlike act of creation: 'I will have to make her [her reconstructed self] as Jewish legend tells how God made the

first man: by moulding a piece of dirt and breathing life into it'
(*GS* 45).

The next four chapters correspond to the larger cross/circle in the
Celtic Cross spread. As Bunning explains, the horizontal line (cards 4
and 6) 'shows time moving from your past on the left into your future
on the right. The vertical line [cards 3 and 5] is your consciousness
moving from your unconscious on the bottom to your conscious
mind on the top.'[38] In keeping with this, Alice in Chapter 3 ('Page of
Swords') and Stella in Chapter 4 ('The Star') tell the parallel stories of
their births and ancestry. Unusually for Wintersonian female characters, Alice and Stella are deeply attached to their fathers and strongly
influenced by them. This influence extends to their prenatal state.
Incapable of making any concessions to himself or to anybody else,
Alice's father, the self-made tycoon, had solemnly vowed 'not to make
love to her [his wife] until he had been made a director of the line' (*GS*
53). Thus, Alice was begotten on the very day he obtained the desired
promotion, as a result of her parent's first lovemaking (*GS* 57). This
is why she describes herself as 'Athene [*sic*] born fully formed from
the head of Zeus' (*GS* 59).[39] Alice means this remark to be ironic.
However, if the irony is ignored, it can be read literally as confirmation that Alice is the child of a god and goddess united by *amor vulgaris*. As such, she has all the potentialities of the *filius philosophorum*,
including androgyny. Ironically, since The Page of Swords is a card
associated with the use of mental powers,[40] and Alice identifies herself with Pallas Athena, the Greek goddess of war, wisdom and the
arts, as a child she was declared 'officially not clever' (*GS* 71). Consequently, unlike her sisters, she attended a local Catholic school from
which she 'was frequently removed to accompany [her] father [on his
journeys]' (*GS* 71). As usually happens with archetypal heroes, this
deficiency in her education was to prove paradoxically beneficial, for
it was during their long transatlantic cruises that Alice could share
with her father his love of the sea and of astronomy. The inability of
common people to recognise her potentiality, her unusual education,
her association with Pallas Athena and the extraordinary circumstances of her begetting, all point to Alice as an archetypal hero. As
such, her birth was also surrounded by extraordinary circumstances.
She was born a week before she was due, on the night her father 'got
the madness on him and told [his wife that] he had to go tugging' (*GS*
57). Alice's mother made the unusual decision of accompanying him,
with the result that she went into labour on the river, on a tugboat

called the *Godspeed*. With uncanny foresight, her grandmother unexpectedly 'stepped out of the shadows' to help them (*GS* 57), bringing with her, among other things, 'a Bible', 'a pile of clean rags' and 'a little blanket from the dog's box' (*GS* 57–8), in what may be read as an allusion to the Fool's tattered clothes and the dog tearing at his leg in the Tarot trump. Alice's grandmother, an illiterate widow who, like her only son, had married a man totally unlike her, has the easygoing faith in the Bible of her Irish ancestors. A hardworking woman, she held, as Alice explains, the title of 'Official Polisher of Brass Plaques and some said that when she had finished her Friday round the shine of it was so bright that it tipped the waves like a skimming stone and could still be seen in the harbour of New York' (*GS* 53). Taking into account the fact that the rags she used for polishing the brass plaques of shipping companies at the quays were the same rags she employed to wrap up the newborn baby, Alice's proud description of her grandmother's capacity to project the light refracted by the brass plaques across the Atlantic may be read as a hint that her polishing art, like that of Aladdin with his brass oil lamp, or like the alchemist's skill of turning base metal into gold, has a magical component. As her important role in Alice's birth and in her later education suggests, she is the Wise Old Woman in charge of passing her inherited, visionary wisdom on to Alice. Ishmael will perform a similar role as Wise Old Man with her daughter Stella.

Stella tells the story of her family and birth in Chapter 4, 'The Star'. The Star is the major arcana that comes after The Tower in the Tarot pack. It symbolises the Star of Hope among the ruins of the Tower, conveying an irrational, intuitive faith that the tower can be rebuilt on a new base.[41] In this card, 'a naked girl is seen kneeling by the edge of a stream or pool, pouring water from two pitchers. Behind her, in most versions, can be seen a tree with a bird hovering over it. In the sky above eight stars are visible. One star is distinctive in size and shape.'[42] As Alfred Douglas explains, the water symbolises 'the *aqua nostra*, the Water of Life or energy of the psyche which is needed to transfer consciousness from the sublunary world to the higher spheres'.[43] The star 'is an emblem of the spirit, the mystical Centre, and of the call of destiny. To the alchemist it was a symbol of the imagination, by which he was linked to the powers of the unconscious and to the material substances that he hoped to transform'.[44] The tree is the 'Tree of Life, symbolising the immortality that lies ahead', and the bird is 'a dove, the symbol of the Holy Spirit, the divine messenger'.[45]

The symbolism of this card perfectly reflects Stella's personality and her anima role. When her mother was expecting her, she felt an urgent longing to eat diamonds (*GS* 86). Ishmael borrowed some from his friends, the Jewish jewellers of New York, and she swallowed them all, with the result that '[h]er belly shone' (*GS* 89). Ishmael's action replicates God's act of breathing his divine spark into a piece of mud when he created the first man. In Stella's own words: 'I saw the light and pressed myself as close as I could to the membrane of my genial prison. The light struck through Mama's belly and fed me' (*GS* 87). The following day, Uta excreted all diamonds but one. When the baby was born, the eager owners of the missing diamond found it mysteriously lodged in the base of her spine (*GS* 93). In keeping with her role of anima, while Alice was born, simply, on a river, Stella is literally surrounded by *aqua nostra*/psychic energy/imaginative power (in the form of snow, a river and the sea) at the time of her birth. After a heavy snowstorm, in the night of a freezing 10 November (Paracelsus's birth date), Alice's mother felt the whim to go alone to her favourite Italian restaurant, Signora Rossetti's. Uta had been following the course of the Hudson river, until, mistaking the reflection of the stars on the water for the city lights, she lost her way in the 'white maze' and unexpectedly found herself near the 'great doors of the Cunard Building', the shipping company directed by Alice's father, who was to become Uta's boss and lover (*GS* 90). Thus, Uta unwittingly found herself at the intangible crossroads formed by the double 'symmetry' connecting her future with David's, and that of Stella with Jove's.

Uta is fascinated by the 'stellated brightness' of a particular star, which she compares to 'a cast jewel', as she sees them move 'one after the other' over the slow water, 'skimming towards her' (*GS* 90). This sight reminds her of her father making flat stones skip over the tops of the waves when she was a child: 'Each one, he had said, flew on to another country, rested at last at a shore beyond the sea. She fancied that these hard bright things were souls like her. Souls joining the bodies that had gone ahead of them, in rags, in sorrow, in haste, unwilling, dead bodies over the sea, leaving their souls behind' (*GS* 90). Her description strikingly recalls Alice's remark that the 'bright shine' of the brass plaques polished by her grandmother 'tipped the waves' across the Atlantic 'like skimming stones' (*GS* 53). David connects both shortly before his death, when, walking along the Liverpool wharf with his mother, he tells her how '[h]is secretary, Uta, had told him a story about her own soul flashing across the waters towards her' (GS 150).

Interpreting the vision in the light of her father's skimming stones, Uta concluded that the particularly bright shooting star was her soul coming to rescue her at last from her living death in this wasteland. However, at the end of the novel, Alice questions this interpretation: 'Her soul? Stella's? The Jews believe that the soul comes to inhabit the body at the moment of birth. Until then, until the image of itself becomes flesh, it pursues its crystal pattern, untied. Wave function of life scattered down to one dear face' (GS 217). The critic David Lloyd Sinkinson has cogently interpreted Uta's vision as an example of 'synchronicity' in Jung's understanding of the term as 'the simultaneous occurrence of two meaningfully but not causally connected events'.[46] As he explains, Jung's main interest was 'to study the non-causal correspondences between the inner world of the unconscious and the outer world of reality'.[47] Water is a symbol of the unconscious often used in the novel, but Uta's vision is much more complex, since it materialises a double Paracelsian 'correspondence' between events taking place simultaneously in heaven and on earth ('above' and 'below') and to self and world ('within' and 'without'). In 'The Tower', Stella points to the correspondence between heaven and earth when she says that, as a child, she 'imagined love as a glass well. I could lean and dabble my hands in it and come up shining. I knew it was flowing by the noise of the water over the subterranean pebbles' (GS 39–40).[48] As the association with love suggests, the 'glass' well is a mirror of heaven, just as the pebbles are a mirror of the stars, expressing the fundamental complementarity and reversibility of spirit and matter. Stella points to this reversibility when she describes both the stars and the pebbles as diamonds coming respectively from 'the stellar wall' and 'the earth's crust' to the middle ground represented by her 'gem-stole body': 'On the night I was born the sky was punched with stars. Diamonds deep in the earth's crust. Diamonds deep in the stellar wall. As above, so below. Uniting carbon mediated in my gem-stole body' (GS 187). The correspondence between self and world is meant to express a similar reversibility between micro and macrocosm. From this perspective, the events signify the merging of Stella's astral, spiritual and material bodies at the moment of her birth – that is, as the configuration of her 'inner heaven', 'corresponded' externally by the macrocosmic movement of the stars and pebbles to unite themselves with the Mother earth/Uta. From this double perspective,

Alice's and Uta's interpretations are *both* right. Needless to say, the *cosmocrator* or Universal Architect capable of performing this unique act of creation is Stella's Cabbalistic father, Ishmael.

After her tantalising vision, Uta unexpectedly went into labour and lost consciousness. With the same prescience that had brought Alice's grandmother to the *Godspead* at the moment of her birth, Ishmael, who was at home, realised what was happening and began to call for help. Miles away, Raphael, a Polish tea seller with a pack of husky dogs and sled, heard Ishmael's preternatural call and, following his directions, found Uta and the nearly born baby in the snow. The episode can be interpreted realistically, as Uta later did, as the product of sheer chance (*GS* 92). However, the fact that Ishmael's envoy is named Raphael, like the Archangel of love and joy, driving an 'Angel Car' (*GS* 85) led by dogs (Alice's totem), reinforces the symbolic interpretation and the association of Ishmael with God, as does the fact that Raphael completes the intangible symmetry Uta had initiated that night, by making the awkward decision of taking mother and baby to the door of Signora Rossetti's, where, sure enough, little Jove is waiting for Stella.

As a child, Stella had a squint. Her realist mother considered this a defect of vision. However, like Alice's supposed dullness, Stella's physical defect is in fact a token of her uniqueness, the confirmation of her spiritual and imaginative potential, as Ishmael suggests when he interprets it as a sign that she 'will be a poet' (*GS* 77). Pondering on her parents' divergent interpretations, Stella reflects on how certain art critics misinterpreted the innovations in the treatment of light made by Picasso, Matisse and Cézanne as 'an optical confusion. Nothing but a defect of vision', just as earlier critics had thought that El Greco's 'elongations and foreshortenings [. . .] were an eye problem' (*GS* 81). Her conclusion is that perhaps 'art is an eye problem [. . .]. What you see is not what you think you see' (*GS* 81).[49] The paradox in this statement points to Stella as a visionary, like her father, whose favourite mantra is 'Shadows, signs, wonders' (*GS* 80, *passim*). For Stella, as for Jeanette Winterson, the discourse of art is more truth-revealing than traditional science, geography or history precisely because of its capacity to focus reality from different perspectives, including intangible ones. Alice extends this idea to the New Physics when she points to the abandonment of the 'either-or' perspective of traditional science for the 'both-and' formula stemming from Werner Heisenberg's indeterminacy principle. As she notes, every quantum physical measurement depends on the position of the observer, so that, as Schrödinger's cat experiment demonstrates, before opening the box, the cat is both dead and alive (*GS* 207). In this sense, each measurement 'is an individual act of creation, an incarnation of potential being into concrete being in our world, limited by space and time'.[50]

Chapter 5, 'Ten of Swords', is narrated by Alice. In the Tarot, this minor trump represents the naked body of a youth floating on water with ten knives stuck into his torso, abdomen and legs. This card, symbolising desolation, disruption and ruin, 'marks the lowest point in [the] cycle of fortune. From now on things can only get better. The worst has already been experienced.'[51] In keeping with this symbolism, Alice centres her narration on her relationship with Jove. Drawing on a *topos* Winterson developed at length in *Sexing the Cherry*, Alice says that she and Jove had expected their relation to be 'the lightest of things, he and I, lifting each other up above the heaviness of life'. However, they 'knew that gravity is always part of the equation', and they were 'soon snared by the ordinariness we set out to resist' (*GS* 102). Alice attributes the 'heaviness' that hampered their 'volatile experiment' (*GS* 102) to Jove's inconstancy, which, in what may be read as another significant symmetry, she compares to that of her father: 'His interest in me pendulumed from hot intensity to cool indifference. Weeks together would be followed by months apart. Then he would woo me again and each time I was determined to resist' (*GS* 105). Alice summarises their unequal relationship with a double archetypal metaphor: 'I did not think of us as one man and his dog. [. . .] If I had turned into a dog he had always been a dark horse' (*GS* 105). Alice's identification with a dog reinforces her association with the Fool in the Tarot and therefore with her symbolic ego role, while the description of Jove as a dark horse, with its connotations of sexual potency, promiscuity and instinctual knowledge, points to his condition of 'shadow'.[52] Consistent with this role, Jove displays a wholly materialistic outlook on reality: 'Matter is energy. Of course. But for all practical purposes matter is matter. Don't take my word for it. Bang your head against a brick wall' (p. 191).[53] Thus, although theoretically he is ready to accept the existence of 'a parallel universe somewhere near here' (*GS* 191), he dismisses Stella's intimations of other realities as the dreamwork and fantasies of unhealthy individuals (*GS* 190), women in particular: 'My wife believed that she had a kind of interior universe as valid and as necessary as her day-to-day existence in reality. [. . .] She refused to make a clear distinction between inner and outer. [. . .] At first I mistook this pathology as the ordinary feminine' (*GS* 191).

The improvement heralded by 'Ten of Swords' materialises in the next chapter, 'Page of Cups'. This card represents Narcissus, the beautiful youth who fell in love with his own reflection and killed himself when he realised the impossibility of fulfilling his love.[54] In keeping with this symbolism, Alice describes her relationship with Stella in terms of equality and mutual love that closely follow Nicole Brossard's definition of lesbian love as a relation between 'desiring subject/subject of desire':[55] 'Desiring her I felt my own desirability. [. . .] Her breasts as my breasts, her mouth as my mouth, were more than Narcissus hypnotised by his own likeness' (*GS* 119). Both Alice and Stella make constant use of mirror images to refer to their relations. For example, Alice describes herself and Stella lying next to each other as 'a mirror confusion of bodies and sighs, undifferentiated, she in me, me in she and no longer exhausted by someone else's shape over mine' (*GS* 119), while Stella sees, surfacing in her dreams from her unconscious, 'a tall mirror hinged into a case. The woman in the mirror has an unknown face' (*GS* 41–2). At this stage, Stella does not recognise the face of the woman in the mirror – 'I looked in the mirror. Was that my face?' (*GS* 34) – just as Alice failed to recognise her face when, after a bad dream, she looked at herself in the mirror: 'There was a small mirror in my room. When I looked into it I did not see Alice' (*GS* 22). Needless to say, the woman in Stella's mirror is Alice, ready to leap through the looking glass to unite herself with her, just as the woman in Alice's mirror is Stella, but the complete figure of their unified self is more complex than that, since, as Stella eventually realises, it is a compound of three juxtaposed faces: her own and those of an 'older woman' and a younger 'shadow man' (*GS* 45–6). This reflected image of three-persons-in-one is an emblem both of the complex nature of each individual (Paracelsus's three bodies in man/Jung's division of the self into ego, shadow and anima/animus) and of 'The Eternal Triangle' (*GS* 200) constituted by Alice, Stella and Jove, whose archetypal model is the Holy Trinity.[56]

Chapter 7, entitled 'Death', marks the beginning of the second phase in Alice's individuation process. This card represents the hero's descent to the underworld and, as such, symbolises the necessary death of the old self, 'to be replaced in due course by something new and totally different'.[57] In this chapter, Alice narrates the declining years and death of her father. Drawing a symmetry with Ishmael's Cabbalistic practices, she recalls how David 'used to do magic tricks' (*GS* 158), and how, watching him make every object on the table disappear by 'whipping the table-cloth off the table' (*GS* 158), she learnt to believe that '[p]erhaps the firm surface of order and stability is as much an illusion as a silk handkerchief over a non-existent glass' (*GS* 159). Associating his death with his disappearing tricks, Alice consoles herself with the thought that her father, 'at the moment of physical death, may simply have shifted to an alternative point of his wave function' (*GS* 161). With neat symmetry, in the next chapter, 'The Moon', Stella narrates the death of her father in terms that substantiate Alice's wish-fulfilment. Ishmael, who 'had been close to Werner Heisenberg', is struck by the similitude between the paradoxes of Jewish Cabbala and the 'strange notions of the simultaneous absence and presence of matter' in quantum physics (*GS* 168). Stimulated by it, he starts a year-long experiment to increase his body's revolutions: 'Papa wanted to discover whether or not he could move himself along his own wave function, at will, whilst alive in his body. If gross matter is reducible to atoms, and the atom itself subject to unending division, then the reality of matter is conceptual. [. . .] Could Papa escape himself by himself? Could he be his own gateway?' (*GS* 168). Eventually, Ishmael's experiment is successful and he dematerialises himself into a wave function while holding in his hand a copy of Muriel Rukeyer's poetry collection, *Body of Waking*, opened at the page containing 'King's Mountain', a poem about the search for 'the other city' (in the novel's context, a Paracelsian mountain), where 'drifts and caves dissolve' into 'a new form', as do 'the limitations of our love' (*GS* 170).

'The Moon' is a card representing the descent of the dead to the underworld. 'At the foot of this Tarot card lies a deep, mysterious pool, out of which a crayfish is attempting to crawl on to the dry land. A path leads up from the pool and wends its way to the horizon.'[58] The path is guarded by two dogs (or a dog and a wolf). In the background can be seen 'a pair of forbidding towers which form a way to the mysterious regions beyond. Above, a full moon hangs in the night sky'.[59] As Douglas explains, 'the Moon was often believed to be the abode of the dead. [. . .] Its negative aspect was symbolized by Hecate, the guardian of the gates of Hades, one of whose main attributes was the dog.'[60] The crayfish crawling out of the pool is the 'symbol of the primitive devouring forces of the unconscious which have to be over-come' if the dead are to enter Hades, 'where they would be kept safe until the time of rebirth'.[61] In keeping with this symbolism, the chapter begins with an item of news reporting the disappearance of Jove and Stella's yacht off the coast of Capri after a series of storms (*GS* 165). Alice, who had been prevented from accompanying them by the illness and death of her father, reads it while she is with her bereaved mother on the *QE*2 (*GS* 197) (the same ship and the same cruise on which she met Jove for the first time), and she immediately starts a desperate search for them.

As Stella's first words suggest – 'Am I dead? Dead as in doornail. Dead as in to the world. Dead as in gone. Dead as in buried. Dead as a dodo, dead as a herring, dead as mutton, dead as in left for?' (*GS* 165) – this chapter consists of her direct interior monologue as she lies dying on the deck of the yacht. Her thoughts move from the memory of her father's extraordinary death to an association of Jove with Mozart's opera, where 'Don Giovanni, unrepentant, [is] dragged down into Hell' (*GS* 171). She then distinctly recalls having been 'temporarily knocked out when the storm hit the boat off horizontally' and feeling strangely calm when she 'regained consciousness in the expectation of death' (*GS* 175). At this point she loses control over chronological time – 'It seemed that days had passed, not dead, not alive, in the cat's paw of the storm' (*GS* 176) – and thinks that 'I was a child again at the mercy of larger forces' (*GS* 175). Her words neatly follow an archetypal symbolism of rebirth whose origins go back to the Pythagorean *kouros*, the youth who 'stands at the borderline between the world of the human and the world of the divine; has access to them both, is loved and recognised in both. It's only as a kouros that the initiate can possibly succeed at the great ordeal of making a journey into the beyond.'[62] Like the *kouros*, then, Stella is at the borderline between this world and the world of the dead, in an in-between realm she describes as a wormhole: 'It was as though we had floated off the world's edge into a science-fiction sea. [. . .] Maybe we've sailed through one of your [Jove's] wormholes and come up in a parallel universe' (*GS* 179, 180). Literally, this wormhole is the eye of the storm that keeps the yacht spinning around and connects sky and sea within its funnel structure. Figuratively, it is the archetypal brink of Stella's childish 'glass well' from where she could see by reflection the subterranean world of love she yearned to enter (*GS* 41).

In Greek mythology, the souls of the deceased are led by Hermes to Charon, the ferryman, who takes them across the river Acheron to Hades.[63] Those who cannot afford the passage, or are not admitted by Charon, are doomed to wander on the banks of the Styx, a marshy lagoon formed by the river. In the symbolism of The Moon, this may mean that, if Stella is to complete her initiation process, she must fight 'the primitive devouring forces of the unconscious' symbolised by the crayfish and must bypass the dogs that guard the entrance to Hades. Stella identifies the boat with consciousness and the sea with the unconscious: 'The boat is a blade, knife-edge of consciousness precarious on the unconscious sea' (*GS* 185). She associates Jove with the crayfish when she says, '[i]n the moonlight I might have mistaken him for a knight in shining armour' (*GS* 184), implying that the armour is in fact a carapace; compares herself and Jove with the guardian dogs – 'a pair of jackals we were crouched and baying at the moon' (*GS* 185); and identifies Jove with Lucifer (*GS* 186). Psychologically, the danger Jove represents is the extinction of Stella's sense of self, which Ishmael warns her to preserve ('Learn to remember your real face' (*GS* 186)); and she feels herself wavering: 'The sense of who I am is strengthening and weakening simultaneously' (*GS* 186).

According to Jung, the shadow is materialistic, intuitive and wholly ruled by *concupiscencia effrenata*, irrepressible sexual cupidity.[64] In keeping with this definition, Jove separates love and sex (*GS* 184, 205) and imposes a sadomasochistic pattern on his relationship with Alice (*GS* 204–5). His sadomasochistic drive develops into paranoia after eight days of deprivation at sea: he starts fantasising about devouring himself: 'How much of me could we eat and still say that I am alive? Arms. Legs. Slices of rump' (*GS* 184). He goes on 'making little cuts in [his] arms with a filleting knife' (*GS* 194); he forces Stella to have sex with him (*GS* 185) and, as he himself explains in 'Knave of Coins', ends up killing Stella and eating fillets carved from her buttocks and hip (*GS* 195–6). At the same time, however, Jove's thoughts have significant similarities to those of Stella. He starts to believe her when 'she said that we might have slipped through a kink in time' (*GS* 194) and, falling into a trancelike dream, he is struck by the thought that 'I was a child again' (*GS* 195). This similarity in their thoughts points to their anima/shadow complementarity as well as to the unavoidability of Jove's role, since the rescue of Stella/the anima by Alice/the ego necessarily involves the alienation of Jove/the shadow. Jove seems to intuit the unavoidability of his role when he reflects, 'Quite often I had the disagreeable sensation that I was being thought' (GS 194–5), but his materialism prevails and he dismisses the idea as 'a common effect of attenuation' (GS 195).

In the last chapter, 'Judgement', Alice explains how, after being rescued, 'Jove was able to avoid criminal charges on the grounds of temporary insanity' (GS 215). Like Henri in *The Passion*, then, he is left in hospital at the end of the novel. However, unlike Henri, who, in keeping with his ego role, was articulate enough to try and reconstruct/heal himself by means of his storytelling, Jove only narrates one chapter and he exclusively employs it to justify his murderous action. Thus, like the cook in *The Passion*, who is never allowed to offer his own perspective on the events, Jove is condemned to alienation by his own inarticulacy.

At the beginning of 'The Moon' Stella associated her father with Coleridge's friendly albatross (GS 176) and called to him for help (GS 177). At the end of the chapter she is rewarded with a vision of Ishmael/Charon, 'rowing towards [her] with Alice/Hermes, his dark figure upright in a moon-scooped boat', while her own voice simultaneously rushes to meet them 'over the water, skimming in a bright curve' (GS 186), in what may be interpreted as yet another variation on the stars/pebbles motif. Watching them come to her rescue, Stella realises '[h]ow simple it is now' (GS 186) and she abandons herself to the cathartic experience of her second, cosmic birth: 'I seem to be tumbling over myself, ready to tunnel out of the womb of the world, my hands and feet bouncing off its warm wall' (GS 186). When Ishmael and Alice arrive, Stella is already dead. With impeccable symmetry, the separation of her physical and astral bodies is symbolised by the traumatic liberation of the diamond lodged in her spine by the action of Jove's knife. Ishmael restores her daughter to life by rubbing the diamond over her eyes and face and putting it in her mouth – that is, by feeding her physical body with *spiritus mundi*, as he had done many years before when she was still in Uta's womb (GS 209). Ishmael's godlike act restores Stella to life, with the difference that, since her second birth takes place at the end of her quest for individuation and cosmic integration, she is now *filius* and *Anthropos*, child and god, an alchemical magus in her own right, ready to celebrate her 'chymic wedding' with Alice, her paired opposite.

This stage takes place in Chapter 10, 'The Lovers'. As Alice explains, Stella showed her this Tarot card, representing a young man 'trying to choose between two women, Cupid, arrow-borne, over his head' (*GS* 200). According to Douglas, '[t]he youth is caught in the dilemma of having to choose between loyalty to his mother and desire for his beloved, between traditional authority and independent action. [. . .] Only by withdrawal from the influence and authority of the mother can the quest proceed and the treasure hard to attain, immortality, be won at last.'[65] Stella redefines the roles of these characters in lesbian terms when she tells Alice that, perhaps, 'the women are trying to decide for themselves and the man is taking no notice' (*GS* 201). This, of course, is the situation in which Alice and Stella find themselves, having to choose between love for each other or loyalty to Jove, the representative of patriarchal authority. At the end of the chapter Alice explains how, after her recovery from plastic surgery, Stella took the diamond back to the descendant of its owner. Watching it in the jeweller's upraised hand, Alice is struck by the thought that 'I too was in the red kitchen on that snowy night when Uta had escaped and seen her soul skimming towards her across the impassive sea' (*GS* 217). In the light of this remark, Alice's real name 'Alluvia: the deposit collected and jetted by the river' (*GS* 121), acquires its full dimension, identifying Alice with Stella's skimming stone/star/diamond/astral body. Needless to say, once Alice and Stella are united, there is no need for Stella to keep the diamond.

In this chapter, Alice attributes to her childhood experiences the pattern of inequality she had always felt with her male lovers – 'a heroes/villain psyche of He loves Me He loves Me Not' (*GS* 204) – and draws a symmetry between her father's triangular relationship with his wife and lover, on the one hand, and her own relationship with Stella and Jove, on the other: 'As I half slept, I could not fully distinguish which was my father/myself, Stella/Uta, whether the distance we imagine separates one event from another had folded up, leaving the two clock faces to slide together, plates of time, synchronous' (*GS* 199). This suggested round of identities brings to mind the Hermetic idea that the individual forms part of a vast system, or huge family, each one constituting a link in a chain reaching back to the beginning and projecting itself into the future. As Ishmael confides to Alice: 'Since the beginning of time you and I have been sitting here [. . . .] What do you not know that there is in you now, a Caesar, a Raphael, a tear of Mozart, the ended bowel problems of Napoleon at Waterloo?' (*GS* 209–10). Thus, Ishmael defines himself as a 'temporary imprint in a temporary place' (*GS* 209) and describes life in holistic terms as a flux of energy incessantly changing shape: 'This is not the afterlife. This is no after life. There is life, constantly escaping from the forms it inhabits, leaving behind its shell' (*GS* 212). With these words Ishmael endorses the belief in the unitary nature of the cosmos held by Paracelsus and the New Physicists. Before dissolving again into antimatter as mysteriously as he had materialised, the old Cabbalist made a last remark: 'Everything possible to be believed is an image of truth' (*GS* 213). His words echo both William Blake's belief in the godlike creativity of the human imagination and the contention of quantum physics that the observer's perspective determines the shape of reality, projecting symmetries between non-causally and non-locally related events.[66]

The symmetries Alice and Stella perceive between their lives and the lives of their ancestors are equally imaginative and non-causal, the result of their attempts to impose meaning and coherence over the chaotic flood of their memories and desires. Likewise, the symmetries offered by the author to the reader depend for their perception on a subjective act of interpretation. For example, the fact that the novel begins by situating the birth of Paracelsus on 'November 10 1493' (*GS* 1), goes on to place Stella's birth on 'November 10 1947' (*GS* 75) and ends by locating Alice's present on 'November 10 19:47' (*GS* 219) hints at a symmetry between the three events, which is in fact more visual than real: in the first two dates, the last three figures of the years do not coincide and, in the third, it is the time of the day, not the year.

The reluctance of some reviewers to grant coherence to *Gut Symmetries* is understandable, since appreciation of the novel's structure depends wholly on the reader's choice of perspective. At first sight, the division into eleven chapters named after Tarot cards imposes on *Gut Symmetries* the deceptive linearity of the hero's quest. This forward movement is complicated by the alternation of narrative voices and the achronicity of the narrators' accounts, which freely combine memories of the past with present events. Further, the fact that Alice narrates eight chapters, Stella two and Jove only one points to a narrative asymmetry that is echoed thematically by the multiplication of similarly asymmetric love triangles. Alice offers an explanation for the logic underlying this pattern when, trying to puzzle out her complex feelings for Jove and Stella, she says: 'One plus one is not necessarily two. I do the sum and the answer is an incipient third. Three parts of two: Jove and Stella, Jove and Alice, Alice and Stella, and under the surface of each the head of the other' (*GS* 119–20). Her words, which echo Pythagoras's speculations on the mathematical formula underlying the mystery of the Holy Trinity,[67] presuppose the rejection of the either-or logic of Aristotle's principle of the excluded middle, synthesised in the axiom: *tertium non datur*. Like the measurement of subatomic particles in quantum physics, the composition of this 2+1 triangle is rather unstable, yielding different compositions according to the perspective of the observer: Jove and Stella+Alice; Jove and Alice+Stella; Alice and Stella+Jove. The love triangles formed by the members of the earlier generation allow for similar arrangements: David and his wife+Uta; Uta and David+his wife; Ishmael and Uta+David. This variability introduces an element of randomness in the 'symmetrical' multiplication of the triangles that brings to mind the multiplication of fractals in dynamic models like the 'zooming Sierpinski', reproduced below, or, more appositely, the 'dancing triangles', whose elements move in spirals.[68]

At the end of the novel, Alice makes a reflection on time which perfectly summarises the structural complexity of *Gut Symmetries*: 'If the universe is movement it will not be in one direction only. We think of our lives as linear but it is the spin of the earth that allows us to observe time' (*GS* 218). Correcting Heraclitus's *panta rei*, Alice compares this spinning movement to the whirlpools in a river: 'the river moves on, never step in the same river twice, time surging forward and sometimes leaving a caracol, its half-turn backwards that mocks the clock' (*GS* 218). And, echoing *Art & Lies*, she uses the train and the rose – 'The Freight train and the rose garden' (*GS* 219) – to respectively symbolise Newton's time arrow and the cyclical time of myth. The combination of both time schemes expresses the paradox of life in time and eternity, what Alice describes as 'infinity and compression caught in the hour. [. . .] The universe curving in your gut' (*GS* 219).

Like the earlier novels, then, *Gut Symmetries* has the form of a spiral or whirlpool, whose basic components are unstable triangles. Thematically, the triangle that stands at the centre and generates the others is the love story of Alice, Stella and Jove. This thematic centre is mirrored structurally in Chapter 5, where, undercutting Alice's narration, there is an italicised section containing the tale of three friends in search of '*That which cannot be found*' (*GS* 140–1). With the only difference of the italics, this tale is literally reproduced in Winterson's short story 'Three Friends' (*WOP* 47–51). As such, it constitutes a metalepsis, or unlawful trespassing on ontological levels, adding to the confusion of Alice's identity with that of the writer. As an allegory of the hero's quest, it is also a *mise en abyme* of *Gut Symmetries*, compressing into a nutshell the various versions of the quest developed throughout the novel (the Fool's journey along the Tarot trumps/the alchemical search for the Philosopher's Stone/the Jungian quest for individuation/the quest for the Holy Grail) under the medieval *topos* of 'the Ship of Fools', defined in the glossary as 'Lunatics/saints sailing after that which cannot be found' (*GS* 6). In this sense, this story of three friends is the microcosmic circle/cross within the larger circle/cross of Winterson's textual macrocosm, or, in Alice's terms, the 'contemplative' 'sister universe' 'curled up on the Planck scale' (*GS* 4, 3) that she described as 'the symbol behind all symbols [. . . .] the mandala of the East and the Grail of the West' (*GS* 4). Structurally, the fact that this archetypal story is situated at the approximate centre of *Gut Symmetries* (*GS* 140–1) points to its condition of *umbilicus* or *axis mundi*, both the centre of the narrative whirlpool and the wormhole connecting the fictional world of the characters with the real world of author and readers. The unification of both worlds carried about by this tale reveals *Gut Symmetries* as the *unus mundus*, Paracelsus and Jung's unified psychophysical reality.

Winterson's following novel, *The.PowerBook*, appeared in 2000. The Jeanette Winterson Readers' Site described it as 'a stripped version of *Art & Lies* and *Gut Symmetries* [which are] massive texts, packed with sidetracks and poetic extravagance. The PowerBook is the opposite, with all the extravagance peeled off'. The simplicity specifically referred to the structure and language, which were defined as 'very precise', so that '[n]othing, except what is needed is there'.[69] This description is echoed in the novel by the narrator's repeated remark that she likes 'structures without cladding' (*PB* 34, 38, 41). By contrast, the reviewers did not see its structural simplicity and cohesion. Thus, Jeannine DeLombard complained that 'Winterson's insistent fracturing of conventional storytelling techniques leaves us yearning for the completeness of a traditional narrative, however illusory it may be;'[70] while Jenny Turner said in a mixed review that '*The.PowerBook* isn't really a novel anyway. It's more like a set of short stories being marketed as a novel [. . .]. Except that it isn't even a set of short stories. It's more like a bundle of bits and pieces, nicely laid out, signed, numbered and bound in home-splodged cardboard and sold as an artist's book at a private gallery in the West End.'[71]

As Elaine Showalter has noted, *The.PowerBook* is designed 'to suggest the appearance and the technique of virtual reality, with a cover like a computer handbook and chapter divisions of hard drives, icons and documents'.[72] These features, as well as the dots in the title and in the author's name (Jeanette.Winterson), point to the interactive logic of the internet as the novel's organising principle. The main narrative line takes the form of a chat between a young woman called 'Ali' or 'Alix' (*PB* 138) and a customer, an older, upper-middle-class married woman whose alias is 'Tulip' (*PB* 25). In the earlier novels the protagonists achieved self-individuation and wholeness by rewriting/imagining their life stories. By contrast, Ali/x seems to have commodified the self-healing capacity of writing into a way of earning a living. She owns an old shop in Spitalfields called VERDE,[73] which is full of period disguises, from where she ships e-stories on command, meant to grant her internet customers, '[j]ust for one night the freedom to be somebody else' (*PB* 4). However, for all its apparent commodification, the writing task of this 'language costumier' (*PB* 2) still has the old shamanistic power to heal. She makes sure that what her customer wishes is 'to be transformed' (*PB* 4), and she explicitly says that the potential for self-transformation lies in the very act of storytelling: 'The alphabet of my DNA shapes certain words, but the story is not told. I have to tell it myself' (*PB* 4). In the earlier novels, the protagonists' maturation process invariably followed the linearity of the hero's quest. By contrast, Ali/x's storytelling is ruled by the internet principle that 'there is always a new beginning, a different end' (*PB* 4). Thus, the story of Ali/x and Tulip is arranged as a web of thematically related stories that can be accessed, interacted upon, abandoned and reopened at will by narrator and narratee, as if they were links in a hypertextual network. From this perspective, their apparent fragmentariness, inconclusiveness and chaotic arrangement may be said to respond to the same logic J. Hillis Miller detected in computer compositions, where '[w]hatever is printed is always just one stage in a potentially endless process of revision, deletion, addition, and rearrangement'.[74]

This structure is already suggested by the index, called 'MENU', which differentiates graphically between the chapters belonging to the frame narrative (the internet chat) and the embedded stories invented by Ali/x on Tulip's command. Following the fashion of e-mail addresses, the chats are written in small print and the embedded stories in capitals. In principle, this graphic difference points to a structure as old as *The Arabian Nights*, where Sheherezade lures the sultan into keeping her alive 'just for one night' by telling him a story. Like Sheherezade, Ali/x tells Tulip a story every night that is interrupted when narrator and narratee resume their chat, to be later continued or abandoned for another story. In the traditional tale-within-the-tale structure, the first-level narration 'frames' the other tales by opening and closing the embedded narratives. By contrast, in *The.PowerBook* the frame narrative is left open, as is suggested by the fact that the last four chapters have their titles written in capitals, as would be appropriate for embedded stories. This structural openness is echoed thematically by the fact that the virtual love affair initiated by Ali/x and Tulip through their internet chat progressively moves from the past to the present and is left inconclusive at the crucial moment when Tulip has to choose between taking a train to Oxford, where her husband is waiting for her, or leap out of the train and start a new life with Ali/x. In keeping with the interactivity of the narration, Ali/x offers Tulip both 'links' for her to actualise, that is, she narrates both possible endings (*PB* 205–6). This double ending has been compared to 'those of Fowles and Hardy'.[75] Another intertext that comes to mind is Jorge Luis Borges' 'The Garden of Forking Paths'. This is the story of a man called Ts'ui Pen who decided to devote his life to the composition of a book and a labyrinth. Thirteen years later, when he was murdered, the only thing that was found in his rooms was a bulky manuscript containing 'a vague heap of contradictory drafts', that allowed for all kinds of alternative reading combinations. The narrator eventually discovered the labyrinth nobody had been able to find when he realised that the book and the labyrinth were a single object and that the book was 'a labyrinth of labyrinths'.[76] Ts'ui Pen's circular book, in which all conceivable endings are possible, multiplies *ad infinitum* Ali/x's offer of freedom to Tulip, since it gives the reader the possibility of reading, and so living, endless variations on the same events. In this sense, Ts'ui Pen's book-as-labyrinth constitutes a formidable materialisation of the infinite potentiality of virtual reality.

In classical tale-within-the-tale fictions narrator and narratee belong to a 'real' world sharply differentiated from the unreal world of the embedded tales. By contrast, in *The.PowerBook* the 'real' world of the frame and the 'unreal' world of the embedded narratives – what Ali/x ironically calls 'meatspace' and 'cyberspace' (*PB* 161) – are progressively blurred until they entirely merge in 'QUIT', where the protagonists of two embedded stories, Ali the Turk and Alix from the Muck House, identify with the narrator (here called Ali/x). This willed indeterminacy of the narrator's identity is further enhanced by the fact that Ali/x constantly identifies herself with Jeanette Winterson: both are Virgo (*PB* 48); both have red hair (*PB* 27, 157, 174); both were born in the industrial North and given in adoption (*PB* 137); both come from a family of weavers (*PB* 155); both live in the same house in Spitalfields and both enjoy an international reputation as writers of fictions (*PB* 33) about 'Boundaries. Desire' (*PB* 35).[77] The confusion of real and unreal ontologies and of fictional and flesh-and-blood writers points to Winterson's conception of reality as unitary and many-sided. Like Alice in *Gut Symmetries*, Ali/x defines it as a virtual reality of multiple possibilities, only some of which are provisionally actualised by an effort of the individual imagination:

> In quantum reality there are millions of possible worlds, unactualised, potential, perhaps bearing in on us, but only reachable by wormholes we can never find. [. . .] I can't take my body through space and time, but I can send my mind, and use the stories, written and unwritten, to tumble me out in a place not yet existing – my future. (*PB* 53).

In keeping with this, in the first instalment, 'NEW DOCUMENT', Ali/x compares stories with '[M]aps of journeys that have been made and might have been made. A Marco Polo route through territory real and imagined' (*PB* 53_4);[78] and she explains that her purpose is to make the real and the imaginary stories/worlds merge: 'I was typing on my laptop, trying to move this story on, trying to avoid endings, trying to collide the real and the imaginary worlds. [. . .] It used to be that the real and the invented were parallel lines that never met. Then we discovered that space is curved, and in curved space parallel lines always meet' (*PB* 93–4). Given the identification of Ali/x with Jeanette Winterson, these words may be read as a metacomment on the overall structure of the novel. From this perspective, the alternation of frame and embedded stories and the progressive merging of the two parallel narrative lines in the 'curve' formed by the last four chapters confer on *The.PowerBook* the same whirlpool structure we found in the earlier fictions.

The first chapter, 'language costumier', is preceded by an icon consisting of the letters X and Y engulfed within circles. In the light of Ali/x's remark that '[h]ere we take your chromosomes, twenty-three pairs, and alter your height, eyes, teeth, sex' (*PB* 4), the presence or absence of the letter X in the narrator's name may be read as a hint of her capacity to change her sex and that of her e-customers by means of her storytelling. Ali/x herself suggests as much when she instructs Tulip to '[t]ake off your clothes. Take off your body. Hang them up behind the door. Tonight we can go deeper than disguise' (*PB* 4). The first embedded story, 'OPEN HARD DRIVE', materialises this possibility. Set in the late sixteenth century, it is the story of a Turkish girl called Ali, who was brought up as a boy by her mother as the only way to preserve her life. The story, which has the exotic and marvellous charm of an *Arabian Nights* tale, begins with Ali's perilous journey from Turkey to Holland to bring the first tulip bulbs to 'Suleiman's friends, the Dutch' (*PB* 11). Crossdressed as a boy with two embalmed bulbs and a stalk hidden in her crotch, Ali undertakes a sea journey in the course of which she is kidnapped by pirates and sold to the Italian envoy to the Turks, ending up as sexual trainer to a princess (*PB* 18). This ending actualises Ali/x's promise to Tulip, since the 'tulip girl' is 'transformed' into a man by the sheer force of her desire: 'As the Princess kissed and petted my tulip, my own sensations grew exquisite, [. . . and] I felt my disguise come to life' (*PB* 22).[79]

Ali's marvellous capacity to change her sex without loss of identity and the fact that she is a Turkish transvestite undertaking a journey across Europe in 1591 (*PB* 10) points to this story as a rewriting of Virginia Woolf's *Orlando*: Ali's sea journey, including the captain's invitation to eat (*PB* 13),[80] replicates Orlando's voyage from Turkey to England dressed as a gypsy woman, after her change of sex.[81] Likewise, Ali's initiation into sex of the virginal princess inverts Orlando's sexual initiation by Elizabeth I, the Virgin Queen.[82] Orlando kept updating her outfits according to the period she was living in. Echoing this, Tulip is asked to transvest/transform herself by putting on the period disguises Ali/x keeps in her shop. Besides suits of armour, wimples and field boots, these include 'wigs on spikes, like severed heads' (*PB* 3), in clear allusion to the 'head of a Moor' hanging from the rafters in Orlando's family palace that he used to play with as a boy.[83]

Besides sharing these traits with Turkish Ali, Orlando is, like Ali/x, the author of a multilayered and labyrinthine single text. Orlando's originally was a 'very short' poem entitled 'The Oak Tree', the only survivor of 'the great conflagration' in which she had burnt her juvenilia at the age of thirty.[84] Orlando had started writing it in 1586,[85] and had continued adding to it in the course of nearly three centuries, altering it according to the spirit of the age and the influence of the canonical writers in each period, 'till the manuscript looked like a piece of darning most conscientiously carried out'[86] – that is, until it looked very much like Ali/x's hypertextual network. As she started to think that it was time to make an end of it, Orlando, 'to her astonishment and alarm', suddenly saw that the pen in her hand 'began to curve and caracole with the smoothest possible fluency'.[87] The result was a 'most insipid verse', whose first stanza ran:

> I am myself but a vile link
> Amid life's weary chain,
> But I have spoken hallow'd words,
> Oh, do not say in vain![88]

This description of herself as a link in a weary chain of writers transmitting the hallowed words of past masters is as ironic as the fate of 'The Oak Tree': Nicholas Greene, the critic who had framed Orlando into burning all her creative works, praises it as a masterpiece three centuries later, when the poem has become a huge patchwork of earlier voices and styles without a trace of 'the modern spirit' in it.[89] Woolf's description of writer and work as interdependent is echoed by Ali/x's succinct remark: 'I am the story' (*PB* 5), while her picture of authorship as derivative and of writing as intertextual foreruns the unison of soprano voices Handel contributed to at the end of *Art & Lies* and brings to mind Borges' concept of a supra-individual spiritual Voice, a composite of the voices of all the dead poets, joyously contributing endless variations on the same, all-enveloping text.[90]

This conception of writer and writing provides the theoretical framework for the instability and reversibility of Ali/x's and Tulip's identities as well as for the intertextual relation between *Orlando* and *The.PowerBook*. Further, from Woolf's and Borges' perspective, the fact that Ali/x's words constantly echo those of earlier Wintersonian characters, from the Jeanette of *Oranges* to the Alice of *Gut Symmetries* (whose name is quasi-homophone to Alix), enhances the palimpsestic nature of Ali/x's identity. Alix thus becomes the latest reincarnation of Winterson's single, prototypical narrator-character, just as *The.PowerBook* is the latest variation on what Winterson herself has described as 'one long continuous piece of work [. . . .] from *Oranges* to *The PowerBook*'.[91] Ali/x refers to this several times, for example, when she says 'I keep telling this story – different people, different places, different times – but always you, always me, always this story' (*PB* 119), and when she compares Turkish Ali's storytelling to Rembrandt, who 'painted himself at least fifty times [. . . as] a record, not of one life, but of many lives – lives piled in on one another, and sometimes surfacing through the painter and into paint' (*PB* 214).

The second tale that Ali/x offers Tulip, entitled 'NEW DOCUMENT', tells of a lesbian love affair initiated after a chance encounter by a single and a married woman simply identified as 'I' and 'you' (*PB* 32). This story is situated in Paris in the narrator's present. The single woman is, like Ali/x, a writer of fiction, who thinks, with Henri and Villanelle, that 'I risk more than I should' (*PB* 38) and that '[o]nly the impossible is worth the effort' (*PB* 55).[92] In keeping with this, she wishes to experience 'the real thing, the grand passion, which may not allow affection or convenience or happiness' (*PB* 51). By contrast, the married woman is, like Tulip, reluctant to change her lifestyle. She thinks (like Jove in *Gut Symmetries*) that 'you can have as much sex as you like but love is taboo' (*PB* 51), and she does not mind lying to her husband in order to enjoy casual sex without putting her marriage at risk (*PB* 38–9). Her outlook on marriage echoes that of the narrator's married lovers in *Written on the Body* as well as Bartholomew and the Victorian couples' obsession with marriage in *Orlando*.[93] The story ends with a gratifying sexual encounter followed by the abrupt disappearance of the married woman: 'No difficulties. No complications. Not even goodbye. So that's the end of it then' (*PB* 58). In *Written on the Body*, this would have put an end to the relation, with the narrator trying to assuage her/his acute pain by moving on to another lover. By contrast, Ali/x leaves the story open and, confronted with Tulip's silence at the other end of the computer (*PB* 63–4), tries to lure her into the chat again by telling her the story of the archetypal triangle formed by King Arthur, Lancelot and Guinevere. The story, narrated in 'SEARCH', ends tragically because, as Lancelot explains, the fact that she was 'married to someone else meant nothing to me' (*PB* 68), but Guinevere refused to break her 'marriage vow' (*PB* 71). Thus, Arthur's wife sacrificed herself and Lancelot, opting for the seclusion and penance of a convent. In the ensuing chat, Ali/x makes a list of equally 'great and ruinous lovers', including Vita and Violet; Oscar and Bosie; and Burton and Taylor (*PB* 77). She explains that, in this type of love story, there are only 'three possible endings: Revenge. Tragedy. Forgiveness' (*PB* 78), and goes on to describe their own love in the same terms: 'My search for you, your search for me, goes beyond life and death into one long call in the wilderness. I do not know if what I hear is an answer or an echo. [. . .] It doesn't matter. The journey must be made' (*PB* 79).

Ali/x's words bring to mind Eliot's contention in 'East Coker' that 'the fight to recover what has been lost [involves] neither gain nor loss, / For us there is only the trying'.[94] Like Eliot, Ali/x envisions love as a life quest, a perilous journey of uncertain outcome that she overtly compares to the journey of the 'The Three Friends' (see above): 'My search for you, your search for me, is a search after something that cannot be found. Only the impossible is worth the effort. What we seek is love itself, revealed now and again in human form' (*PB* 78). This idea is exemplified in 'SPECIAL' with the story of George Mallory and Andrew Irvine's last ascent to Everest. Like that of the Ship of Fools (*PB* 6), their enterprise was considered a lunatics' endeavour: 'Mallory argued for a final attempt. His colleagues thought he was in poor condition and mentally unstable' (*PB* 149). However, Mallory and Irvine climbed on and on until, like the Three Friends in the tale, they met with Death. Mallory's death at the top of Everest, like that of Ishmael in *Gut Symmetries*, is described as an essential transformation and cosmic integration, literally, in his case, into a Paracelsian man/mountain: 'Mallory had played the game and won. Only it didn't feel like a game, it felt like music. The mountain was one vast living vibration. Again he heard the piercing sound in his head, and underneath them his pulse. [. . .] time had stopped long since and there was no time' (*PB* 151, 152). Thus, when he was found by Odell (the third 'friend' in this version of the tale), 'Mallory was lying face down, his back and shoulders naked and white and changed into a part of the mountain' (*PB* 152).

After her long silence following the Paris story, Tulip eventually responds to Ali/x in 'open it', by showing her 'a plane ticket on the screen, destination Naples' (*PB* 83). Encouraged by this, Ali/x imagines a second meeting of the single and the married women, this time on the island of Capri. The single woman, who now explicitly calls herself Ali (*PB* 96), has brought her laptop with her and is, like the narrator of the frame narrative, 'trying to move this story on, [. . . .] trying to collide the real and the imaginary worlds' (*PB* 93). In keeping with this, she defines Capri both as 'an imaginary island and a real one' (*PB* 87) – that is, both as the historic place and as the symbolic lesbian space where she hopes to fulfil her love.[95] Thus, she describes her entrance into the city as a ritual penetration into the womb of the island: 'As I stand in the front car [. . .] feeling the train move down through the sunlight towards the tunnel, I feel like I am being born. [. . . The track] divides into a curved diamond, a vulva, a dark mouth – one of the many caves on the island where a rite of passage is observed' (*PB* 89). The narrator finds Tulip and her husband occupying room number 29 (*PB* 93, 94, 115), the same room she had occupied in Paris with a male lover (*PB* 58). But they are now staying at 'The Quisiana. The hotel where Oscar Wilde came after his release from prison' (*PB* 91), a fact that casts the ominous shadow of this 'grand and ruinous lover' on Ali's expectations of happiness. The encounter culminates in Anacapri, a village 'high up on the hillside overlooking the sea' (*PB* 97), where Tulip's original reluctance to renew their relation melts in a kiss (*PB* 100). Echoing the scene in *The Passion* where a troupe of acrobats steal kisses from the onlookers as they fly across the square (*P* 59), their kiss is accompanied by the improvised acrobatics of some Italian kids and an Australian tourist, who build a human ladder to rescue a frisbee that has landed on the head of the Madonna presiding over the square from her shrine (*PB* 102). The 'lightness' of the child at the top of the ladder, who 'jumps into the air as if he were a thing of air, weightless, limitless, untroubled by gravity's insistence' (*PB* 102), materialises Ali/x's dream of freedom from the tyranny of gravity/the physicality of her body.[96] Later, in bed, while Tulip is asleep, she points to her malleability in Tulips' hands when, echoing Julia Kristeva, she describes her body as 'a map that you redraw' (*PB* 109).[97] This thought leads Ali/x to associate love with the 'buried treasure' waiting to be found at the end of the quest, at 'the place where time stops. Where death stops. Where love is' (*PB* 109–10). This place between '[w]hat exists and what might exist' (*PB* 110) is the *axis mundi* Mallory found at the top of Everest, the point of confluence between time and eternity that Handel, Picasso and Sappho reached at the end of *Art & Lies*; the 'wormhole' leading Ishmael and Stella to the world of antimatter in *Gut Symmetries*, or, as Eliot put it in 'The Dry Salvages': 'The point of intersection of the timeless / With time [. . . . where] the impossible union / Of spheres of existence is actual'.[98] In what amounts to a metacomment on Winterson's writing practice in general, in the next chat, 'night screen', Ali/x will add fiction to this list of Eliotean 'still points': 'a story is a tightrope between two worlds' (*PB* 119).

For all their happiness together, the meeting in Capri ends like the earlier one, with the abrupt return of Tulip to her husband (*PB* 116). This is a cataclysmic event for Ali, which is fitfully echoed by the thunderstorm that shatters the island (*PB* 110). In the next embedded tale, 'VIEW AS ICON', Ali/x narrates the story of another 'great and ruinous' couple, Paolo and Francesca. This archetypal story of impossible love differs from that of Lancelot and Guinevere in that, instead of exemplifying tragedy, this story exemplifies revenge. Unlike Lancelot and Guinevere, Paolo and Francesca choose to fulfil their love against all odds and so meet with violent death at the hands of Francesca's husband, who is also Paolo's elder brother, a spiteful and revengeful 'strange swarthy misshapen man' (*PB* 126). Before their twined souls fly 'hand in hand' (*PB* 129) out of their torn bodies towards eternal bliss, Francesca, like Villanelle, equates their suffering for love to Christ's passion: 'There is no love that does not pierce the hands and feet' (*PB* 128).

In the ensuing chat, 'blame my parents', Tulip says that she finds the two options 'absolutist' and asks for a more practical middle way: 'isn't there a better ending than either/or?' (*PB* 133). Ali/x's answer is that she cannot accept Tulip's terms because her parents taught her 'that the treasure is really there' (*PB* 134). This sentence is further elaborated in two embedded tales, ᴇMᴘTY TRASH' and 'SHOW BALLOONS', as well as in the chat entitled 'own hero'. In the tales, Ali/x tells the story of her own adoption by Mr and Mrs M, in terms that are strongly reminiscent of the stories of Jeanette in *Oranges* and of the little girl in 'Psalms' (*WOP* 219–30),[99] while in 'own hero' the details of Ali/x's birth and family background rather resemble those of Jeanette Winterson.

The Ms are the owners of 'a Muck Midden', a parodic *hortus conclusus* in the middle of 'the Wilderness' (*PB* 137), surrounded by a high fence that protects the family against 'Temptations' (PB 138) but also prevents them from reaching 'The Promised Land' that lies beyond the wilderness, where the 'buried treasure' is (PB 194). Mr and Mrs M believed that a baby is a treasure and therefore adopted a little girl and called her 'Alix because they wanted a name with an X in it, because X marks the spot' (PB 138). Thus, besides the chromosomic mark of her femaleness, the X in the narrator's name symbolises her condition as child/treasure. In the analysis of *Gut Symmetries* we saw how alchemy identifies the Philosopher's Stone with a child, born out of *amor vulgaris*, the type of love capable of unifying paired opposites. This is the ancient wisdom that, unknown to them, informs Mr and Mrs M's belief, for they are simply 'superstitious people' (PB 137). Indeed, Mr M behaves like an alchemist who has forgotten that the real aim of the alchemical process is spiritual illumination, not the refinement of base metals into gold. Thus, he tries to find treasure by digging 'so fiercely at the end of the rainbow that part of the kitchen subsided' (PB 139), and he has 'a supply of large glass jars with lead seals' containing chemicals in a cellar forbidden to Alix (PB 141). Like the Queen of Spades, who stole Villanelle's heart and kept it in a glass phial (P 120), Mr M has 'an opaque jar with a heart drawn on it and a dagger through the heart' containing 'Love' (PB 142). Also like the Queen of Spades, he is associated with the evil aspect of the underworld, as his smell of 'sulphur' suggests (PB 142). As an alchemist's piece of land, the Muck Midden is full of metals (PB 139) and the house is clogged with exotic and rare objects associated with occultism, including a 'bevelled mirror on its chain [. . .whose] scrollwork was angels and streamers' (PB 145).

However, with love bottled up and sealed off in the cellar, Mr M has no chance of finding the Philosopher's Stone. As a child, Mrs M acquired the power to attract metals like a magnet by crawling inside the trunk of a tree that had been struck by lightning, and she used this power to find a key and many foreign coins; but the key does not fit any door (PB 195–6),[100] and the money is worthless, so she keeps it in 'a tin bucket' (PB 145, 196) that is reminiscent of Jove's bucket of stale water in *Gut Symmetries*, and uses it to feed the fire, in what can be read as a parody of the alchemical process. As Alix significantly observes, the burning of the coins still produces the effect sought by the alchemists: 'The best coins were the true copper pennies that burned from orange to blue – an Aladdin's lamp blue, or the underside of dragon's wings, or the green you get from goblins' (PB 145).

Looking at the burning coals, which she considers her 'books' (*PB* 146), Alix has a vision of 'the road winding through the flames', showing her the way to '[a]nother world' where the treasure lay (*PB* 146).

When Alix told her mother about this vision, she was angry. Unlike her husband, Mrs M could write and read and she liked telling Alix 'stories from her youth' in her distant birthplace, a bountiful Land of Cockaigne fairyland on the bank of a river, from where 'the fish would jump into the pan, tame as fleas' at the housewives' command (*PB* 143). However, after many years in the enclosure, Mrs M had become as shortsighted as her husband: 'My mother and father both wore spectacles. I took my mother's off her nose and tried to see through them. The world was blurred and strange' (*PB* 145). In order to avoid lapsing, like them, into what Blake would call 'Single vision & Newton's sleep',[101] Alix kept reminding herself: 'I had to stay young. I had to look in the right place. I had to keep the fire going. I had to believe in the treasure. I had to find the treasure too' (*PB* 146). In a characteristic pendular swing, Ali/x will exemplify the contrary type of alchemist in 'REALLY QUIT', where she tells the story of Giovanni da Castro, a young man with the insight to find treasure in the white stones that covered the barren mountains around Rome. Taking some of them home, he 'smelted them, experimented and produced alum', the precious Turkish dye for wool (*PB* 221).

The story of Ali/x and Tulip, left open in 'VIEW', is continued in 'meatspace', with Tulip e-mailing Ali/x to announce her arrival in London. As Tulip says, this time she wants their meeting to take place in '[m]eatspace not cyberspace' (*PB* 161). Consequently, in the next chat, 'spitalfields', Ali/x draws a brief picture of this area of East London. Her shop, VERDE, is situated near Christ Church – 'the Hawksmoor church' (*PB* 235) – and the meatmarket, in an area frequented by tourists seeking to retrace the bloody paths of Jack the Ripper and Count Dracula (*PB* 3, 235–6). Reminiscing of the dark lanes and dead-end canals of Venice in *The Passion*, Ali/x describes this ancient part of the London as 'an emperor maze of streets that darken into alleys, and alleys that blank into walls' (*PB* 165). And, echoing the London of Peter Ackroyd's novels and biographies, she describes the area as a living palimpsest of successive generations of Londoners stretching back to their millenarian origins. Its symbol is the body of a woman found in a richly decorated stone sarcophagus that 'had been there for one thousand eight hundred years' (*PB* 167).

In the next embedded story, 'HELP', Ali/x and Tulip at last meet in the flesh. As Ali/x ironically says when Tulip kisses her: 'Meatspace still has some advantages for a carbon-based girl' (*PB* 174). Like Alice in *Gut Symmetries*, Ali/x uses mirror images to describe their love: 'Sex between women is mirror geography. [. . .] You are a looking-glass world. You are the hidden place that opens to me on the other side of the glass. [. . .] You are what the mirror reflects and inverts. I see myself, I see you, two, one, none' (*PB* 174). Surprised by her own feelings, Tulip tells Ali/x at this stage that she feels as if she had been caught in her own net (*PB* 178). As an answer, Ali/x tells her the Story of the Red Fox (*PB* 179–81), which is the marvellous tale of the fox/hunter who willingly gives up his life to fulfil his beloved princess's whim. With this story, Ali/x exemplifies unconditional and all-forgiving love, the third possible ending for the stories of 'great and ruinous lovers'. Characteristically, Tulip's comment is that Ali/x's demand is 'too intense. We'd wear each other out in six months' (*PB* 181). Also characteristically, Ali/x replies that '[t]his love exists' (*PB* 187). It is what Dante called 'the love that moves the sun and the other stars' (*PB* 187), the buried treasure, the Grail at the end of Lancelot's quest (*PB* 187–8). In keeping with this, in the next instalment of their love story, 'CHOOSER', Ali/x will offer Tulip two endings for her to interact with, a 'daring' and a 'cowardly' one. Only if she dares to risk all can she expect to find the treasure of true love.

In the following chat, 'strange', Alix makes an oblique reference to *Orlando* when she says that the reason she began her narration with 'Ali and the tulip' was that she wanted 'to make a slot in time. To use time fully I use it vertically. One life is not enough' (*PB* 209). The story of Orlando, then, provides the model for the development of the main storyline. However, as in the earlier fictions, the linearity associated with this pattern only provides the axis for the embedded stories to spin around. In keeping with this, in the next embedded story, 'QUIT', Ali/x goes back to the sixteenth century to retake the story of Turkish Ali, who now turns out to be a teller of 'tall' stories, like Ali/x and Jeanette Winterson: 'As he knots himself into a history that never happened and a future that cannot have happened, he is like a cross-legged Turk who knots a fine carpet and finds himself in the pattern' (*PB* 215). Caught with Ali/x and Jeanette Winterson, then, within the unstable and all-encompassing virtual network, 'Ali the storyteller is no longer sure when the things happen. The happening and the telling seem to be tumbling over and over each other, like the acrobats who used to visit his village, turning their red and blue legs like the spokes of the wheel, round and round, faster and faster' (*PB* 216). Like the wild gyrations of Fortunata and her pupils in the dancing school (*SC* 72), the spinning around of these Turkish acrobats constitutes an apposite visual icon of the spiralling structure of Ali's storytelling and, by extension, of *The.PowerBook*.

In the last two chapters, 'RESTART' and 'SAVE', Ali/x adds a second loop to the spiral initiated in 'QUIT' by returning to the beginning of her narration. These two chapters are separated from the rest by a blank page on which is written in bold type: '**The world is a mirror of the mind's abundance**' (*PB* 223). This sentence, which seems to be a variation on Thomas Traherne's famous meditation beginning 'The world is a mirror of infinite Beauty, yet no man sees it',[102] synthesises the basic idea around which the novel develops, namely, that the world can be 'a cosmic dustbin' (*PB* 142), as Mrs M believed, or a marvellous place to live in, depending on how we imagine it. In this sense, this sentence is both a *mise en abyme* of *The.PowerBook* and its thematic core.

In the first embedded story, the captain of the ship that took Ali to Europe broached this subject during their conversation over breakfast. The captain, who had seen the rise and fall of Antioch (*PB* 15–16) and therefore entertained no illusions about the permanence of material things, told Ali, in words that Ali/x would later endorse (*PB* 79), that 'there is no wrong road. There is only the road you must travel' (*PB* 14). When Ali asked him, 'And if the road leads nowhere?', he retorted, 'Turn your Nowhere into a Somewhere' (*PB* 14). In 'RESTART' Alix from the Muck House has a similar conversation with her mother. The child, who had tried to climb out of the enclosure to see the Wilderness, is told by her mother that there is nothing outside and that '[n]othing is the most dangerous thing [because if] there is nothing there, you can invent something' (*PB* 228). Mrs M's mistrust of the imagination is consistent with her realist conviction that 'This is real life' and that 'nothing can change it' (*PB* 228). By contrast, the captain considers reality the illusory product of our dreams:

> You are young [. . .]. You do not know that the guilded palaces and the souks do not really exist. [. . .] You will live in the world as if it is real, until it is no longer real, and then you will know, as I do, that all your adventures and all your possessions, and all your losses, and what you have loved – this gold, this bread, the green glass sea – were things you dreamed as surely as you dreamed of buffalo and watercress. (*PB* 14–15)

The captain's contention that 'the guilded palaces and the souks do not really exist' brings to mind the exemplary tale of 'The Prince and the Magician' in John Fowles's novel, *The Magus*. In this tale, a young prince is told by the king, his father, that princesses, islands and God do not exist. The prince then meets a stranger who presents himself as God and convinces him that his father lied. He returns to the king, who retorts that in reality the stranger is only a magician, and that all kings and gods are merely magicians. On hearing this the prince is distressed and wants to die. But when he sees the awful face of death and remembers 'the beautiful but unreal islands and the unreal but beautiful princesses',[103] he decides that he can bear the burden of unreality. As soon as he decides to accept as real the unreal reality of magic, the prince himself is transformed into a magician.

In the last chapter, 'SAVE', Ali/x will find herself at the same critical juncture as Fowles's prince. Like the first, 'language costumier', this last chapter is situated on the day of Ali/x's arrival at VERDE, thus adding a third loop to the spiralling structure initiated in 'QUIT'. Adding to her identification with Orlando, Ali/x says that the old house was haunted by a gentle ghost who held hands with her (*PB* 236), and she describes the house as yet another point of intersection between time and eternity: 'If you were to come here, forgetting about time, and ringing the bell as the afternoon ends, you would find the shop as it has always been – keeping its secrets, offering you something that money can't buy – freedom just for one night' (*PB* 236).[104] Sitting at her computer, Ali/x then starts telling the story of Orlando (*PB* 236–7). At the end of Woolf's fiction, the protagonist, on realising that 'I am sick to death of this particular self. I want another', starts calling to herself, 'as if the person she wanted might not be there, "Orlando"'.[105] She then concludes that 'she had a great variety of selves to call upon',[106] and imagines herself at the far end of a long gallery of ancestors stretching back to the beginning of time and the cowled figure of a severe monk with a book in his hands.[107] This fancy comes to an abrupt end when 'the stable clock struck four [and t]he gallery and all its occupants fell to powder'.[108] The spell thus broken, Orlando recovers her old sense of self: 'Her own body quivered and tingled as if she suddenly stood naked in a hard frost. Yet, she kept [. . . .] complete composure (for she was now one and entire [. . .])'.[109]

Ali/x rewrites these passages in her story of Orlando. Struck by similar thoughts of self-dissolution, as she realises that 'my outline was beginning to blend with other outlines' in the 'liquid forest' where she finds herself, the Orlando in Ali/x's tale also calls to herself: 'I said my name again and again – 'ORLANDO! ORLANDO!' (*PB* 237). Her hope is that 'my name would contain me, but the sound itself seemed to run off my tongue, and drop, letter by letter, into the pool at my feet' (*PB* 237). Like Narcissus, she looks for herself in the water, but when she puts '[her] hand down into the pool of water, [her] name was gone' (*PB* 237–8). At this point she is seized by the same death wish that drove Narcissus to suicide and led Woolf's Orlando to entertain thoughts of 'flinging herself on the spongy turf and there drinking forgetfulness' on the brink of the 'silver pool [where] Sir Bedivere flung the sword of Arthur'.[110] Woolf's Orlando is revived from the deathly slumber that eventually overcomes her by the timely arrival of a romantic and chivalrous horseman, 'Marmaduke Bonthrop Shelmentine, Esquire', soon recognised by her as her twin soul and lover.[111] Echoing this, Ali/x Orlando tries to find the traces left in the forest by the horsemen who carried off 'the woman she loves' (*PB* 238). Eventually she reaches the gate of a palace where she 'heard her calling my name – ORLANDO, ORLANDO!', but when she enters it, the palace is deserted (*PB* 238). She then realises that the palace is full of searchers, like her, and she comprehends that '[e]ach of us, solitary, intent, had made the palace into a personal labyrinth' (*PB* 239), with the shape of their own desires. The exception is Astolfo, 'a different kind of man', who is 'chasing a peasant boy who had stolen his horse' (*PB* 240). Like Mrs M to Alix, Astolfo tells Orlando and the other searchers that what they are searching for does not exist. No sooner has he revealed this than '[t]he palace was gone, or rather, it was no longer outside myself. [. . . It] had folded up again into the hiding places of the mind' (*PB* 241).

The ending of this story suggests that, unlike the prince in Fowles's tale, Ali/x has finally opted for realism. However, after writing this story, she leaves the shop and goes for a walk along the Thames. She then sees, shining up from the silt in the water, a light 'making a vertical shaft from the bottom to the surface' (*PB* 243), in what may be read as a variation on Uta's vision of the stars/pebbles rising from the bottom of the sea in *Gut Symmetries* (see above). Struck by the connectedness symbolised by this vertical shaft, Ali/x realises that the river is a historical palimpsest – 'This is a Roman river, an Elizabethan river. This is the route to the Millennium Dome' (*PB* 242) – expressing the fluidity of time and identity: 'The end of one identity, the beginning of another' (*PB* 242). Then, reversing Woolf's

Orlando's recovery of her sense of self by the clock's striking the hour, Ali/x throws her watch into the water and makes up her mind to '[g]o home and write the story again. Keep writing it because one day she will read it' (*PB* 243). Thus, the novel ends with Ali/x reaffirming her visionary stance and with the promise of new fictional variations on the only possible subject: a single story of love, which, as she now realises, 'is the true history of the world' (*PB* 244). Learning to tell this story of love is the lesson little Silver will be taught by her wise old master in the next novel, *Lighthousekeeping*.

Notes

 1 Katy Emck, 'On the High Seas of Romance: Review of *Gut Symmetries*', *Times Literary Supplement* (3 January 1997): 21.
 2 David Sexton, 'A Serious Case of Solipsism: Review of *Gut Symmetries*', *Spectator* (4 January 1997): 27, 30; 27.
 3 Helena Grice and Tim Woods, 'Grand (Dis)unified Theories? Dislocated Discourses in *Gut Symmetries*', in Grice and Woods (eds), *'I'm telling you stories'*: 117–26; 118.
 4 Jove's words are deceptive, since organicism also excludes randomness in nature. Based on Aristotle's principle of teleology or final causation, it contends that organisms develop according to predetermined patterns in order to fulfil the 'Idea' of the entire organism. See Davies, *The Cosmic Blueprint*, 6–7.
 5 'philosopher, demon, hero, god and all things'. Carl G. Jung, 'Paracelsus', *The Spirit in Man, Art, and Literature* (1929), in *The Collected Works*, 15.(1985): 3–12; 8.
 6 *Ibid.*, 7.
 7 Remo F. Roth, *The Return of the World Soul: Wolfgang Pauli, Carl Jung and the Challenge of the Unified Psychophysical Reality* (2004) [2002]: III 3.8. www.psychovision.ch/synw/platinfertilityhermincarnp3.htm. Consulted on 8 July 2004.
 8 *Ibid.*, III 3.8.
 9 *Ibid.*, IV 3, V 1.2.
 10 Frances A. Yates, *Giordano Bruno and the Hermetic Tradition*. London: Routledge and Kegan Paul; Chicago: University of Chicago Press (1977) [1964]: 437–44, 446–7.
 11 Jung, 'Paracelsus', 11.
 12 Yates, *Giordano Bruno*, 151.
 13 Jung, 'Paracelsus', 9.
 14 Carl G. Jung, 'Paracelsus the Physician', in *The Spirit in Man, Art, and Literature*: 13–30, 22n. See Chapter 3 on this.

15 *Ibid.*, 26, 27n.

16 *Ibid.*, 16.

17 *Ibid.*, 16.

18 'So odd was the anatomy of this mis-bodied *bel esprit* that some hazarded his sex as female' (*GS* 1).

19 Davies and Gribbin, *The Matter Myth*, 233, 229.

20 *Ibid.*, 245–6.

21 Although, as an atheist, Jove does not believe in an afterlife, as a scientist he is currently 'working on a new model of the cosmos, dimensionality in hyperspace, ghost universes, symmetrical with ours' (*GS* 15). The lecture he gives on the cruise is entitled 'The World and Other Places' (*GS* 15), like Winterson's collection of stories (1988) and the title story in it (*WOP* 87–100).

22 Roth, *The Return of the World Soul*, II 4.1. According to Pauli, this intermediate realm was the really innovative aspect of Hermetic alchemy, since it made possible the consideration of psychophysical reality as empirically observable, which was the final goal of depth psychology. *Ibid.*, II 2.8.

23 Cavendish, *The Magical Arts*, 4.

24 *Ibid.*, 4.

25 See Yates, *Giordano Bruno*, 84–116.

26 Sanford L. Drob, 'The Sefirot: Kabbalistic Archetypes of Mind and Creation', *CrossCurrents: The Journal of The Association for Religion & Intellectual Life* 47.1 (Spring 1997). www.crosscurrents.org/Drob.htm. Consulted on 7 July 2004.

27 Douglas, *The Tarot*, 117–24.

28 See Remo F. Roth, *Some Thoughts about the Relationship of Carl Jung's Depth Psychology to Quantum Physics and to Archetypal Psychosomatics*, Parts I and II, (2003) [1994]. www.psychovision.ch/synw/gslecture_rome_e_p1a.htm. Consulted on 11 June 2004.

29 Susana Onega, 'Science, Myth and the Quest for Unity in Jeanette Winterson's *Gut Symmetries*', *Anglistik. Mitteilungen des Deutschen Anglistenverbandes* 15.1 (2004): 93–104.

30 Joan, Bunning 'The Celtic Cross', 2002 (1995). www.learntarot.com/ccross.htm. Consulted on 11 June 2004.

31 Douglas, *The Tarot*, 43, 44.

32 *Ibid.*, 43.

33 *Ibid.*, 44.

34 *Ibid.*, 93–4.

35 Stella's reaction also echoes that of Jacqueline in *Written on the Body*. See Chapter 3.

36 Hélène Cixous and Catherine Clément, 'Sorceress and Hysteric', in *The Newly Born Woman*, 3–39.

37 This symbology echoes that of the Queen of Spades and her husband in *The Passion*.

38 Bunning, 'The Celtic Cross'.

39 Jeanette uses the same words to describe her mother's decision to adopt her (*O* 10).

40 Sharman-Burke and Greene, *El tarot mítico*, 202.

41 *Ibid.*, 92–3.

42 Douglas, *The Tarot*, 96.

43 *Ibid.*, 96–7.

44 *Ibid.*, 96.

45 *Ibid.*, 97.

46 David Lloyd Sinkinson, '"Shadows, signs, wonders": Paracelsus, Synchronicity and the New Age of *Gut Symmetries*', in Helena Bengston, Marianne Borch and Cincide Maagaard (eds), *Sponsored by Demons: The Art of Jeanette Winterson*. Odense: Scholars' Press (1999): 81–92; 82.

47 *Ibid.*, 82–3.

48 Opposed to Stella's deep 'well of love' is Jove's shallow bucket of stale water (*GS* 40–1). In *Sexing the Cherry*, the eldest of the Twelve Dancing Princesses lives happily with a mermaid at the bottom of a well (*SC* 47).

49 Stella's words bring to mind Jeanette's complaint that her 'needlework teacher suffered from a problem of vision' (*O* 45).

50 Roth, *Some Thoughts*, III 3.9.

51 Douglas, *The Tarot*, 181.

52 Carl G. Jung, 'The Battle for Deliverance from the Mother', *Symbols of Transformation* (1911–12/1952), in *The Collected Works* V (1981): 274–35 280.

53 Jove's remark echoes Einstein's defence of nature's objectivity with the famous statement: 'The moon is also there when nobody looks'. In Roth, *The Return of the World Soul*, IV 2.3. It also recalls Jeanette's dream of the City of Lost Chances 'full of those who chose the wall' (*O* 112–13).

54 Sharman-Burke and Greene, *El tarot mítico*, 135–6.

55 In Parker, 'Nicole Brossard', 310. Louise and the nameless narrator of *Written on the Body* enjoy a similar relation.

56 A similar, though exclusively male, trinitarian game is played in the 'Ithaca' chapter of *Ulysses*, when the fusion of Bloom's and Stephen's faces in a mirror results in the features of Shakespeare. James Joyce, *Ulysses*. Harmondsworth: Penguin (1972) [1922]: 628–9.

57 Douglas, *The Tarot*, 84.

58 *Ibid.*, 99.

59 *Ibid.*, 99.

60 *Ibid.*, 100.

61 *Ibid.*, 100.

62 Peter Kingsley, 'In the Dark Places of Wisdom: The Forgotten Origins

of the Western World', *Parabola* (Winter 1999). www.goldensufi.org/ PKarticles.html. Consulted on 25 July 2004.

63 Dante's 'Inferno' also provides a standard version of the classical myth. On the main functions of the underworld, see Chapter 2.

64 Jung, 'The Battle for Deliverance from the Mother', 280.

65 Douglas, *The Tarot*, 63.

66 Zhen Wang, 'The Time's Arrow within the Uncertainty Quantum' (20 May 1998). http://arxiv.org/abs/quant-ph/9806071. Consulted on 27 July 2004.

67 See Carl. G. Jung, 'A Psychological Approach', 107–200.

68 See both dynamic models at work in Robert L. Devaney, 'The Dynamical Systems and Technology Projects at Boston University' (2004) [1999]. http://math.bu.edu/DYSYS/index.html. Consulted on 18 July 2004.

69 Anna Troberg, The Jeanette Winterson Reader's Site (2000) [1997].www.uni-koeln.de/phil-fak/englisch/kurse/wintersn.htm. Consulted on 14 January 2002.

70 Jeannine DeLombard, 'Control Option Delete', *Lambda Book Report* 9.5 (December 2000): 24–5; 24.

71 Jenny Turner, 'A Tulip and Two Bulbs', *London Review of Books* 22.17 (7 September 2000): 10.

72 Elaine Showalter, 'Eternal Triangles', *Guardian* (2 September 2000): 9.

73 The building really exists; it is a Georgian house refurbished by Jeanette Winterson, who bought it when she discovered that the derelict greengrocer's in the basement was called 'JW Fruits'. Deborah Ross, 'Tea with the Holy Terror', *Independent* (8 April 2002). http://enjoyment. independent.co.uk/music/interviews/story.jsp?story=282750. Consulted on 3 August 2004.

74 J. Hillis Miller, 'The Ethics of Hypertext', *Diacritics* 25.3 (Fall 1995): 27–39; 27.

75 Kate Kellaway, 'She's Got the Power', *Observer* (27 August 2000). http://books.guardian.co.uk/print/0,3858,4055646-99930,00.html. Consulted on 14 January 2002.

76 Borges, 'El jardín de senderos que se bifurcan', *Ficciones*: 472–80; 476, 475, my translation.

77 Reynolds, 'Interview', 25.

78 Her words echo Jordan's real and imaginary journeys.

79 Doll Sneerpiece has a similar experience when her porcelain codpiece comes to life (*AL* 129–30).

80 Captain Bartolus helped dainty Orlando to a slice of corned beef. Virginia Woolf, *Orlando. A Biography*. London: Vintage (2000) [1928]: 98. By contrast, Ali is offered chicken, in what may be interpreted as an allusion to Napoleon's passion for chicken.

81 *Ibid.*, 73.
82 *Ibid.*, 10.
83 *Ibid.*, 3.
84 *Ibid.*, 58.
85 *Ibid.*, 153.
86 *Ibid.*, 153.
87 The 'caracole' movement of Orlando's pen is echoed by Alice's description of time as a 'caracol' in a river, in *Gut Symmetries* (see above). Since Orlando applies it to writing, this metaphor constitutes a significant antecedent of Winterson's structural whirlpools.
88 Woolf, *Orlando*, 154.
89 *Ibid.*, 183.
90 In 'Tlön, Uqbar, Urbis Tertius', for example, Borges imagines a world called Tlön where supra-individual spiritual authorship is the rule: 'The books are seldom signed. The concept of plagiarism does not exist: it has been established that all the works are the work of a single author, who is atemporal and anonymous [. . . .] The [books] of fiction deal with a single argument, with all imaginable permutations'. Borges, 'Tlön, Uqbar, Urbis Tertius', *Ficciones*: 431–43; 439, my translation.
91 In Reynolds, 'Interview', 25.
92 Both protagonists of *The Passion* live according to the motto: 'what you risk reveals what you value' (*P* 43, 73, 91).
93 Woolf, *Orlando*, 156.
94 Eliot, 'East Coker', 203.
95 Winterson has employed this symbol several times, for example in *Written on the Body* and in 'The Poetics of Sex'. See Chapter 3.
96 As Paulina Palmer has noted, the association of homosexual love with bodies in movement is related to Bakhtin's concept of carnival and his definition of the grotesque body as 'a body in "the act of becoming", in the process of being "continually built, created"'. Palmer, '*The Passion*: Story-telling, Fantasy, Desire', 111. See Chapter 2.
97 Julia Kristeva has described the process of abjection, through which the child differentiates itself from the mother, as 'a primal mapping of the body'. Kristeva, *Powers of Horror*, 71. Thus, Ali/x's words point to Tulip's role in the construction of herself as subject.
98 Eliot, 'The Dry Salvages', 212–13.
99 Their name echoes that of 'Mr. M'., one of Orlando's prospective husbands. Woolf, *Orlando*, 159.
100 This is an allusion to the key and door in Rapunzel's lonely tower that Winterson further develops in *Lighthousekeeping*. See Chapter 5.
101 Blake, 'Letter to Butts'.
102 Thomas Traherne, 'The First Century', in *Centuries of Meditations* (2004) [1908]. www.ccel.org/t/traherne/centuries/htm/TOC.htm. Con-

sulted on 7 August 2004.

103 John Fowles, *The Magus: A Revised Version*. London: Jonathan Cape (1977): 552.

104 Ali/x's words combine echoes from Eliot's description of the open field in 'East Coker', 196–7 and of the river in 'The Dry Salvages', 205.

105 Woolf, *Orlando*, 201.

106 *Ibid.*, 202.

107 *Ibid.*, 208–9.

108 *Ibid.*, 209.

109 *Ibid.*, 209.

110 *Ibid.*, 260.

111 *Ibid.*, 262.

5

Only connect . . .

In the last four years, Jeanette Winterson has considerably increased the range of her already notable public activity. She has lectured, interviewed other writers, given talks on the radio, written book introductions, essays on art, short stories, poems 'of the month' and what one reviewer has described as 'plenty of opinionated journalism'.[1] Most of these articles, poems and short stories are accessible on her website, launched at the publication of *The.PowerBook*. In 2000 Winterson undertook with Margaret Reynolds the job of editing the new Vintage reprintings of Woolf's novels. According to a columnist of the *Independent*, on 10 September 2001 she secluded herself with the theatre director Deborah Warner in 'an isolated hut with no heating or water' in order to work undisturbed on the adaptation of *The.PowerBook* into play-form for the National Theatre.[2] In 2002 she worked on a script of *Sexing the Cherry*, conceived as twenty-four short pieces for BBC and Internet, and on a documentary on *Orlando* for BBC4's 'Art that Shook the World' series. In 2003 she published a book for children, *The King of Capri*, and on 25 February 2004 she launched *Lighthousekeeping* with an energetic promotional campaign. The writer is at present working on a new 'play about fanaticism [which] will be directed by Warner at the Theatre de Chaillot in France, where Winterson, who is taking French lessons, is thinking of living. She finds the Continent "more open to ideas" [than Britain or America]'.[3]

In 2003 Jeanette Winterson said that all the books she had written from *Oranges* to *The.PowerBook* 'make a cycle or a series' and should be seen as 'one long continuous piece of work'.[4] This statement has been contradicted by D. J. Taylor, who sees *Lighthousekeeping* as confirmation that 'everything she writes is essentially a variation on the same thing' and firmly concludes that what the new novel offers is 'more of the same'.⁵ Most reviewers, however, have described the new novel in very positive terms, as 'a light and lovely thing'⁶ and as 'a brilliant, glittering piece of work, the kind that makes you gasp out loud at the sheer beauty of the language';⁷ while Lucy Daniel has suggested that, rather than signalling a new departure, '*Lighthousekeeping* returns us to the beginning of the cycle, offering an elegiac, fantastical setting for the naïve, blunt, genial voice of *Oranges Are Not the Only Fruit* (1985)'.⁸ This is an interesting suggestion that transforms Winterson's return to HarperCollins into a case of Jungian synchronicity.⁹ Another reviewer, Delia Falconer, concurs with Daniel in thinking that *Lighthousekeeping* shows Winterson moving away from the 'weighty' ideological complexities and arty sophistications of her 1990's fiction, and back to the 'lightness' of fantasy and storytelling characteristic of the 1980s, and she hails the move as something long awaited by Winterson's readers: 'As a lapsed fan, I approached *Lighthousekeeping* with trepidation – only to be delighted and surprised. Winterson's new novel is a return to the clever, clear-eyed, deceptively easeful fairytales of her earlier work.'¹⁰

As we saw in the Introduction, in *Art Objects* Jeanette Winterson rejected Victorian realism as 'essentially anti-art' and said that she was 'not particularly interested in folk tales or fairy tales', that she used them simply as 'a trap for the reader's attention' (*AO* 30–1, 189). The publication of *Lighthousekeeping* nine years after these provocative statements shows Winterson reconsidering them, since *Lighthousekeeping* is a novel about learning the art of storytelling and the story that Silver, the protagonist, tells is fully indebted to key Victorian texts, both real and fictional. Thus, Silver's story of the Revd Babel Dark, 'the most famous person ever to come out of Salts' (*L* 11), is presented as the story of the real person who inspired Robert Louis Stevenson to write *Dr Jekyll and Mr Hyde* (*L* 186–7), and Winterson devotes a whole chapter to 1859, the year 'Charles Darwin published *On the Origin of Species*, and Richard Wagner completed his opera *Tristram and Isolde*' (*L* 23, 169). Further, as Samantha Matthews has pointedly remarked, readers of *Treasure Island* 'will recognise in the narrator's opening words – "My mother called me Silver. I was born part precious metal part pirate" – a play on the anti-hero Long John Silver'.¹¹ Similarly, Pew, the lighthousekeeper, is named after 'the sinister pirate Blind Pew who brings "the black spot", while the boy-hero Jim Hawkins is recalled here as Silver's wonky-legged terrier DogJim'

(*L* 21).[12] Besides these nineteenth-century authors and texts, the novel acknowledges many other literary hypotexts. For instance, the title suggests an intertextual relation with Virginia Woolf's *To the Light-house*, while 'the epigraphs are from Muriel Spark's *Memento Mori* ("Remember you must die") and Ali Smith's *Hotel World* ("Remember you must live")'.[13] Yet another example of what Daniel calls Winterson's 'literary magpie-ism' is provided by Silver's stealing of Thomas Mann's *Death in Venice*, a novel that 'is itself highly allusive, incorporating translations of Homer and Wagnerian references which connect with Winterson's use of *Tristram and Isolde*'.[14]

At the beginning of the novel Silver explains that she had never met her seafaring father, that her 'mother was a single parent and she had conceived out of wedlock. [. . .] So she was sent up the hill, away from the town' (*L* 4–5). The expulsion from the community of a sinful woman and the fruit of her sin is a well-known romance *topos* that came to a climax of popularity in the nineteenth-century stories of 'seduced and abandoned maidens'. In Nathaniel Hawthorne's *The Scarlet Letter* (1850), for example, Hester Prynne and her baby daughter Pearl are cast out of the Puritan village to an archetypal wilderness overtly associated with witchcraft. In Silver and her mother's case, their exile is from the Scottish village of Salts to an oddly slanting house 'cut steep into the bank. The chairs had to be nailed to the floors, and we were never allowed to eat spaghetti' (*L* 3). This description is reminiscent of the floorless house Jordan visits in 'the city of words', whose furniture had to be 'suspended on racks from the ceiling' and whose inhabitants 'must travel by winch or rope from room to room' so as to avoid falling into the 'bottomless pits' below (*SC* 21). At the same time, this quasi-vertical house, built on the hill 'at an angle' (*L* 4), constitutes a formidably imaginative variation on Jim Hawkins's climactic adventure in *Treasure Island*, when the daring boy manages to pilot the *Hispaniola* to shelter with the help of the pirate Israel Hand. As it beached, 'suddenly the *Hispaniola* struck, staggered, ground for an instant in the sand, and then, swift as a blow, canted over to the port side, till the deck stood at an angle of forty-five degrees'.[15] The adventure ends with the villainous Hands 'loos[ing] his grasp upon the shrouds, and plung[ing] head first into the water' to his death, and a terrified Jim clinging to the cross-trees 'with both hands till [his] nails ached', since, '[o]wing to the cant of the vessel, the masts hung far out over the water, and from my perch on the cross-trees I had nothing below me but the surface of the bay'.[16] Equally terrified by the possibility of falling into the abyss, Silver and her mother 'had to rope us together like a pair of climbers, just to achieve our own front door. One slip, and we'd be on the railway line with the rabbits' (L 4). Thus, mother and child lived literally 'strapped together like it or not' (L 6), like the Italian fighters in *Written on the Body*, or rather, like Louise and the nameless narrator, whose bodies were held together in a 'single loop of love' (*WB* 88). When one day the wind suddenly blew her mother off the hill, she quickly had to undo the harness as she fell, thus preventing Silver from following her to her death (L 6–7).

The loss of her mother situates the ten-year-old child in the position of a Dickensian orphan, as Miss Pinch, the schoolteacher, is commissioned by the local authorities to take her under her provisional charge. As her name suggests, Miss Pinch is a troublesome and niggardly spinster, who (echoing Muriel Spark's epigraph), lives according to the motto 'Life is a Steady Darkening Towards Night' (L 48). Like Mr Gradgrind's definition of a horse in *Hard Times*, which is incomprehensible for Sissy Jupe although she lives at the circus in daily contact with horses,[17] Miss Pinch's geography lessons are absurdly factual and Utilitarian, and so uninspiring for children that, as Silver observes, '[t]he way she described the world, you wouldn't want to visit it anyway' (L 10). In Dickens's novels the characters and their habitats usually mirror each other. In keeping with this, Miss Pinch lives in Railings Row, a deserted terrace of black-bricked and salt-stained houses, in a house she keeps boarded up like the rest, its front door covered with a 'rain-soaked marine-ply' and secured by a triple lock and bar, for fear of burglars (L 9). Indeed, Miss Pinch and her house are equally impenetrable and solitary and they share a similarly diminished brilliant past: the derelict terrace had once belonged to prosperous tradesmen (L 8), and she is the proud 'direct descendant of the Reverend Dark' (L 10). Or so she likes to think, for one of the ironies of the novel is that she is in fact an orphan (L 230). Echoing Oliver Twist's foul treatment at the workhouse, Silver describes her first meagre supper of pickled herrings 'while she fried herself an egg' (L 9) in the gloomy light of the inimical house. With the characteristic deadpan humour of earlier Wintersonian heroines in distress, she reports her sleepless night in an improvised bed made of 'two kitchen chairs end to end, with a cushion on one of them' and a 'one-duck' eiderdown with most of the feathers outside and so full of lumps that it seemed to have been stuffed with the whole duck: 'So

I lay down under the duck feathers and duck feet and duck bill and glassy duck eyes and snooked duck tail, and waited for the daylight' (*L* 9). Thus finding herself at this crucial juncture in life between the two options represented by Spark's and Smith's epigraphs, little Silver courageously opts for the life-enhancing one, since she finishes the chapter with a consoling thought that she will repeat at the end of the novel: 'We are lucky, even the worst of us, because daylight comes' (*L* 9, 231).

The next day, Miss Pinch puts up a note on the Parish notice board with a description of Silver, to be given 'free to any caring owner' (*L* 10). Pew, the old and blind lighthousekeeper, is the only one to respond, so Silver and DogJim begin a new life in the lighthouse, with Silver to be apprenticed to Pew. Referring to the intertextual relationship between *Treasure Island* and *Lighthousekeeping*, Samantha Matthews has argued that 'Winterson inverts her model: Silver's quest is for the metaphysical treasure of self discovery and love'.[18] From this perspective, the fact that Silver is named after a precious metal points to her condition of child/treasure – like Alix in *The.PowerBook* – someone with the inborn capacity to read the signs nobody else is able to spot and to find the treasure of illumination/the Philosopher's Stone/the Holy Grail/true love. In the earlier novels, the protagonists' acquisition of these visionary powers was invariably achieved at the end of their individuation process and directly related to their own ability to shape their fragmentary memories and repressed desires into a coherent life-narrative. Only in *Art & Lies* are Handel and Picasso assisted in this task by Sappho, the mother of love poetry, who, as we saw in Chapter 3, personifies the writer as shaman – that is, someone capable of shaping and giving overall significance to the anarchy and futility of particular phenomena by the use of myth. As a 'mediator' between the two worlds, Sappho was associated with Hermes, the guide of souls to the underworld. As such, she accompanied Handel and Picasso in their archetypal journey from London (the world of common day) to Lesbos (the underworld). *Lighthousekeeping* fictionalises a variant of this supernatural aid: the initiation of Silver into this mediating role by Pew, the quintessential storyteller, whom Silver herself calls 'Mercury', that is, by the Latin name of Hermes (*L* 229).

At the end of *Orlando*, the protagonist imagines herself at the head of a long line of writers, going back to 'some one older, further, darker, a cowled figure, monastic, severe, a monk, who went with his

hands clasped, and a book in them'.[19] This monk, like Thomas
Chatterton's fictional *alter ego*, the medieval blind monk and bard
Thomas Rowley, is a personification of the archetypal storyteller
embodied by Pew, whose blindness, as he himself explains, is com-
pensated for by the 'gift of Second Sight, given to me on the day I went
blind' (*L* 47). Each day following her arrival, Pew tells Silver a story
about the lighthouse, beginning with that of Josiah Dark, the Bristol
merchant who commissioned the building of this and many other
lighthouses along the Scottish coast after one of his ships suffered a
terrible shipwreck in 1802 (*L* 11–12), an episode that is reminiscent of
Stevenson's short stories of wreckages, especially 'The Merry Men'
(1887). Pew's lighthouse was completed in 1829, its light lit with
uncanny synchronicity at the very moment Josiah's first son was
born. Therefore, '[t]hey called him Babel, after the first tower that ever
was' (*L* 15). Pew tells Silver these and related stories as if he had been
an eyewitness even though the events narrated took place more than
a century before, since Silver was born (like Jeanette Winterson) in
1959 (*L* 11). When Silver objects that 'You weren't there then. You
weren't born', Pew simply retorts: 'There's always been a Pew in the
lighthouse at Cape Wrath' (*L* 46).

Pew's suggested agelessness echoes that of Long John Silver's
parrot in *Treasure Island*, who, according to its owner, 'is, may be,
two hundred years old';[20] this agelessness is also in keeping with his
condition of shaman. When the lighthouse was automated, he disappeared in the sea in his mackerel boat, taking DogJim with him (*L*
123). Man and dog reappeared many years later when Silver visited the
lighthouse, now turned into a tourist attraction (*L* 219). When she
asked him where he had been, Pew shrugged and gave Silver the
same answer the first Pew had given Josiah Dark on the day he hired
him as lighthousekeeper: 'Here, there, not here, not there, and sea-
sonally elsewhere' (*L* 231, 204). This sentence points to Pew as a
mediator between the two worlds, since he changes places according
to the seasons, like Persephone, the queen of the underworld, who
spent six months on earth and six months with her husband, Hades.
The fact that Pew has a barge and appears and disappears from the
sea at will further associates him with Charon, the ferryman, who
takes the souls of the deceased to Hades, while his function of lighthousekeeper and his attachment to DogJim associate him with
Hecate, the guardian of the gates of Hades, one of whose main attributes is the dog.[21] Further still, the day Josiah Dark made Pew's

acquaintance, 'the first thing [he] noticed about the man was his fingers long like a spider's legs, and articulated at the joints. The man was lifting webs from the hedgerows and stretching them inside a frame he had cut from hedgerow timber. He had invented a way of preserving the webs and sold them for good money to sailors' (*L* 204). Pew's appearance and job associate him with Arachne, the spider, or rather, given his collective identity, with the Fates or Moirai, the three Greek goddesses who spin the strands of a human destiny closely bound to hazard and death.

When Pew invited Silver to the lighthouse and started telling her stories the old lighthousekeeper situated himself and the child in an archetypal master–pupil relationship. The initiation of a purblind hero/ine by an old wise wo/man is an archetypal *topos* that Winterson had already used in *Oranges*, in the tale of 'the princess and the old hunchback' and in its countertale, 'Winnet Stonejar and the Wizard'. As we saw in Chapter I, the latter is a version of 'Rapunzel', the fairy-tale of a little girl who was taken from her parents by a witch and kept in a stone tower until a valiant prince came to her rescue. Silver overtly compares the door to the lighthouse with 'The forbidden door that can only be opened with a small silver key. The door that is no door in Rapunzel's lonely tower' (*L* 219). In *The.PowerBook*, Alix's mother, Mrs M, found what she believed to be the key to 'buried treasure', but the materialistic and loveless life she led at the muck house prevented her from finding the door that matched that key (*PB* 195–6). As Alix and Rapunzel well knew, and as Silver makes clear, only love can open this door, which is 'the door at the top of the stairs that only appears in dreams', the door that led Perceval 'into the Chapel of the Grail' (*L* 219).

Like *Oranges* and *Great Expectations*, Silver's narration is structured as the adult protagonist's retrospective account of her life story. However, unlike Jeanette and Pip, Silver tells her story to an explicit narratee, a nameless woman simply addressed as 'you' (like Ali/x's narratee in *The.PowerBook*) with whom she has fallen in love at first sight in a remote convent on the Greek island of Hydra (*L* 192). The narrating act takes place in the novel's present in a solitary hut on the edge of a forest near the lighthouse (*L* 209), in a situation that is strongly reminiscent of Winterson's own seclusion with Deborah Warner to write the script of *The.PowerBook* described above, thus suggesting the identification of the fictional narrator-character with her flesh-and-blood creator. This narrative structure has the deceptive linearity of the hero's quest, since while Silver's narration progresses from birth to adulthood, the act of narrating is itself retrospective. As we saw in Chapter 2, the quest for individuation is usually symbolised by a physical and spiritual journey that takes place in two phases. In the first, the child apprehends the difference between self and world. In Silver's case, this phase begins with her early years with her mother and her training by Pew at the lighthouse and her journey to Bristol in search of Pew after his disappearance. In Bristol, Silver finds herself utterly alone in a hostile, alien world that she regards as 'A NEW PLANET', and where Pew's 'doubloons' have no value (L 136). Her marginalisation increases during her next journey to Capri, where she tries to assuage her loneliness by stealing a mechanical parrot that calls her by her name, a ludicrous episode that combines echoes of The.PowerBook and Treasure Island (L 154–7). At this stage, Silver has not yet found the treasure of true love, only a 'partner' who went to Italy to visit her while she was in quarantine (L 157). Her ensuing arrest and internment in the Tavistock Clinic in London on a diagnosis of a nervous breakdown symbolises the turning point when the heroine's ideals and values are reversed, giving way to the inward-looking phase in her individuation process, when the ego has to confront the depths of its own psyche and establish links with the inner self. This second phase corresponds to the journey that Silver (like Sappho, Handel and Picasso in Art & Lies) undertakes from London to the Aegean, and which comes to an end when she finds the nameless lady in the convent, an episode that subverts the unhappy ending of Perceval and Genevere's impossible love and reveals Hydra as the 'Treasure Island' hiding the 'buried treasure' of true love/gnosis.

This double-loop quest structure provides the longitudinal axis around which the novel unfolds. Like Treasure Island, Lighthousekeeping is divided into sections, with chapters whose first lines provide their titles, in which Silver alternates the narration of her life story with the retelling of the stories Pew told her during her apprenticeship, including the story of the Revd Babel Dark and the building of the lighthouse. The alternation of these two narrative strands, suggesting the interdependence of the private and the public, is reflected structurally in the undercutting of Silver's narration by ten dialogues. The first five, between Silver and Pew, show Silver as a curious and attentive child, eager to learn. Thus, they begin either with Silver's entreaties to Pew to tell her a story: 'Tell me a story, Pew' (L 49, 73,

109), or with the child's questions about her own past, or Babel Dark's, or Pew's: 'Pew, why didn't my mother marry my father? [. . . .] Why didn't Babel Dark marry Molly?' (*L* 85); 'How were you born, Pew?' (*L* 91). By contrast, in the other five dialogues, Silver has taken up Pew's position as addressee: she is now the wise storyteller being questioned by the nameless woman. Four of these dialogues begin: 'Tell me a story, Silver' (*L* 129, 173, 189, 225), while the remaining one (nearly) ends with the same sentence (*L* 151) and begins: 'I sometimes think of myself up at Am Parbh' (*L* 149). The interpolation of these ten dialogues and the fact that they can be arranged in two sets of five mirroring each other may be said to reflect at the narrative level the double-loop structure of Silver's individuation process and her trans-mutation from treasure-child into visionary storyteller.

On the day of her arrival, the lighthouse must have seemed as awe-inspiring to little Silver as the witch's tower to Rapunzel, since '[o]ur business was light, but we lived in darkness. The light had to be kept going, but there was no need to illuminate the rest. Darkness came with everything. It was standard' (*L* 20). However, unlike Rapunzel, Silver soon began to enjoy her new lifestyle, since the darkness out-side helped her see her own internal darkness: 'I learned to see in it. I learned to see through it, and I learned to see the darkness of my own' (*L* 20). Echoing Paracelsus's micro/macrocosm correspon-dence, Silver realises at this point that 'There were two Atlantics: one outside the lighthouse. And one inside me. / The one inside me had no string of guiding lights' (*L* 21). The first stage, then, in Silver's transmutation from apprentice lighthousekeeper to Hermetic mediator between the two worlds is the illumination of her internal darkness. As Pew observes, to accomplish this she would have to over-come the 'handicap of sight' (*L* 205) – the equivalent of Mr and Mrs M's myopia, or Blake's 'Single vision'. Thus, he asks her never to rely on what she sees and to close her eyes and watch the vision inside (*L* 205–6). Silver's training is completed the day her vision of 'Babel Dark coming towards the lighthouse' lingers on with eyes wide open: 'I opened my eyes, and saw the waves and the ships and the birds. Pew let go of my hand. "Now you know what to do"' (*L* 206).

Pew's role as Hermetic mediator between the two worlds is matched by the symbolism of the lighthouse as *umbilicus* or *axis mundi*, that is, as the 'wormhole' connecting life-in-time with eter-nity.[22] This interpretation is enhanced by the association of the light-house with the Tower of Babel, destroyed by God precisely because it

threatened to connect heaven and earth. In keeping with this symbolism, the lighthouse stands at 'the north-western tip of the Scottish
mainland [in] a wild, empty place, called in Gaelic *Am Parbh* – the
Turning Point' (*L* 11). That is, it stands at *finis terrae*, the world's end,
at what Eliot calls in 'Burnt Norton' 'the still point of the turning
world',[23] or, in Winterson's own terms, at the point of entrance for
Gulliver's 'sailing beyond the compass, [to a place] where no one has
ever been, [and] knowledge is dearly bought'.[24] 'Made of granite, as
hard and unchanging as the sea is fluid and volatile' (*L* 17), this lighthouse was the first of many more to be 'built over 300 years' (*L* 17)
along the coasts of Scotland. When they were all lit at night, they
projected a 'string of lights' (*L* 17) signalling both the physical edge
between land and sea and the mythical boundary between the realms
of the living and the dead. In keeping with this, Silver establishes a
Hermetic correspondence between the lighthouses and the stars
when, looking at the only star visible through the tiny window of her
room, she reflects: '*Only connect.* How can you do that when the
connections are broken?' 'That's our job, Pew had said. These lights
connect the whole world' (*L* 107). The italics leave no doubt that Silver
is here quoting E. M. Forster's epigraph ('*Only connect . . .*') to
Howards End (1910), a novel that fictionalises the characters' struggle
to make connections in a Victorian liberal-humanist period that preceded the First World War. In A. S. Byatt's *Babel Tower*, Frederica, the
protagonist, obsessively repeats this phrase.[25] She believes that she
married Nigel, her possessive and violent ex-husband, because she
'was beglamoured' by Margaret Schlegel's entreaties to Mr Wilcox to
build a 'rainbow bridge' connecting 'the prose in us with the passion',[26] that is, reconciling the seemingly incompatible spiritual and
material drives of the self. Frederica quotes at length from Chapter 22
of *Howards End*, where Margaret reflects:

> It did not seem so difficult. She need trouble him [Mr Wilcox] with no
> gift of her own. She would only point out the salvation that was latent in
> his own soul, and in the soul of every man. Only connect the prose and
> the passion and both will be exalted, and human life will be seen to be
> at its height. Live in fragments no longer. Only connect, and the beast
> and the monk, robbed of the isolation that is life to either, will die.[27]

Byatt's Frederica, who is preparing a lecture on love and marriage in
Howards End and *Women in Love*,[28] goes on to compare Forster's ideal
of Oneness with that of D. H. Lawrence, concentrating her analysis on

Chapter 27, where Birkin experiences the mystic dissolution of his self's identity and his merging with Ursula through the experience of love. Frederica finds Lawrence's idea of fusion with someone else 'a little sickening, I am a separate being'.[29] She concludes that, for all their differences in tone – 'Forster was uneasily mocking, whereas Lawrence was in deathly earnest'[30] – the two writers' goal of unification and wholeness is imbued by a similarly strong religious aspiration of transcendence, and that although she had always tried to experience it herself, this goal cannot be achieved in the present (the late 1960s): 'Why, thinks Frederica, does it seem so impossible, so far away, so *finished*, this Oneness, Love, the Novel? [. . . .] Or perhaps, it's only me, who can't do it.'[31] This is a key question that brings to mind Winterson's rejection of the novel as an exhausted literary form and situates Frederica in the shadow of Doris Lessing's *The Golden Notebook* (1962), whose protagonist, Anna Wulf, is similarly struck by the impossibility of achieving Forster and Lawrence's goal, in her case in the 1950s. Anna tries to overcome the writer's block caused by her feeling of self-fragmentation by writing four separate notebooks: 'a black notebook, which is to do with Anna Wulf the writer; a red notebook, concerned with politics; a yellow notebook, in which I make stories out of my experience; and a blue notebook which tries to be a diary'.[32] Written in the first person and forming the bulk of the novel, these notebooks contain the different facets of Anna Wulf's 'real' life, which she tries to reconcile in a fifth 'golden notebook'. At the same time, however, the notebooks are undercut and their value is called into question by five sections entitled 'Free Women', written in the third person and containing Wulf's fictional accounts of the 'real' events described in the notebooks. Anna's compartmentalisation of her life is taken a step further by Frederica, who takes for granted the impossibility of unifying the various facets of her life and sees them as independent strands in a structure of 'laminations':

> And she, Frederica, had had a vision of being able to be all the things she was: language, sex, friendship, thought, just as long as these were kept scrupulously separate, *laminated*, like geological strata, not seeping and flowing into each other like organic cells boiling to join and divide and join in a seething Oneness. Things were best cool, and clear, and fragmented, if fragmented was what they were.[33]

As the reader finds out in Byatt's next novel, *A Whistling Woman*, Frederica eventually materialises this idea into a 'book of jottings, cut-ups, commonplaces and scraps of writing, which she called *Laminations*',[34] where she freely combines reality and fiction: 'she had begun to put in passages from the books with which she was trying to teach him [her son Leo] to read'.[35] As the narrator reminds the reader, Frederica 'had had the word, *Laminations*, before the object. It referred to her attempts to live her life in separated strata, which did not run into each other. Sex, literature, the kitchen, teaching, the newspaper, *objets trouvés*'.[36]

After her arrival in Bristol in search of Pew, Silver, ironically following Miss Pinch's advice, starts frequenting the public library and soon becomes obsessed with reading every book in it. Frustrated by the impossibility of finishing any of them, she starts buying herself 'shiny silver notebooks with laminated covers' [. . .]. I copied the stories out as fast as I could, but all I had so far were endless beginnings' (L 139). When, after the incident with the speaking parrot in Capri, a therapist asks Silver if she keeps 'a diary' (L 160), she answers that she has 'a collection of silver notebooks' and when the therapist wants to know if the notebooks are 'consistent', she admits feeling that she has 'more than one life' and that it would be impossible to tell one single story [with a] beginning, a middle, and an end' (L 160–1). These 'silver notebooks with laminated covers' juxtaposing fragments of fiction and reality situate Silver in Anna and Frederica's shadow, still trying, like them, to respond to Forster and Lawrence's entreaties on behalf of unification, even though she is living at the end, rather than at the middle, of the twentieth century.

Structurally, Frederica's unfinished and multilayered book of *Laminations* constitutes a *mise en abyme* of *Babel Tower*, since Byatt's novel is itself similarly built on the juxtaposition of various apparently unconnected real and fictional narrative strands, including the events of Frederica's private life; the life of her widowed bother-in-law, the Vicar Daniel Orton; the life of a couple of scientists gathering snails on the moors of Frederica's native Yorkshire; and the life of the unkempt and charismatic Jude Mason, the author of *Babbletower*, a utopia about a Saint Simonian falanstery that progressively turns into a Sadeian horror castle. *Babbletower* resembles *Laminations* in form. When Frederica first saw it, it was 'only scribbled heaps of notes; and a swarm of scenes, imagined and re-imagined'.[37] However, the totalitarian ideology endorsed by the community, with its annihilation of individual choice and its utopian yearning for the end of history, represents the counterdiscourse of *Laminations* and, as its title suggests, of *Babel Tower* as well, bringing to the fore the basic dialectics between determinism and freedom on which Byatt's novel develops. Set against the totalitarian discourse of Mason's bloodcurdling dystopia, Frederica's difficulty in unifying the various facets of her life constitutes an affirmation of freedom, a refusal to see human life as predetermined. Her defence of complexity, freedom and hazard is reflected by the external narrator's hesitancy about which narrative line of *Babel Tower* to tell first: 'It might begin [with the story of the scientists in Yorkshire]';[38] 'Or it might begin with Hugh Pink [a friend of Frederica's] in Herefordshire in the autumn of 1964';[39] 'Or it might begin in the crypt of St Simeon's Church [where Daniel Orton works]';[40] 'Or it might begin with the beginning of [Jude Mason's *Babbletower*]'.[41]

When Pew tells Silver that their job is to make 'connections', then, he situates the little girl in Anna Wulf and Frederica's position, simultaneously wishing to unify the various facets of their lives and incapable of reducing them to a single, all-embracing and coherent narrative. Like them, Silver feels the need to establish the relation between her private life and that of her community.[42] Therefore, she decides to start the narration of her life one century before her birth, at the time when the lighthouse was built. But, like the narrator of *Babel Tower*, she is immediately struck by the arbitrariness of her attempt and constantly wonders where she should begin (*L* 11–12, 14). She summarises her options in a chapter fittingly entitled 'A beginning, a middle and an end is the proper way to tell a story. But I have difficulty with that method':

> Already I could choose the year of my birth – 1959. Or I could choose the year of the lighthouse at Cape Wrath, and the birth of Babel Dark – 1828. Then there was the year Josiah Dark first visited Salts – 1802. Or the year Josiah Dark shipped firearms to Lundy Island – 1789.
> And what about the year I went to live in the lighthouse – 1969, also the year that Apollo landed on the moon? (*L* 23)

She finally opts for 1789. That year the young Joshua Dark had idealistically risked his life smuggling muskets to the supporters of the French Revolution (*L* 13) and 'had intended to escape to France with his mistress and live in the new free republic' (*L* 14). However, like the communards in *Babbletower*, Joshua was soon disenchanted by the difference between the revolutionary ideals and their realisation: 'When the slaughtering started, he was sickened [. . .]. To escape his own feelings, he joined a ship bound for the West Indies and returned with a 10% share in the treasure. After that, everything he did increased his wealth' (*L* 14). Thus, Joshua's wealth was the fortuitous product of his idealism (*L* 14), just as Silver herself 'was a child born of chance' (*L* 32). Pondering on these and other examples of hazard, Silver concludes that there is a great difference between the complexity of real life, ruled by chance, and the artificial cause-and-effect simplicity of narrative: 'There was a story: the story of Molly O'Rourke and Babel Dark, a beginning, a middle, and end. But there was no such story, not that could be told, because it was made of a length of braid, an apple, a burning coal, a bear with a drum, a brass dial, his footsteps on the stone stairs coming closer and closer' (*L* 102). Years later, Pew summarises Silver's life story in similar terms: 'A book, a bird, an island, a hut, a small bed, a badger, a beginning . . .' (*L* 230). These descriptions are strikingly reminiscent of Frederica's definition of her life as a number of '*objets trouvés*'.

Before disappearing in the sea with DogJim, Pew leaves Silver a chest that is strongly reminiscent of Captain Flint's chest in *Treasure Island*. Silver finds in it, among other things, several types of old foreign coins; two identical pins; two first editions (*On the Origin of Species* and *Dr Jekyll and Mr Hyde*), and two sets of manuscripts: a series of notebooks containing 'Dark's diary of his life in Salts', and 'a scuffed folder' wrapped in paper and tied with a brown ribbon, holding 'an untidy pile of papers' written in a big and uncertain hand; several 'drawings of himself, always with the eyes scored out; and [. . .] watercolours on cartridge paper of a beautiful woman always half-turned' (*L* 124–5). As is suggested by the difference between 'his neat brown notebooks, and his wild torn folder' (*L* 161), the notebooks record in an orderly fashion Babel Dark's public life as the Vicar of Salts with his legal wife and son, while the torn folder with the loose leaves constitutes the chaotic record of Dark's secret life in Bristol, where he founded a bigamous second family under the name of Lux (*L* 186) after a chance encounter with his former lover, Molly O'Rourke, at the Great Exhibition of 1851 (*L* 78 ff.).

Silver overtly associates Babel Dark's duplicitous life as Dark/Lux with Dr Jekyll and Mr Hyde. As she explains, Robert Louis Stevenson, who came from the 'dynasty' of engineers that built the Scottish lighthouses (*L* 25), came to Salts in 1886, and he heard Babel Dark's story from his own lips 'just before his death' (*L* 26). After reading *The Strange Case of Dr Jekyll and Mr Hyde* (*L* 184), Dark describes Dr

Henry Jekyll, in terms that pun with his own Christian name, as 'an upright beacon, a shining example, a fellow of penetrating intellect and glowing humanity' (*L* 184), and the 'stunted dark creature by the name of Edward Hyde' (*L* 184–5) as his opposite: 'The one is all virtue and the other is all vice' (*L* 185). However, as Dark does not fail to realise, 'while they seem to be entirely separate, the dreadful and disturbing part, is that they are the same person' (*L* 185). Like Dr Jekyll, the Revd Dark publicly led a pious and socially acceptable life in Salts, where he lived in self-imposed exile with his wife and son. The model middle-class Victorian woman, Mrs Dark was deeply religious and charitable, self-denying to the point of stinginess, 'as dull as a day at sea with no wind' (*L* 54), and as frigid as her breakfast and her bedroom were cold (*L* 52, 55). A constant source of irritation for Dark, she acted as a catalyst for his growing sadomasochism, which materialised in ever more frequent and barely motivated episodes of physical violence against her and were invariably followed by equally violent acts of self-punishment. Dark had married her because she met the social requirements of a vicar's wife: she was 'the one lady of good blood in the place – a cousin of the Duke of Argyll [. . .]. She was no beauty, but she read German fluently and knew something of Greek' (*L* 44). With this choice of wife and vicarage Dark sought atonement for having yielded to the temptations of the flesh incarnated by Molly, the red-haired working-class girl he was passionately in love with but could not trust because she did not behave according to the received standards of morality: she had willingly yielded her virginity to him without the sacrament of marriage and, far from being afraid of her body, she enjoyed her sexuality as much as he did (*L* 28–9). Their love, symbolised by the pair of ruby and emerald pins Silver finds in Pew's chest (*L* 30, 221), is a prelapsarian perfect fusion of twin souls in Lawrence's sense of the term, stemming from the same cosmic force that created the world:

> 'My seahorse', Molly had called him, when he swam towards her in their bed like an ocean of drowning and longing.
>   The sea cave and the seahorse. It was their game. Their watery map of the world. They were at the beginning of the world. A place before the flood. (*L* 80–1)

When Molly told Babel that she was pregnant, he hit her repeatedly, causing the blindness of their unborn daughter, Susan (*L* 81), who was later to marry the first Pew (*L* 205). After this, Dark aban-

doned his seduced lover, gave up his loose lifestyle as a 'ladies' man'
and a 'dandy' (*L* 27, 28), dressed 'all in grey' (*L* 30), and took up the
post of vicar of Salts. Significantly, his mistrust of Molly was founded
on a tragic error of vision: by chance he had seen her embracing a
stranger and jumped to the conclusion (confirmed by a treacherous
acquaintance, Price, who was later to blackmail him) that she had
another lover, when in fact he was her brother: '[a] smuggler, a fugi-
tive, but still her brother' (*L* 222). This fact explains why all the
self-portraits in his folder have the eyes scored out, and why the only
time Molly visits him in Salts she adopts the name of Mrs Tenebris
(*L* 186), for, as Silver learnt in the pitch darkness of the lighthouse,
true insight lies beyond the soul's internal darkness and is obscured
by eyesight.

Babel Dark's rejection of passion brings to mind both the fear of
self-annihilation through fusion with the other often felt by
Lawrence's male characters and Mr Wilcox's refusal to 'connect' 'the
monk' and 'the beast' in him in *Howards End*. Indeed, Margaret
Schlegel's description of Mr Wilcox could easily be applied to Babel
Dark:

> Outwardly he was cheerful, reliable and brave; but within, all had
> reverted to chaos, ruled, as far as it was ruled at all, by an incomplete
> asceticism. Whether as boy, husband or widower, he had always the
> sneaking belief that bodily passion is bad, a belief that is desirable only
> when held passionately. Religion had confirmed him. [. . .] He could not
> be as the saints and love the Infinite with a seraphic ardour, but he could
> be a little ashamed of loving a wife.[43]

However, where Mr Wilcox's sexual repression is motivated by religion, that of Babel Dark also has, as we have seen, a crucial social
component, a feature that, as David Punter has pointed out, is a determinant in the split between Jekyll and Hyde: 'The original tendency
of Jekyll's *alter ego*, so he claims, was by no means towards the vicious,
but rather towards the "loose", a neutral desire for certain kinds of
personal freedom which has been repressed by the "imperious" need
not only to conform to, but also to stand as a public example of, strict
virtue.'[44] It is a fear of personal freedom, then, that forces Dark to
choose the anonymity of regulated behaviour. His first sermon in
Salts, entitled 'Remember the rock whence ye are hewn, and the pit
whence ye are digged' (*L* 43), is significant in this respect, since it is
based on the biblical passage 'The Lord Comforts Zion', in Isaiah 51.1,

in which God reassures the Israelites that they are His chosen people and that their sufferings will soon be at an end, provided that they abide by His law.[45] Babel synthesises the comforting feeling of spiritual and social superiority he derives from the Bible in the hymn entitled '*Fastened to the rock*' (*L* 121), where the Church (as rock) provides a reassuring image of stability against the chaos and impermanence of life in time: '*We have an anchor that keeps the soul steadfast and sure while the billows roll. Fastened to the rock which cannot move, grounded firm and deep in the Saviour's love*' (*L* 121, original italics). However, in Dark's tormented imagination, this Christian image is soon transformed into a pagan counterimage of unendurable and everlasting torment: 'Fastened to the rock. And he thought of Prometheus, chained to his rock for stealing fire from the gods' (*L* 121).

In the light of Nietzsche's contention that 'all the famous characters of the Greek stage, Prometheus, Oedipus, etc., are only masks of [Dionysos]',[46] the comparison of Dark to Prometheus gives an archetypal dimension to his situation, transforming it into a tragic struggle between the archaic forces of wild, naked nature, symbolised by Dionysos and expressed in wild emotion or sensation, and the Apollonian forces of reason and ideation, associated with culture, art and subjectivity, that prescribe the mortification and sublimation of these impulses. From a Nietzschean perspective, Babel Dark's story is comparable to that of Aschenbach, the protagonist of Thomas Mann's *Death in Venice* (1911), the novel that obsessed Silver so much. Aschenbach is a distinguished member of the middle class, a conservative writer of conventional bourgeois morality, who is, however, increasingly troubled by homosexual impulses that he systematically represses and sublimates in his writings. As Vagelis Siropoulos notes, 'He invents and inhabits a disinfected Apollonian universe where the body as the locus of symbolic excess is mortified and *jouissance* is prohibited. [. . .] Nevertheless, homosexual desire becomes the d/evil within Aschenbach's system [, . . .] a path leading to an abjected physicality where *jouissance* and death collide.'[47] With the only difference that Babel Dark's Dionysian impulse is heterosexual, the behaviour of both characters is strikingly similar. Like Aschenbach, Dark tries to sublimate the passion he feels for Molly by transforming it into a perfectly innocent, prelapsarian relationship. Thus, on feeling 'the breath of her on him' while she is asleep, Dark compares himself to Adam, feeling 'God breathing first life into his sleeping body' (*L* 68), and he recalls how after their first meeting, 'he had taken her apple picking in his father's garden' (*L* 68). Unlike Adam, however, he does not dare to eat this Edenic fruit. In his family home in Salts he keeps a bucket of rotting apples that he is willing neither to eat nor to give away to the poor (*L* 56–7).

Dark's faith undergoes a final test the day his dog Tristram accidentally falls over the cliff on to an inaccessible ledge. In his attempt to rescue the animal, Dark discovers a cave whose walls are made entirely of sea fossils (*L* 116). Darwin himself came to inspect this cave, whose existence gainsaid the biblical account of the creation of the earth, suggesting 'all kinds of new possibilities' (*L* 119). Characteristically, Dark is unable to accept this evidence: 'He had always clung to the unchanging nature of God, and the solid reliability of God's creation. Now he was faced with a maverick God who had made a world for the fun of seeing how it might develop. Had he made Man in the same way?' (*L* 120). The troubled vicar finds the answer to this question in the cave itself when, tracing with 'his fingers the hollow spirals of the fossils [, h]e remembered his fingers in her [Molly's] body' (*L* 120), but he stubbornly dismisses the association (*L* 120). Thus, where Dr Jekyll's scientific experiments were meant to prove that, if evolution is a ladder, it may be possible to bring about an artificial reversion of the species, Darwin's evolutionist model of the universe triggers off Vicar Dark's anguished leap into agnosticism: 'Perhaps there was no God at all. He laughed out loud. Perhaps, as he had always suspected, he felt lonely because he was alone' (*L* 120).

His realisation that the universe might not be following a predetermined, divine plan, and that he might be in fact free to choose his destiny, inexorably leads Dark to existentialist angst and a vision of the void that he resolves by putting an end to his life. Thus, in an episode that brings to mind the association of the sea with dissolution and death in *Death in Venice* and Virginia Woolf's *The Waves*, Babel Dark makes his own experiment in artificial reversion; he unclothes himself and walks slowly out to sea, tightly holding in his hand the seahorse fossil he identified himself with: 'They would both swim back through time, to a place before the flood' (*L* 122). Pew's version of Dark's life ends here. However, one hundred pages later, Silver provides confirmation that the experiment was successful when she adds that, after drowning, Babel Dark saw the pattern of the stars reflected on water and saw himself 'patterned in stars' (*L* 222). Dark's

vision of this Hermetic correspondence expressing the overall unity
of the cosmos is followed by a vision of himself and the seahorse
swimming 'into the cone of light' cast by the lighthouse, 'signalling
the way to the bottom of the world. His body was weightless now. His
mind was clear. He would find her' (L 223). Thus, Dark is left revert-
ing to the time before the Flood when, free from social and religious
constraints, he can acknowledge the 'other within', his Jungian
shadow, his life-enhancing, Dionysiac drive, and unite himself with
his twin soul or his anima, thus bringing about his essential transformation and integration with the cosmos. This is an optimistic
ending that has, however, the escapism of a wish-fulfilment dream,
since Babel Dark's unification and healing takes place by virtue of
Silver's act of imaginative creation – that is, in the Apollonian world
of art that had caused Dark and Aschenbach's self-fragmentation.

Silver's life story ends similarly with herself and her beloved
addressee in the Edenic hut by the forest, sitting in front of the fire
and trying to 'recognise each other in the place that is ours', which is
the place of love (L 232). That is, it ends with an attempt at recreating
the fusion of twin souls experienced by Birkin and Ursula and
Tristram and Isolde, and stubbornly refused by Mr Wilcox, Babel
Dark and Aschenbach. Silver makes this attempt, however, knowing,
as Anna, Frederica and Perceval did, that success is impossible, since
'[t]here is so little life, and it is fraught with chance. We meet, we
don't meet, we take the wrong turning, and still bump into each other.
We conscientiously choose the "right road" and it leads nowhere' (L
214). The difference between Silver and Perceval, on the one hand,
and Anna and Frederica, on the other, is that the former believe with
other Wintersonian characters that only the impossible is worth the
effort and that, as the drowning sailor in Pew's tale well knew, 'stories
are like prayers' (L 40) and can work miracles, provided that the
storyteller tells them properly and the listener is ready to believe
them.

On 24 March 2005 Jeanette Winterson told me in an e-mail that
she was working on a book entitled *Tanglewreck*, 'about a world where
time is distorting'. As she explained in the 'March' entry of *The
Jeanette Winterson Column, Tanglewreck* is a children's book she
intended to publish in mid-March 2005, coinciding with the birthday
of her godchildren, who 'will be nine and six this month'.[48] At the time
of writing, this project remained unfulfilled; according to Amazon,
the book is scheduled to be published by Bloomsbury on 1 January

2006. The synopsis of *Tanglewreck* that appears on the Amazon web-site runs as follows:

> In a house called Tanglewreck lives a girl called Silver and her guardian Mrs Rockerbye. Unbeknown to Silver there is a family treasure in the form of a seventeenth century watch called The Timekeeper and this treasure holds the key to the mysterious and frightening changes in time. When Silver goes on the run to try and protect herself and The Timekeeper a remarkable and compelling adventure unfolds full of brilliance and wit, as is befitting an author with the imagination and style of Jeanette Winterson.[49]

This description shows the book as a sequel to *Lighthousekeeping* with orphaned Silver living an adventure that involves her learning how to make good use of keys to treasures. The fact that the treasure is a watch that holds the key to the control of time shows the tale growing around two of the most significant recurrent *topoi* in Winterson's fiction, namely, the question of time and the search for that which cannot be found.

The other forthcoming book Winterson mentioned to me in her e-mail is a novella entitled *Weight: The Myth of Atlas and Heracles*, which she was commissioned to write by Canongate for a new series called 'The Myths'. Winterson's story was scheduled for publication in September 2005, in a boxset with stories written by Karen Armstrong and Margaret Atwood. In the excerpt from the foreword to *Weight* that appears in the Canongate book catalogue for July–December 2005, the writer explains:

> When I was asked to choose a myth to write about, I realised I had chosen already. The story of Atlas holding up the world was in my mind before the telephone call had ended. If the call had not come, perhaps I would never have written the story, but when the call did come, that story was waiting to be written. Re-written. The recurring language motif of Weight is 'I want to tell the story again'.

The opposition of lightness and weight, like that of time and eternity, is a recurrent key *topos* in Winterson's fiction in general and in *Sexing the Cherry* in particular. As the writer implicitly acknowledges, the novella is also thematically indebted to *Lighthousekeeping* – for, as she further explains: 'Weight moves far away from the simple story of Atlas's punishment and his temporary relief when Heracles takes the world off his shoulders. I wanted to explore loneliness, isolation, responsibility, burden, and freedom too.'

In conclusion, the Amazon synopsis of *Tanglewreck* and the writer's foreword to *Weight* both point to Winterson's continuing interest in the same *topoi* that recur in the earlier novels, thus confirming the suggestion made in the Introduction that she is a 'hedgehog' type of writer, constantly approaching the same subjects and ideas from different perspectives while trying to relate everything to a single central vision. The thematic recursiveness of Winterson's work necessarily qualifies her declaration that, with *Lighthousekeeping*, she is initiating a new cycle, since not only this novel but also her forthcoming children's story and novella clearly stem from the same imaginative source that gave the earlier fictions their distinctive Wintersonian character.

Notes

1 Caroline Baum, 'Review of *Lighthousekeeping*', *Sydney Morning Herald* (6 March 2004). www.smh.com.au/cgi-bin/common/popupPrintArticle. pl?path=articles/. Consulted on 31 March 2004.
2 Ross, 'Tea with the Holy Terror'.
3 Jaggi, 'Redemption Songs'.
4 In Reynolds, 'Interview', 25.
5 D. J. Taylor, 'The Solace of Solitude: *Lighthousekeeping*', *Literary Review* (May 2004): 49.
6 Katherine England, 'Jeanette Winterson: *Lighthousekeeping*', *The Advertiser* (2004). www.theadvertiser.news.com.au/printpage/0,5942,886 0071,00.html. Consulted on 2 April 2004.
7 Christina Patterson, 'Of Love and Other Demons'. Review of *Lighthousekeeping, Independent* (7 May 2004). http://enjoyment.independent.co.uk/ books/interviews/story.jsp?story=518837. Consulted on 3 August 2004.
8 Lucy Daniel, 'Snooked Duck Tail'. Review of *Lighthousekeeping, London Review of Books* (3 June 2004): 25–6; 25.
9 In the introduction to the Vintage edition of *Oranges*, Winterson said that she had removed the book from Pandora because the imprint had been bought by Rupert Murdoch. Winterson, 'Introduction' to *Oranges*, xv. Yet, as Maya Jaggi observes, 'with *Lighthousekeeping*, she followed her publisher Caroline Michel to Fourth Estate, an imprint of the Murdoch-owned HarperCollins. "Typical me that I had to put that in writing," [Winterson] shakes her head, amused'. Jaggi, 'Redemption Songs'.
10 Delia Falconer, 'Review of *Lighthousekeeping*', *The Age* (20 March 2004). www.theage.com.au/articles. Consulted on 31 March 2004.
11 Samantha Matthews, 'Jeanette Winterson's Personal Fables of the Writer's Vocation: *Lighthousekeeping*', *Times Literary Supplement* (May 2004): 21.

12 At the same time, the fact that DogJim is a terrier associates it with Jeanette's dog in *Oranges*, just as Silver is linked with Jeanette through their orphanhood.

13 Daniel, 'Snooked Duck Tail', 25.

14 *Ibid.*, 25.

15 Robert Louis Stevenson, *Treasure Island*. Cambridge: Cambridge University Press (1995) [1883]: 171.

16 *Ibid.*, 172, 173.

17 Charles Dickens, *Hard Times*. London: Penguin (1994) [1854]: 4.

18 Matthews, 'Jeanette Winterson's Personal Fables', 21.

19 Woolf, *Orlando*, 209.

20 Stevenson, *Treasure Island*, 74.

21 Douglas, *The Tarot*, 100.

22 See Chapter 4 on this.

23 Eliot, 'Burnt Norton', 191.

24 Jeanette Winterson, 'Introduction: Gulliver's Wound', to *Gulliver's Travels, by Jonathan Swift*. Oxford: Oxford University Press (1999): v–xii; xii.

25 A. S. Byatt, *Babel Tower*. London: Chatto & Windus (1996): 18, *passim*.

26 *Ibid.*, 308.

27 *Ibid.*, 308–9.

28 *Ibid.*, 306.

29 *Ibid.*, 312.

30 *Ibid.*, 310–11.

31 *Ibid.*, 311.

32 Doris Lessing, *The Golden Notebook*. New York: Simon & Schuster (1962): 406.

33 Byatt, *Babel Tower*, 312, original emphasis.

34 A. S. Byatt, *A Whistling Woman*. London: Chatto & Windus (2002): 39. This is the last novel in a quartet on English life from the early 1950s to 1970 written by Byatt with Frederica as a protagonist. The first two are *The Virgin in the Garden* (1978) and *Still Life* (1986).

35 *Ibid.*, 39.

36 *Ibid.*, 38–9.

37 Byatt, *Babel Tower*, 10.

38 *Ibid.*, 1.

39 *Ibid.*, 2.

40 *Ibid.*, 4.

41 *Ibid.*, 10.

42 In an essay entitled 'Only Connect', Selma R. Burkom convincingly argued that Doris Lessing was one of the first writers to handle the individual consciousness in its relation to the collective. Selma R. Burkom, '"Only Connect": Form and Content in the Works of Doris Lessing', *Critique* 11 (1969): 51–68.

43 In Byatt, *Babel Tower*, 308–9.

44 David Punter, *The Literature of Terror: A History of Gothic Fictions from 1765 to the Present Day*. London and New York: Longman (1980): 241.

45 The Dog Woman carved this passage on a medallion and hung it round Jordan's neck the day she found him, but later on he exchanged it for a pair of tiny dancing shoes Fortunata had given him, to his mother's indifference (*SC* 10, 130).

46 Friedrich Nietzsche, *The Birth of Tragedy and the Genealogy of Morals*, trans. Francis Golffing. New York: Doubleday Anchor Books (1956): 65.

47 Vagelis Siropoulos, 'The Dionysian (Gay) Abject: Corporeal Representation in *The Birth of Tragedy* and *Death in Venice*', in Ruth Parkin-Gounelas (ed.), *The Other Within. Volume I: Literature and Culture*. Thessaloniki: Athanasios A. Altintzis (2001): 93–103; 97.

48 Jeanette Winterson, *The Jeanette Winterson Column* (March 2005). www.jeanettewinterson.com/pages/content/index.asp?PageID=315. Consulted on 24 March 2005.

49 Anon, 'Synopsis of Jeanette Winterson's *Tanglewreck*', 2005. www.amazon.co.uk/exec/obidos/tg/browse/-/274842/026-4914605-0465245. Consulted on 24 March 2005.

Conclusion

In the span of thirty years, Jeanette Winterson has achieved international recognition as one of the leading present-day British writers. No longer of exclusive interest for the lesbian readership that launched her to fame in the 1980s, her novels are read, enjoyed and hotly discussed both by the general public and academia. Thus, while film and theatre versions have been made of her most popular novels, the most experimental ones often appear in the syllabuses of university courses on contemporary British fiction and are the subject of an increasing number of dissertations and critical essays both in Britain and elsewhere. In this sense, the recent publication in France of an introductory book on Winterson's work in a collection aimed at university students is proof of her presence in academic circles outside the English-speaking world.[1]

In the last two decades, critics' efforts to situate Winterson's work within the general panorama of contemporary writing have more often than not delved into the question of subjectivity. Thus, as early as 1994, Paulina Palmer situated Jeanette Winterson with Margaret Atwood and Angela Carter in a postmodernist trend characterised by 'the delineation of subjectivity as fractured and decentered' as well as by the 'treatment of genre'.[2] In the following decade, Andrea L. Harris placed Winterson with Virginia Woolf, Djuna Barnes and Marianne Hauser in 'a particular group of twentieth-century women novelists that question the way in which the sex/gender binary works to conceal rather than reveal difference [. . . ,] explore the border between masculine and feminine, [and analyse] the place where these terms overlap and intersect,'[3] while Lauren Rusk saw her as belonging in an international trend, also exemplified by Woolf, James Baldwin and Maxine Hong Kingston, representing what Rusk calls *The Life Writing of Otherness.*[4] Although different in many respects, these essays share a crucial concern with the analysis of subjectivity in Winterson's work, perceived as marginal and/or fragmented, no matter whether the marginality and fragmentariness stem from the characters' lesbianism or simply from their condition as women. This perception is given a further turn of the screw in a recent essay on 'Jeanette Winterson's Evolving Subject', written by Kim Middleton Meyer,[5] which appears, together with essays on Angela Carter, Kazuo Ishiguro and Martin Amis, in a section devoted to 'Pathological Subjects'.[6]

Although there is no denying that the identity of Winterson's characters is marginal, unstable and fragmentary, to describe it as permanently fractured or pathological would be to obliterate the crucial fact that the novels invariably show the protagonists' evolution from self-fragmentation and ignorance to unification and gnosis. Similarly, to describe Winterson's delineation of subjectivity as exclusively representative of women-as-other, whether lesbian or heterosexual, would be to ignore the fact that the maturation process undergone by her characters invariably follows an archetypal quest pattern and is, therefore, representative of the human condition at large. Thus, while in *Oranges* the purblind heroine is Jeanette, a lesbian girl, and in *Boating for Beginners* it is Gloria, a heterosexual girl, in *The Passion* and *Sexing the Cherry*, the characters bound on their self-quest are two young men, Henri and Jordan, with Villanelle and Fortunata personifying the anima qualities they must acquire in order to round off their individuation process. In a predictable development, in the next novel, *Written on the Body*, the hero/ine's gender is never stated, thus pointing to a bisexuality that is wholly in keeping with the programmatic differentiation by French feminists in the 1970s between sexual orientation and gender and the denunciation of traditional gender roles as the cultural constructions of patriarchy. As we saw in Chapter 3, the evolution of Winterson's protagonists from lesbianism to bisexuality involves the rejection of the 'invert' model associated with early lesbian novels like Radclyffe Hall's *The Well of Loneliness* and the adoption of the 'friendship' model inaugurated by Virginia Woolf's *Orlando* and further developed by Maureen Duffy in her later fiction. In Winterson's case, this move from one model to the other is progressive and is accompanied by significant changes in the representation of the protagonists. Thus, while the Jeanette of *Oranges* is a physically normal lesbian woman, Villanelle and the Dog Woman are hybrid or 'grafted' beings ('monstrous', according to patriarchy). Their physical abnormality symbolises an androgyny that, like that of the pineapple in Andrew Marvell's poem 'Bermudas', is seen as exceptional in nature. In *Written on the Body*, the bisexuality of the narrator is made representable at the cost of omitting her/his name and of suppressing any references to his/her gender. Handel's androgyny, in *Art & Lies*, is the artificial product of a castration. Doll Sneerpiece's porcelain codpiece, in the same novel, and Turkish Ali's embalmed tulip stalk, in *The.PowerBook*, which are stirred into life by the force of their owners' desire, are parodic variants on this type of artificial androgyny. Indeed, Sappho is the first character in Winterson's fiction to enjoy a natural bisexuality wholly unrelated to the specificities of her body. After her come Alice and Stella in *Gut Symmetries*, and Ali/x and Tulip in *The.PowerBook*, all of whom are physically normal women with a bisexual orientation. In keeping with this, when Ali/x, who identifies herself with Orlando, makes a list of 'great and ruinous lovers' (*PB* 77), she places homosexual and heterosexual couples on the same footing. Her list foreshadows the characterisation of Silver, the protagonist of *Lighthousekeeping*, whose bisexuality, though implicit, is hinted at by the fact that she sets the heterosexual passions of Tristram and Isolde, and of Babel Dark and Molly, on a par with her own homosexual passion for the (bisexual) nameless lady, thus suggesting that she takes bisexuality for granted and considers the question of sexual orientation totally irrelevant.

The force that drives Winterson's protagonists on their life quests, then, is an acute feeling of lack and incompleteness that produces in them a consuming desire for the other, expressed in archetypal images such as the search for buried treasure/the Philosopher's Stone/the Holy Grail/that which cannot be found/death. The fulfilment of this desire is described as the embrace of identical twins, tied-up fighters, the intertwined strings of flying kites, Solomon's knot, or the merging of a face and its reflection in a mirror, Narcissistic images all of them, meant to express the reversibility of the patriarchal equation 'desiring object/object of desire'. The archetype underlying these images is that of the biblical and mythical androgyne. As Aristophanes explains in Plato's *Symposium*, when they are torn from each other, the androgynes' suffering is so intolerable that they devote the rest of their lives to searching for their split halves and, once they are reunited, they prefer to starve to death rather than separate themselves again. The love that drives these androgynes together is *amor vulgaris*, procreative sexual love, the cosmic power capable of reconciling all opposites: spirit and matter; man and cosmos; god and goddess. In this sense, the Dog Woman's preternatural lack of desire is paradigmatic of her godlike self-sufficiency and wholeness.

In keeping with its archetypal nature, the protagonists' process of maturation and cosmic integration is invariably presented as a double physical and spiritual journey, constantly compared to Perceval's quest for the Holy Grail, the Fool's quest through the arcana of the Tarot, the alchemist's search for the Philosopher's Stone, or the medieval Ship of Fools. At the narrative level, this quest structure is echoed by the fact that – with the only exception of *Boating for Beginners*, where the narrative role is assumed by an external narrative instance that parodies the omniscient narrator-author of Genesis – all the narrators are autodiegetic, that is, they are both narrators and protagonists, reporting their life stories in retrospect in a manner characteristic of the *Bildungsroman*. Thus, the novels simultaneously develop in two opposite directions. On the one hand, the physical journey of the narrator-characters progresses from past to present along a chronological 'time's arrow' symbolised by the Newtonian train in *Art & Lies* and *Gut Symmetries*. On the other, their minds move backwards as they try to recover the lost memories and repressed desires of a past that seems fragmentary and incomprehensible to them. This antithetical movement, which can be represented as a recumbent eight, the symbol of the infinite, expresses the eternal recurrence of mythical time (the Dantean rose, as opposed to the train, in *Art & Lies* and *Gut Symmetries*).

Further, while in *Oranges* and *Written on the Body* the narrative role relies on a single character, in the later novels this role is shared by two or more characters whose lives are interdependent: by Henri and Villanelle in *The Passion*; by the Dog Woman, Jordan and their alter egos, the nameless ecologist and Nicolas Jordan in *Sexing the Cherry*; by Handel, Picasso and Sappho in *Art & Lies*; by Alice, Stella and Jove in *Gut Symmetries*; by Ali/x and Tulip in *The.PowerBook*; and by Silver and Pew in *Lighthousekeeping*. This alternation of narrative voices complicates the basic structural pattern of the novels, as does the undercutting of the narrative flow by the interpolation of additional texts that offer what may be compared to symphonic variations on the events narrated, producing a characteristically Wintersonian baroque effect of repetition and excess. In these metanarratives, 'fictional' discourses such as fairytales, fragments of romance, of poems, and of religious and mythical texts (from the Bible, Greek mythology, the Tarot, Hermetic and alchemical magic, the Cabbala, etc.), are juxtaposed with the 'objective' discourses of history, medicine, psychology, critical theory, Greek philosophy, Newtonian science, the New Physics and the new technologies, while, in a self-conscious countermovement, they are simultaneously levelled to the sole and all-encompassing category of textual construct by means of metafictional mechanisms, such as the willed confusion of fictional narrator and flesh-and-blood author, the metaleptic trespassing on narrative and ontological boundaries, and the use of a poetic style that is both characteristically Wintersonian and overflows with intertextual echoes from earlier writers and texts.

Structurally, the alternation of narrative voices and the juxtaposition of realistic, fictional, mythical and biblical 'variations' on the same events has the effect of expanding vertically the basic cyclical pattern described above as a recumbent eight into a spiral or vortex, what Alice depicts in *Gut Symmetries* as a 'whirlpool' in the Heraclitean river, or following Woolf's *Orlando*, as a 'caracol' (*SG* 218).[7] As the analysis has shown, every novel manages in one way or another to display this spiralling structure, whose emblem is both Fortunata and the dancers' cosmic dance in *Sexing the Cherry* and the cardinal's book/world in *Art & Lies*, a textual microcosm whose macrocosmic counterpart is the Library of Alexandria that appears in the same novel. This Borgesean conception of the world as a book or as a textual labyrinth is a key Modernist *motif* that points to Winterson's visionary outlook on art and her belief, with William Blake and the Romantic poets, in the godlike creativity of the human imagination. From this visionary perspective, the protagonists' act of reshaping the fragmentary memories of their past into a coherent narrative becomes a therapeutic act of creation/ self-healing, bringing about what Jeanette describes in *Oranges* as her evolution from 'priest' to 'prophet' – that is, from subservient follower of received dogmas to godlike creator of her own reality. In this sense, the novels are all *Künstlerromane*. Read in these terms, the writing activity of Winterson's protagonists becomes the means for their essential transmutation into poets-as-prophets or shamans, Hermetic magi with the ability to transform the particular into the archetypal and so bridge the gulf between the material and the spiritual worlds. In this light, their striving for unity and wholeness expresses a fundamental human need to reconcile time and eternity, matter and spirit, the

Dionysian forces of wild nature expressed in emotion and sensation, and the Apollonian forces of reason and ideation associated with culture and art, what E. M. Forster described in *Howards End* as the need to 'connect' the prose in us with the passion, the beast and the monk in us.

This essential need is already apparent in *Oranges Are Not the Only Fruit* and *Boating for Beginners*, where the self-fragmentation of Jeanette and Gloria is expressed as a series of hallucinations in the course of which the two girls are confronted with their 'orange demon', the personification of their id, who asks them to choose between conforming to the social norms upheld by their mothers/ superegos, or following the promptings of their unconscious and fulfilling their repressed desires (*O* 108; *BB* 67). In the following novels, the self-fragmentation of the protagonist is taken to extremes, since each facet of the self – in Jungian terms, ego, shadow and anima – is personified by a different character. These are the respective roles of Henri, the cook and Villanelle in *The Passion*; of the nameless narrator, Elgin and Louise in *Written on the Body*; and of Alice, Jove and Stella in *Gut Symmetries*. In *Lighthousekeeping*, Molly plays the role of anima to a Babel Dark irreparably fragmented by his determination to keep his ego and shadow facets 'unconnected'. His sadomasochism is the symptom of his split self, as it is also of other characters with a materialistic and patriarchal ideology, who conceive love in terms of inequality and bondage, like the cook in *The Passion*, the Puritans in *Sexing the Cherry*, the nameless narrator in *Written on the Body*, Jove in *Gut Symmetries*, or Picasso's brother and father in *Art & Lies*. In this novel, the relationship between the protagonists, Handel, Picasso and Sappho, does not really conform to the threefold pattern of the earlier novels and is best understood as the duplication of a binary master/pupil relationship between Sappho and Handel, on the one hand, and between Sappho and Picasso, on the other, comparable to that of Pew and Silver in *Lighthousekeeping*. Finally, the relationships of Jordan and Fortunata in *Sexing the Cherry*, of Ali/x and Tulip in *The.PowerBook*, and of Silver and the nameless lady in *Lighthousekeeping* conform to a binary ego/anima pattern from which the figure of the shadow has been excluded.

As we saw in Chapter 5, Frederica, the protagonist of A. S. Byatt's *Babel Tower*, saw her life as complex and fragmentary, but instead of attempting to unify it, she took complexity and fragmentariness for granted and fiercely defended her sense of self from the intrusion of others, including her husband. Her position contrasts with that of Birkin, in D. H. Lawrence's *Women in Love*, who is willing to relinquish his sense of self in order to achieve fusion with Ursula. Frederica sees Birkin's attitude to love as the expression of a Romantic death drive with a strong religious component. The Romantic and religious elements are also clear in Winterson's conception of love. However, her protagonists' obsessive search for unification with the other does not imply the dissolution of the self, but rather, as we have seen, the reconciliation (in Forster's terms, the 'connection') of opposites and the abolition of patriarchal distinctions such as man/woman; self/ other; or subject/object of desire.[8]

In keeping with this, the individuation process of Winterson's characters is invariably presented as a vital choice between destiny and freedom. Thus, if Jeanette is to fulfil her desire for other women, she will have to give up religious community and family home and abjure the dogmas taught her by her mother, just as Gloria has to leave her bossy mother, Mrs Munde, to drown in the Flood, if she is herself to survive. These are traumatic experiences that the wise Dog Woman spares Jordan by giving him a river name that, as she herself explains, is meant to symbolise his freedom. In *Lighthousekeeping*, Babel Dark's self-fragmentation is directly related to his choice of Victorian morality and dogma over the existential freedom offered him by Darwin's evolutionist model of the world. Henri and Villanelle's love of gambling in *The Passion* is the material expression of their belief that human life is ruled by hazard. Their intuition is scientifically demonstrated by Alice in *Gut Symmetries*, who envisions her life, that of Stella and Jove, as well as the lives of their parents as an intricate net of Jungian synchronicities, or significant casual occurrences comparable to the chaotic arrangement of subatomic particles in quantum physics. For Stella's father, Ishmael, these synchronicities are rather Hermetic 'correspondences' expressing the fundamental unity of self and world. From Ishmael's holistic perspective, self and world stand in a micro/macrocosmic relationship, so that every human being can alter not only the course of his or her own life, but also the events in the universe. In *Lighthousekeeping*, Silver, who describes herself as a child born of chance, sees her life as a series of hazardous occurrences, constantly forcing her to make a new start in a different direction. For her, as for Pew, Ishmael, Sappho and other visionary characters who have opted for the difficult freedom of the prophet crying alone in the wilderness, instead of abiding by the collective dogmas of the priest, there is no doubt that the cosmic force capable of granting significance to their lives is *amor vulgaris* in all its manifestations, defined as a relationship of equality and mutual love, not only between sexual partners, but also between (foster) parents and children (the cotton reel connecting Jeanette and her mother; the harness tying Silver to hers; the intangible bonds between the Dog Woman and Jordan; Picasso and her mother; Silver and Pew), as well as between friends, whether male or female (between the Dog Woman and the nuns and whores, extended to Jordan and Tradescant; or between Nicolas Jordan and the ecologist).

This definition of love, which allows for individual freedom and rejects dogma, accepts alterity in the other as well as in oneself and refuses to draw social and generic distinctions, is the essential element in the novels that provides the stimulus for the characters' life quests and confers meaning on their existence. In this sense, Jeanette Winterson's insistent 'call to love' may be said to respond to the demand of what Ruth Parkin-Gounelas, following Julia Kristeva, has described as 'a new ethical imperative' for our present age, aimed at replacing 'the ethical imperative of integrity so dear to a humanist tradition' by a new ethics of freedom involving the recognition of alterity in the others as well as in ourselves.[9] After the terrorist attacks by religious fundamentalists on the population of New York (11 September 2001), Madrid (11 March 2004) and London (7 July 2005), and the policy of hatred adopted in response to these attacks, this ethical imperative seems not only necessary but vital for the survival of the human species and the preservation of the earth.

Notes

1   Christine Reynier, *Jeanette Winterson: Le miracle ordinaire*. Pessac: Presses Universitaires de Bordeaux (2004).

2   Paulina Palmer, 'Postmodern Trends in Contemporary Fiction: Margaret Atwood, Angela Carter, Jeanette Winterson', in Jane Dowson and Steven Earnshaw (eds), *Postmodern Subjects/Postmodern Texts* (Postmodern Studies 13). Amsterdam and Atlanta, GA: Rodopi (1994): 181.

3   Andrea L. Harris, *Other Sexes: Rewriting Difference from Woolf to Winterson*. Albany: State University of New York Press (2000): xi, xii.

4   Lauren Rusk, *The Life Writing of Otherness: Woolf, Baldwin, Kingston, and Winterson*. New York & London: Routledge (2002).

5   Kim Middleton Meyer, 'Jeanette Winterson's Evolving Subject', in Richard J. Lane, Rod Mengham and Philip Tew (eds), *Contemporary*

British Fiction. Cambridge: Polity Press (2003): 210–25.

6   Lane, Mengham and Tew (eds), Part IV, 'Pathological Subjects', in *Contemporary British Fiction*, 2003, 191–255.

7   This structural symbolism of the caracol is in keeping with the baroque motif of the shell used to express unlimited movement, excess and the reversibility of real and imaginary worlds. See Hélène Fau, 'The Illusion of the Shell-Formed Microcosm in Jeanette Winterson's Novels', *Études britanniques contemporaines* 23 (2000): 91–8.

8   In a recently published essay, Christine Reynier interestingly points out how, in *Art Objects*, Winterson uses the term 'transpersonality', as different from Eliot's 'impersonality', to characterise the type of individuation of the self her characters strive to achieve through the 'ethical' experience of love. As she explains, 'The term "impersonality," through its negative prefix, underlines the loss or deprivation of personality [. . .] whereas "transpersonality," through the prefix "trans," points to the crossing over or the transgression of the boundaries of the self'. Reynier, 'Jeanette Winterson's Cogito', 304.

9   Ruth Parkin-Gounelas, 'Introduction' to Parkin-Gounelas (ed.), *The Other Within* (2001): 1–8; 6–7.

Bibliography

Select works by Jeanette Winterson

Novels

Oranges Are Not The Only Fruit. London, Boston: Pandora, 1985; New York: Atlantic Monthly Press, 1985.

Boating For Beginners. London: Methuen, 1985.

The Passion. London: Bloomsbury, 1987; New York: Atlantic Monthly Press, 1988.

Sexing the Cherry. London: Bloomsbury, 1989; New York: Atlantic Monthly Press, 1990.

Written on the Body. London: Jonathan Cape, 1992; New York: Alfred A. Knopf, 1992; New York: Vintage Books, 1992.

Art & Lies: A Piece for Three Voices and a Bawd. London: Jonathan Cape, 1994; New York: Alfred A. Knopf, 1994.

Gut Symmetries. London: Granta, 1997; New York: Alfred A. Knopf, 1997.

The.PowerBook. London: Jonathan Cape, 2000; New York: Alfred A. Knopf, 2000.

Lighthousekeeping. London and New York: Fourth Estate, 2004.

Novella

Weight. The Myth of Atlas and Heracles. Edinburgh: Canongate, forthcoming September 2005.

Short stories

1988. 'Orion', *Granta* 23 (Spring): 131–7.

1989. 'The Architect of Unrest', *Granta* 28 (Autumn): 179–85.

1990. 'Psalms', in Patricia Craig (ed.), *The Penguin Book of British Short Stories*. Harmondsworth: Penguin; Agustine Martin (ed.), *Friendship*. London: Ryan Publishing, pp. 24–6.

1990. 'The Lives of the Saints', in Lisa St Aubin de Teran (ed.), *Indiscreet Journeys: Stories of Women on the Road*. Boston: Faber and Faber.

1991. 'The World and Other Places', in Kate Figes (ed.), *The Best of Cosmopolitan Fiction*. London: Serpent's Tail.

1992. 'Newton', in Patrick McGrath and Bradford Morrow (eds), *The New Gothic: A Collection of Contemporary Gothic Fiction*. London: Picador.

1993. 'The Poetics of Sex' (Best of Young British Novelists), *Granta* 43 (Spring): 311–20, reprinted in Margaret Reynolds (ed.), *The Penguin Book of Lesbian Short Stories*. London and New York: Viking, 1993, pp. 412–22.

1994. 'The Queen of Spades', in John Miller and Kirsten Miller (eds), *Venice*. San Francisco: Chronicle Books, pp. 11–51.

1995. 'The Green Man', *New Yorker* Fiction Issue (26 June): 166–9.

1996. 'O'Brien's First Christmas', in Di Speirs (ed.), *Woman's Hour: 50th Anniversary Short Story Collection*. Harmondsworth: Penguin.

1998. *The World and Other Places*. London: Jonathan Cape.

2005. 'The Night Sea Voyage', in *The Brighton Book*. Brighton: Myriad Editions in association with Brighton festival, pp. 7–13.

Children's books
The King of Capri. London: Bloomsbury, 2003.
Tanglewreck. London: Bloomsbury, forthcoming January 2006.

Non-fiction books and essays
Fit for the Future: The Guide for Women Who Want to Live Well. London: Pandora, 1986.

'Dreams and Buildings', in Mark Fisher and Ursula Owen (eds), *Whose Cities?* Harmondsworth: Penguin, 1991.

'Jeanette Winterson', in Antonia Fraser (ed.), *The Pleasure of Reading*. London, 1992. (This essay is an early, and slightly different, version of the essay 'Art & Life' that was later published in *Art Objects*.)

'Virginia Woolf: Monks House, Rodmell, E. Essex', in Kate Marsh (ed.), *Writers and Their Houses: A Guide to the Writers' Houses of England, Scotland, Wales and Ireland*, London: Hamish Hamilton, 1993.

Art Objects: Essays on Ecstasy and Effrontery. London: Jonathan Cape, 1995; New York: Alfred A. Knopf, 1995.

The Psychometry of Books. Westminster, MD: Alfred A. Knopf Inc., 1996. (Signed, limited edition of 2000 books.)

The Dreaming House. London: Ulysses, 1998.

Jeanette Winterson *et al.* 'Revolting Bodies', *New Statesman and Society* 2.8 (1989), pp. 22–9.

Scripts and radio plays
'Static', (radio play), in Jeremy Mortimer (ed.), *Young Playwrights Festival*.

London: BBC Books, 1988.
Oranges Are Not the Only Fruit: The Script. London: Pandora, 1990.
Great Moments in Aviation (Script). London: Vintage, 1994.

Introductions
'Introduction' to *Adeline Mowbray* by Mrs Opie. London: Pandora, 1986.
'Introduction' to *A Simple Story* by Elizabeth Inchbald. London: Pandora, 1987, pp. vii–xi.
'Introduction' to *Oranges Are Not the Only Fruit*. London: Vintage, 1991 (1985), pp. xi–xv.
'Foreword' to Margaret Reynolds (ed.), *Erotica: Women's Writing from Sappho to Margaret Atwood*. London: Ballantine Books, 1992.
'Introduction: Gulliver's Wound' to *Gulliver's Travels* by Jonathan Swift. Oxford: Oxford University Press, 1999, pp. v–xii.
'Jeanette Winterson on *The Waves*', in *The Waves* by Virginia Woolf. London: Vintage, 2000.
2002 'Introduction' to *Essential Acker: The Selected Writings of Kathy Acker*, eds Amy Scholder and Dennis Cooper. New York: Grove Press, 2002, pp. vii-x.

Editions
Passion Fruit: Romantic Fiction with a Twist. London: Pandora, 1986. A collection of short stories.
Jeanette Winterson and Margaret Reynolds (series eds), Vintage series of Virginia Woolf's novels, 2000 ff.

Miscellaneous
Oranges Are Not the Only Fruit; video: Second Sight Television; audio tape: BBC Audio Collection, 1990.
'Work in Progress' BBC Radio 2 (January 2000).
'What Is Art For?', lecture delivered in Seattle (8 November 2000) and Portland (9 November 2000).
'Conversation with Magic Stones', lecture delivered at Tate Modern, London (23 January 2002).
The Official Jeanette Winterson Site. www.jeanettewinterson.com.
The Jeanette Winterson Column (March 2005). www.jeanettewinterson.com/pages/content/index.asp?PageID=315. Consulted on 24 March 2005.
The Jeanette Winterson Reader's Site. Anna Troberg, 1998. http://w1.181.telia.com/~u18114424/index.htm. Consulted on 25 October 2004.

Interviews
Barr, Helen. 'Face to Face: A Conversation Between Jeanette Winterson and Helen Barr', *English Review*, 2.1 (September 1991): 31.

Gerrard, Nicci. 'The Prophet: Nicci Gerrrard Talks with Jeanette Winterson, The Novelist Who Says If It Doesn't Shock It Isn't Art', *New Statesman and Society* 2.65 (1 September 1989): 12–13.

Goody, Felicity. 'Jeanette Winterson in Conversation with Felicity Goody' (Profile) Radio 4 (23 August 1989).

Harthill, Rosemary. 'Jeanette Winterson in Conversation with Rosemary Harthill' (Writers Revealed). Radio 4 (Autumn 1990).

Jaggi, Maya. 'Redemption Songs', Saturday Review: Profile: Jeanette Winterson, *Guardian* (29 May 2004). www.jeanettewinterson.com. Consulted on 1 April 2004.

Miller, Laura, 'The Salon Interview: Jeanette Winterson' (April 1997). www.salonmagazine.com/April97/Winterson970428. Consulted on 31 January 2000.

Reynolds, Margaret. 'Interview with Jeanette Winterson', in Margaret Reynolds and Jonathan Noakes (eds), *Jeanette Winterson: The Essential Guide*. London: Vintage, 2003, pp. 11–29.

Ross, Deborah. 'Tea with the Holy Terror', *Independent* (8 April 2002). www.Independent.co.uk. Consulted on 3 August 2004.

Wachtel, Eleanor. 'Eleanor Wachtel with Jeanette Winterson: Interview', *Malahat Review* 118 (1997): 61–73.

Works cited

Ackroyd, Peter. *Ezra Pound and his World*. London: Thames and Hudson, 1980.

—— *Notes for a New Culture*. London: Alkin Books, 1993 (1976).

Adams, Hazard. *Philosophy of the Literary Symbolic*. Tallahassee: University Presses of Florida, 1983.

Ang, Sinclair Timothy. '(Giving an Other) Reading (of) Hélène Cixous, *écriture* (and) *feminine*', 1998. www.gradnet.de/papers/pomo2.archives/pomo98.papers/rang98.htm. Consulted on 5 March 2004.

Anon. 'Synopsis of Jeanette Winterson's *Tanglewreck*'. 2005. www.amazon.co.uk/exec/obidos/tg/browse/-/274842/026-4914605-0465245. Consulted on 24 March 2005.

Anon. The Noah's Ark Search.com website. www.noahsarksearch.com/ararat.htm.

Bakhtin, Mikhail. *The Dialogic Imagination: Four Essays*, trans. Caryl Emerson and Michael Holquist. Austin: University of Texas Press, 1981 (1934–5).

—— *Rabelais and His World*, trans. Helen Iswolsky. Bloomington: Indiana University Press, 1984 (1965).

Barnes, Julian. *A History of the World in 10½ Chapters*. London: Jonathan Cape, 1989.

Barth, John. 'The Literature of Exhaustion', *Atlantic Monthly* (August 1967): 29–34.

—— 'The Literature of Replenishment: Postmodernist Literature', *Atlantic Monthly* (January 1980): 65–71.

Barthes, Roland. *A Lover's Discourse: Fragments*, trans. Richard Howard. London: Penguin, 1990 (1977).

Baum, Caroline. 'Review of *Lighthousekeeping*', *Sydney Morning Herald* (6 March 2004). www.smh.com.au/cgi-bin/common/popup PrintArticle.pl? path=articles/. Consulted on 31 March 2004.

Bényei, Tamás. 'Risking the Text: Stories of Love in Jeanette Winterson's *The Passion*', *Hungarian Journal of English and American Studies* 3.2 (1997): 199–209.

Berlin, Isaac. *The Hedgehog and the Fox: An Essay on Tolstoy's View of History*. New York: Simon and Schuster, 1970.

Blake, William. *The Marriage of Heaven and Hell* (c. 1790), in John Sampson (ed.), *The Poetical Works of William Blake*. New York and Toronto: Oxford University Press, 1956 (1913), pp. 245–60.

—— 'Letter to Butts' (22 November 1802), in Geoffrey Keynes (ed.), *The Complete Writings of William Blake*. London: Nonesuch; New York: Random House, 1957, p. 818.

Borges, Jorge Luis. *Obras completas* I (1923–49). Barcelona: María Kodama y Emecé (eds), 1989.

—— 'Las ruinas circulares', *Ficciones* (1944), in *Obras completas* I, pp. 451–5.

—— 'La lotería en Babilonia', *Ficciones*, pp. 456–60.

—— 'La biblioteca de Babel', *Ficciones*, pp. 465–71.

—— 'El jardín de senderos que se bifurcan', *Ficciones*, pp. 472–80.

—— 'Tlön, Uqbar, Urbis Tertius', *Ficciones*, pp. 431–43.

—— 'El Aleph', *El Aleph* (1949), in *Obras completas* I, pp. 617–28.

Bowie, Malcolm, *Freud, Proust and Lacan: Theory as Fiction*. Cambridge: Cambridge University Press, 1988 (1987).

Brooks, Libby, 'Power Surge'. The Guardian Weekend (2 September 2000): 10–6.

Bunning, Joan. 'The Celtic Cross', 1995 (2002). www.learntarot.com/ccross. htm. Consulted on 11 June 2004.

Burkom, Selma R. '"Only Connect": Form and Content in the Works of Doris Lessing', *Critique* 11 (1969): 51–68.

Buzbee, Lewis. 'Hidden Journeys, Mythical History', *San Francisco Chronicle* (15 April 1990): 9.

Byatt, A. S. *Babel Tower*. London: Chatto & Windus, 1996.

—— *A Whistling Woman*. London: Chatto & Windus, 2002.

Bynum, Caroline Walker. *Metamorphosis and Identity*. New York: Zone Books, 2001.

Calvo, Mónica. 'A Feminine Subject in Postmodernist Chaos: Jeanette Winterson's Political Manifesto in *Oranges Are Not the Only Fruit*', *Revista Alicantina de Estudios Ingleses* 13 (2000): 21–34.

Campbell, Joseph. *The Masks of God: Primitive Mythology*. New York: Penguin, 1969.

Cavendish, Richard. *The Magical Arts: Western Occultism and Occultists*. London: Arkana, 1984 (1967).

Cheuse, Alan. 'Sating a Passion for High Romance', *Chicago Tribune* (5 July 1988): 3c.

Cixous, Hélène, 'The Laugh of the Medusa' (1976), in Elaine Marks and Isabelle de Courtivron (eds), *New French Feminisms*. Brighton, Sussex: Harvester, 1981, pp. 254–64.

—— 'Coming to Writing', in Deborah Jenson (ed. and trans.), *'Coming to Writing' and Other Essays*, trans. Sarah Cornell, Ann Liddle, Susan Sellers, Susan Rubin Suleiman, Cambridge, MA: Harvard University Press, 1991, pp. 1–58.

—— 'The Last Painting or the Portrait of God', in Jenson (ed.), *'Coming to Writing' and Other Essays*, pp. 104–31.

—— 'Sorties', in Hélène Cixous and Catherine Clément, *The Newly Born Woman*, ed. and trans. Sandra M. Gilbert. London: I. B. Tauris, 1996 (1975), pp. 63–132.

Cixous, Hélène and Catherine Clément. 'Sorceress and Hysteric', in *The Newly Born Woman*, ed. and trans. Sandra M. Gilbert. London: I. B. Tauris, 1996 (1975).

Corbin, B. J. *The Explorers of Ararat*. Highlands Ranch, CO: GCI Books, 1999.

Creed, Barbara. 'Horror and the Monstrous-Feminine: An Imaginary Abjection', *Screen* 27.1 (1986): 63–89.

D. S. 'N. B'., *Times Literary Supplement* (8 July 1994): 14.

—— 'N. B'., *Times Literary Supplement* (14 October 1994): 18.

Dällenbach, Lucien. *The Mirror in the Text*, trans. Jeremy Whiteley and Emma Hughes. Cambridge: Polity Press, 1989 (1977).

Daniel, Lucy. 'Snooked Duck Tail'. Review of *Lighthousekeeping*, *London Review of Books* (3 June 2004): 25–6.

Davies, Paul. *The Cosmic Blueprint*. London: William Heinemann, 1989.

Davies, Paul and John Gribbin. *The Matter Myth: Beyond Chaos and Complexity*. London: Penguin, 1992 (1991).

DeLombard, Jeannine. 'Control Option Delete', *Lambda Book Report* 9.5 (December 2000): 24–5.

Delcourt, Marie. *Hermafrodita*, trans. Javier Albiñana. Barcelona: Seix Barral, 1970 (1958).

Devaney, Robert L. 'The Dynamical Systems and Technology Projects at Boston University', 2004 (1999). http://math.bu.edu/DYSYS/index.html. Consulted on 18 July 2004.

Dickens, Charles. *Hard Times*. London: Penguin, 1994 (1854).

Dirda, Michael. 'A Cornucopia of Earthy Delights', *Washington Post* (13 May 1990): X09.

Douglas, Alfred. *The Tarot: The Origins, Meaning and Uses of the Cards.* Illustrated by David Sheridan. Harmondsworth: Penguin, 1982 (1973).

Drob, Sanford L. 'The Sefirot: Kabbalistic Archetypes of Mind and Creation', *CrossCurrents: The Journal of The Association for Religion & Intellectual Life* 47.1 (Spring 1997). www.crosscurrents.org/Drob.htm. Consulted on 7 July 2004.

Duchêne, Anne. 'After Marengo: Jeanette Winterson's *The Passion*', *Times Literary Supplement* (26 June 1987): 697.

Duffy, Maureen, *The Microcosm*. London: Virago, 1989 (1966).

Duncker, Patricia. 'Jeanette Winterson and the Aftermath of Feminism', in Grice and Woods (eds), *'I'm telling you stories,'* pp. 77–88.

Eco, Umberto. *Postscript to The Name of the Rose* (1983), trans. William Weaver. New York: HBJ, 1994.

EFE. 'El arca de Noé no está en la ladera occidental de Ararat', *Heraldo de Aragón* (28 March 2005): 33.

Eliade, Mircea. *The Myth of the Eternal Return: Cosmos and History*, trans. William R. Trask. London: Arkana, 1989 (1954).

Eliot, T. S. *Collected Poems (1909–1962)*. London: Faber and Faber, 1974 (1963).

—— 'The Love Song of Alfred Prufrock, (1917), in *Collected Poems*, pp. 13–17.

—— 'Portrait of a Lady', (1917), in Collected Poems, pp. 18–22.

—— 'The Burial of the Dead', *The Waste Land*, in *Collected Poems*, pp. 63–5.

—— 'A Game of Chess', *The Waste Land*, pp. 66–9.

—— 'What the Thunder Said', *The Waste Land*, pp. 76–9.

—— 'Notes on the Waste Land', *The Waste Land*, pp. 80–6.

—— 'Burnt Norton' (1935), *Four Quartets*, in *Collected Poems*, pp. 189–95.

—— 'East Coker' (1940), *Four Quartets*, pp. 196–204.

—— 'The Dry Salvages' (1941), *Four Quartets*, pp. 205–13.

—— 'Little Gidding' (1943), *Four Quartets*, pp. 214–23.

—— 'Tradition and the Individual Talent', in M. H. Abrams (general ed.), *The Norton Anthology of English Literature* II. New York: W. W. Norton & Co., 1979 (1919), pp. 2293–300.

Emck, Katy. 'On the High Seas of Romance: Review of *Gut Symmetries*', *Times Literary Supplement* (3 January 1997): 21.

England, Katherine. 'Jeanette Winterson: *Lighthousekeeping*', *The Advertiser* (2004). www.theadvertiser.news.com.au/printpage/0,5942,8860071,00. html. Consulted on 2 April 2004.

Falconer, Delia. 'Review of *Lighthousekeeping*', *The Age* (20 March 2004). www.theage.com.au/articles. Consulted on 31 March 2004.

Fau, Hélène. 'The Illusion of the Shell-Formed Microcosm in Jeanette Winterson's Novels', *Études britanniques contemporaines* 23 (2002): 91–8.

Fisher, Emma. '". . . and before": Jeanette Winterson. *Boating for Beginners*', *Times Literary Supplement* (1 November 1985): 1228.

Fowles, John. *The Magus: A Revised Version*. London: Jonathan Cape, 1977.
—— *The Aristos*. Revised edition. London: Jonathan Cape, 1980 (1964).
—— *The Nature of Nature*. Covelo, California: The Yolla Bolly Press, 1995.
Frazer, Sir James George. *The Golden Bough* (1922). www.bartleby.com/196/
100.html. Consulted on 24 February 2005.
Freud, Sigmund. '*Más allá del principio del placer*' *y otros ensayos* (1940–52),
trans. Luis López Ballesteros y de Torres, in Virgilio Ortega (ed.), *Obras
completas* XIII. Barcelona: Ediciones Orbis S. A., 1988.
Frye, Northrop. *Anatomy of Criticism: Four Essays*. Princeton: Princeton
University Press, 1957.
Fuss, Diana (ed.). *Inside/Out. Lesbian Theories, Gay Theories*. New York and
London: Routledge, 1991.
Ganteau, Jean-Michel. 'Fantastic, but Truthful: The Ethics of Romance',
Cambridge Quarterly 32.3 (2003): 225–38.
—— 'Hearts Object: Jeanette Winterson and the Ethics of Absolutist
Romance', in Susana Onega and Christian Gutleben (eds), *Refracting the
Canon in Contemporary Fiction and Film*. Amsterdam and Atlanta, GA:
Rodopi, 2004, pp. 165–85.
Genette, Gérard. *Figures III*. Paris: Éditions du Seuil, 1972.
Gerrard, Nicci. 'The Prophet: Nicci Gerrard Talks with Jeanette Winterson,
The Novelist Who Says If It Doesn't Shock It Isn't Art', *New Statesman and
Society* 2.65 (1 September 1989): 12–13.
—— 'The Ultimate Self-Produced Woman', *Observer* (5 June 1994): 7.
—— 'Cold Blast of Winterson at the Door', *Observer* (3 July 1994): 11.
Gilbert, Matthew. 'Illuminating the Human Condition', *Boston Globe* (15
June 1988): 79.
Gilbert, Sandra M. and Susan Gubar. *The Madwoman in the Attic: The
Woman Writer and the Nineteenth-century Literary Imagination*. New Haven
and London: Yale University Press, 1984.
Graves, Robert. *The White Goddess: A Historical Grammar of Poetic Myth*. New
York: Farrar, Strauss and Cudahy, 1948. Revised and enlarged edn, New
York: Farrar, Strauss and Giroux, 2000 (1966).
Grice, Helena and Tim Woods, 'Reading Jeanette Winterson Writing', in
Grice and Woods (eds), *'I'm telling you stories,'* pp. 11–16.
—— 'Grand (Dis)unified Theories? Dislocated Discourses in *Gut
Symmetries*', in Grice and Woods (eds), *'I'm telling you stories,'* pp. 117–26.
—— (eds), *'I'm telling you stories': Jeanette Winterson and the Politics of Reading*
(Postmodern Studies 25). Amsterdam and Atlanta, GA: Rodopi, 1998.
Harris, Andrea L. *Other Sexes: Rewriting Difference from Woolf to Winterson*.
Albany: State University of New York Press, 2000.
Hassan Ihab. *The Right Promethean Fire: Imagination, Science and Cultural
Change*. Urbana: University of Illinois Press, 1980.
Hawking, Stephen. *A Brief History of Time: From the Big Bang to Black Holes*.

New York: Bantam Books, 1988.

Hemmings, Clare. 'Lesbian (Anti-)Heroes and Androgynous Aesthetics: Mapping the Critical Histories of Radclyffe Hall and Virginia Woolf', *Revista Brasil de Literatura: Literatures in English Language* Online Journal, Rio de Janeiro, Brazil, 2000. http://members.tripod.com/lfilipe/. Consulted on 18 March 2004.

Hensher, Phillip. 'Sappho's Mate', *Guardian* (5 July 1994): 13.

Hutcheon, Linda. *A Poetics of Postmodernism: History, Theory, Fiction*. New York and London: Routledge, 1988.

Hutton, Elaine (ed.). *Beyond Sex and Romance? The Politics of Contemporary Lesbian Fiction*. London: The Women's Press, 1998.

Innes, Charlotte. 'Rich Imaginings: *Sexing the Cherry*, by Jeanette Winterson', *Nation* (9 July 1990): 64–5.

Irigaray, Luce. 'Sorcerer Love: A Reading of Plato's *Symposium*, Diotima's Speech', *Hypatia* 3 (1989): 32–44.

Jackson, Rosemary. *Fantasy: The Literature of Subversion*. London and New York: Methuen, 1981.

Jaggi, Maya. 'Redemption Songs', Saturday Review: Profile: Jeanette Winterson, *Guardian* (29 May 2004). http://books.guardian.co.uk/departments/generalfiction/story/0,6000,1226858,00.html. Consulted on 5 August 2004.

Jaivin, Linda. '*Lighthousekeeping*. Book Review', *Bulletin* (3 March 2004). www.bulletin.nimensn.com.au/bulletin/EdDesk.nsf. Consulted on 2 April 2004.

Jay, Karla and Joanne Glasgow (eds), *Lesbian Texts and Contexts: Radical Revisions*. London: Onlywomen Press, 1992.

Josipovici, Gabriel. *The World and the Book: A Study of Modern Fiction*. Stanford, CA: Stanford University Press, 1971.

Joyce, James. *A Portrait of the Artist as a Young Man*. Introduction and Notes by J. S. Atherton. London: Heinemann Educational Books, 1969 (1916).

—— *Ulysses*. Harmondsworth: Penguin, 1972 (1922).

Jung, Carl G. *Memories, Dreams, Reflections*. New York: G. P. Putnam's Sons, 1965.

—— 'A Psychological Approach to the Dogma of the Trinity' (1948), trans. R. F. C. Hull, in Sir Herbert Read *et al.* (eds), *Psychology and Religion: East and West. The Collected Works* XI. London: Routledge and Kegan Paul, 1981, pp. 107–200.

—— 'The Battle for Deliverance from the Mother', *Symbols of Transformation* (1911–12/1952), in *The Collected Works* V, 1981, pp. 274–305.

—— 'Paracelsus', *The Spirit in Man, Art, and Literature* (1929), in *The Collected Works* XV, 1985, pp. 3–12.

—— 'Paracelsus the Physician', *The Spirit in Man, Art, and Literature*, pp. 13–30.

Kauer, Ute. 'Narration and Gender: The Role of the First-Person Narrator in
Jeanette Winterson's *Written on the Body*', in Grice and Woods (eds), *'I'm
telling you stories,'* pp. 41–51.

Kaveney, Roz. 'Jeanette Winterson: *Oranges Are Not The Only Fruit*', *Times
Literary Supplement* (22 March 1985): 326.

Kellaway, Kate. 'She's Got the Power', *Observer* (Sunday 27 August 2000).
http://books.guardian.co.uk/reviews/generalfiction/0,6121,359570,00.ht
ml. Consulted on 14 January 2002.

Kemp, Peter. 'Writing for a Fall'. Review of *Art & Lies*, *Sunday Times Books*
(26 June 1994): VII, 1–2.

Kendrick, Walter. '"Fiction in Review." Review of *Written on the Body*, by
Jeanette Winterson', *Yale Review* 81 (1993): 131–3.

Kingsley, Peter. 'In the Dark Places of Wisdom: The Forgotten Origins of the
Western World', *Parabola* (Winter 1999). www.goldensufi.org/
PKarticles.html#anchor1723191. Consulted on 25 July 2004.

Kristeva, Julia. *Powers of Horror: An Essay on Abjection*, trans. Leon S.
Roudiez. New York: Routledge, 1982.

—— 'About Chinese Women' (1974), trans. Seán Hand, in Toril Moi (ed.),
The Kristeva Reader. Oxford: Basil Blackwell, 1989 (1986), pp. 138–59.

Kundera, Milan. *The Unbearable Lightness of Being*, trans. Milan Kundera.
London and Boston: Faber and Faber, 1990 (1984).

Kutzer, M. Daphne. 'The Cartography of Passion: Cixous, Wittig and
Winterson', in Jürgen Kleist and Bruce A. Butterfield (eds), *Re-naming the
Landscapes*. New York and Bern-Frankfurt: Peter Lang, 1994, pp. 133–45.

Lacan, Jacques. 'Le stade du miroir comme formateur de la fonction du Je
telle qu'elle nous est révélée dans l'éxpérience psychanalytique',
(Communication faite au XVIè congrés international de psychanalyse à
Zurich, le 17 juillet 1949), in *Écrits I*. Paris: Seuil, 1966, pp. 89–97.

—— *Encore (Le Séminaire: livre XX)*. Paris: Seuil, 1975.

Lane, Richard J., Rod Mengham and Philip Tew (eds). *Contemporary British
Fiction*. Cambridge: Polity Press, 2003.

Langland, Elizabeth. '"Sexing the Text": Narrative Drag as Feminist Poetics
and Politics in *Sexing the Cherry*', *Narrative* 5.1 (January 1997): 99–107.

Lawrence, D. H. *Sons and Lovers*. Harmondsworth: Penguin Classics, 1987
(1913).

Lessing, Doris. *The Golden Notebook*. New York: Simon & Schuster, 1962.

Lewis, Peter. 'Fiction at the Centre and at the Fringe', *Stand Magazine* 30.3
(1989): 66–73.

Lindenmeyer, Antje. 'Postmodern Concepts of the Body in Jeanette
Winterson's *Written on the Body*', *Feminist Review* 63 (Autumn 1999):
48–63.

Lodge, David. 'Outrageous Things', *New York Review of Books* (29 September
1988): 25–6.

Longrigg, Claire. 'Get Out of My Life – Get One of Your Own', *Guardian* (8 July 1994): 24.

Lyotard, Jean-François. *The Postmodern Condition: A Report on Knowledge*. Manchester: Manchester University Press, 1984 (1979).

Marvell, Andrew. *The Complete Poems*, ed. Elizabeth Story Donno. Harmondsworth: Penguin, 1976 (1972).

Matthews, Samantha. 'Jeanette Winterson's Personal Fables of the Writer's Vocation: *Lighthousekeeping*', *Times Literary Supplement* (May 2004): 21.

Meese, Elizabeth. 'Theorizing Lesbian: Writing – A Love Letter', in Jay and Glasgow (eds), *Lesbian Texts and Contents*, pp. 70–87.

Meyer, Kim Middleton. 'Jeanette Winterson's Evolving Subject', in Lane, Mengham and Tew (eds), *Contemporary British Fiction*, pp. 210–25.

Miller, J. Hillis. 'The Ethics of Hypertext', *Diacritics* 25.3 (Fall 1995): 27–39.

Miner, Valerie. 'At her Wit's End', *Women's Review of Books* 10.8 (May 1993): 21.

Monmany, Mercedes. 'Pasión y muerte de Napoleón', *Insula* 511 (July 1989): 19–20.

Mukherjee, Bharati. 'Beyond Multiculturalism: Surviving the Nineties', *Journal of Modern Literature* 20.1 (Summer 1996): 29–34.

Nagy, Phyllis A. 'Fiction Set in the Fury of Napoleon's Wars', *Philadelphia Inquirer* (5 November 1988): F03.

Newton, Judith and Deborah Rosenfelt (eds), *Feminist Criticism and Social Change*. New York and London: Methuen, 1985, pp. 249–67.

Nietzsche, Friedrich. *The Birth of Tragedy and the Generalogy of Morals*, trans. Francis Golffing. New York: Doubleday Anchor Books, 1956.

Nunn, Heather. '*Written on the Body*: An Anatomy of Horror, Melancholy and Love', *Women: A Cultural Review* 7.1 (1996): 16–27.

Onega, Susana. *Form and Meaning in the Novels of John Fowles*. Ann Arbor and London: U. M. I. Research Press, 1989.

—— '*The Passion:* Jeanette Winterson's Uncanny Mirror of Ink', *Miscelánea: A Journal of English and American Studies* 14 (1993): 112–29.

—— '"Self" and "Other" in Jeanette Winterson's *The Passion*', *Revista Canaria de Estudios Ingleses* 18 (April 1994): 177–93.

——'"A Knack for Yarns": The Narrativization of History and the End of History', in Onega (ed.), '*Telling Histories*', pp. 7–18.

—— '"I'm Telling You Stories. Trust Me": History / Story-telling in Jeanette Winterson's *Oranges Are Not the Only Fruit*', in Onega (ed.), '*Telling Histories*', pp. 135–47.

—— 'Jeanette Winterson's Politics of Uncertainty in *Sexing the Cherry*', in Chantal Cornut-Gentille and José Ángel García Landa (eds), *Gender I-deology: Essays on Theory, Literature and Film*. Amsterdam and Atlanta, GA: Rodopi, 1996, pp. 297–369.

—— 'The Mythical Impulse in British Historiographic Metafiction',

European Journal of English Studies 1.2 (1997): 184–204.

—— 'The "Body/Text" as Lesbian Signifier in Jeanette Winterson's *Written on the Body*', in Marita Nadal and María Dolores Herrero (eds), *Margins in British and American Literature, Film, and Culture*. Zaragoza: Servicio de Publicaciones de la Universidad de Zaragoza, 1997, pp. 119–29.

—— *Metafiction and Myth in the Novels of Peter Ackroyd*. Columbia: Camden House, 1999.

—— 'Postmodernist Re-writings of the Puritan Commonwealth: Winterson, Mukherjee, Ackroyd', in Heinz Antor and Kevin L. Cope (eds), *Intercultural Encounters: Studies in English Literatures*. Heidelberg: Universitätsverlag Carl Winter, 1999, pp. 439–66.

—— 'The Visionary Element in the London Novel: The Case of Iain Sinclair and Peter Ackroyd', *Symbolism. An International Journal of Critical Aesthetics* 2 (2002): 151–82.

—— 'The Descent to the Underworld and the Transition from *Ego* to *Eidos* in the Novels of Peter Ackroyd', in Ramón Plo Alastrué and María Jesús Martínez Alfaro (eds), *Generic and Ontological Boundaries in Literature and Film*. Heidelberg: Universitätsverlag Carl Winter, 2002, pp. 157–74.

—— 'Memory, Imagination and the World of Art in Jeanette Winterson's *Art & Lies*', in Constanza del Río and Luis Miguel García Mainar (eds), *Memory, Imagination and Desire in Contemporary Anglo-American Literature and Film* (Anglistische Forschungen Series). Heidelberg: Universitätsverlag Carl Winter, 2004, pp. 69–80.

—— 'Science, Myth and the Quest for Unity in Jeanette Winterson's *Gut Symmetries*', *Anglistik. Mitteilungen des Deutschen Anglistenverbandes* 15.1 (2004): 93–104.

—— 'Jeanette Winterson's Visionary Fictions: An Art of Cultural Translation and Effrontery', in Jürgen Schlaeger (ed.), *Structures of Cultural Transformation. Yearbook of Research in English and American Literature* (REAL) 20. Tübingen: Gunter Narr Verlag, 2005, pp. 229–41.

—— Onega, Susana (ed.). *'Telling Histories': Narrativizing History; Historicizing Literature* (Costerus, 96). Amsterdam and Atlanta, GA: Rodopi, 1995.

O'Rourke, Rebecca. 'Fingers in the Fruit Basket: A Feminist Reading of Jeanette Winterson's *Oranges Are Not the Only Fruit*,' in Susan Sellers (ed.), *Feminist Criticism: Theory and Practice*. Hemel Hempstead: Harvester Wheatsheaf, 1991, pp. 57–70.

Palmer, Paulina. 'Postmodern Trends in Contemporary Fiction: Margaret Atwood, Angela Carter, Jeanette Winterson', in Jane Dowson and Steven Earnshaw (eds), *Postmodern Subjects/Postmodern Texts* (Postmodern Studies 13). Amsterdam and Atlanta, GA: Rodopi, 1994.

—— '*The Passion*: Story-telling, Fantasy, Desire', in Grice and Woods (eds), *'I'm telling you stories,'* pp. 104–16.

Parker, Alice. 'Nicole Brossard: A Differential Equation of Lesbian Love', in Jay and Glasgow (eds), *Lesbian Texts and Contexts*, pp. 304–29.

Parkin-Gounelas, Ruth. 'Introduction' to Parkin-Gounelas (ed.), *The Other Within*, 2001, 1–8.

Parkin-Gounelas, Ruth (ed.). *The Other Within. Volume I: Literature and Culture*. Thessaloniki: Athanasios A. Altintzis, 2001.

Patterson, Christina. 'Jeanette Winterson: Of Love and Other Demons'. Review of *Lighthousekeeping*, *Independent* (7 May 2004). http://enjoyment. independent.co.uk/books/interviews/story.jsp?story=518837. Consulted on 3 August 2004.

Pearce, Lynne. *Reading Dialogics*. London: Edward Arnold, 1994.

Punter, David. *The Literature of Terror: A History of Gothic Fictions from 1765 to the Present Day*. London and New York: Longman, 1980.

Pushkin, Alexander. 'La dama de espadas' (1834), in *La ventisca y otros cuentos*, trans. Odile Gommes. Madrid: Biblioteca Edaf, 1967, pp. 153–202.

Pykett, Lynn. 'A New Way With Words? Jeanette Winterson's Post-Modernism', in Grice and Woods (eds), *'I'm telling you stories,'* pp. 53–60.

Rabine, Leslie W. 'Romance in the Age of Electronics: Harlequin Enterprises', in Newton and Rosenfelt (eds), *Feminist Criticism*, pp. 248–67.

Raspe, Rudolph Erich. *The Surprising Adventures of Baron Munchausen*. Oxford: Project Gutenberg Literary Archive, 1995 (1793). www.gutenberg.org/etext/3154. Consulted on 7 April 2004.

Reynier, Christine. 'Venise dans *The Passion* de Jeanette Winterson', *Études britanniques contemporaines* 4 (1994): 25–37.

—— *Jeanette Winterson: Le miracle ordinaire*. Pessac: Presses Universitaires de Bordeaus, 2004.

—— 'Jeanette Winterson's Cogito – "Amo Ergo Sum" – or Impersonality and Emotion Redefined', in Christine Reynier and Jean-Michel Ganteau (eds), *Impersonality and Emotion in Twentieth-Century British Fiction*. Present Perfect 1. Montpellier: Publications de L'Université Paul Valéry Montpellier 3, 2005, pp. 299–308.

Reynolds, Margaret. 'Interview with Jeanette Winterson', in Reynolds and Noakes (eds), *Jeanette Winterson: The Essential Guide*, pp. 11–29.

Reynolds, Margaret (ed.). *The Sappho Companion*. London: Vintage, 2001.

Reynolds, Margaret and Jonathan Noakes (eds). *Jeanette Winterson: The Essential Guide*. Vintage Living Texts. Contemporary Literature in Close Up. London: Vintage, 2003.

Rich, B. Ruby. 'In Profile: Jeanette Winterson', *Advocate* (24 June 1997): 105.

Roberts, Michèle. *The Book of Mrs Noah*. London: Minerva, 1993.

Roessner, Jeffrey. 'Writing a History of Difference: Jeanette Winterson's *Sexing the Cherry* and Angela Carter's *Wise Children*', *College Literature* 29.1 (Winter 2002): 102–12.

Ross, Deborah. 'Jeanette Winterson: Tea with the Holy Terror', *Independent* (8 April 2002). http://enjoyment.independent.co.uk/music/interviews/story.jsp?story=2827. Consulted on 3 August 2004.

Roth, Remo F. *Some Thoughts about the Relationship of Carl Jung's Depth Psychology to Quantum Physics and to Archetypal Psychosomatics*. Parts I and II, 2003 (1994). www.psychovision.ch/synw/gslecture–rome–e–pia.htm. Consulted on 11 June 2004.

—— *The Return of the World Soul: Wolfgang Pauli, Carl Jung and the Challenge of the Unified Psychophysical Reality*, 2004 (2002). www.psychovision.ch/synw/platinfertilityhermincarnp3.htm. Consulted on 8 July 2004.

Rowanchild, Anira. 'The State of the Heart: Ideology and Narrative Structure in the Novels of Maureen Duffy and Caeia March', in Hutton (ed.), *Beyond Sex and Romance?*, pp. 29–45.

Rubinson, Gregory J. 'Body Languages: Scientific and Aesthetic Discourses in Jeanette Winterson's *Written on the Body*', *Critique* 42.2 (Winter 2001): 218–32.

Rushdie, Salman. *Midnight's Children*. London: Picador, 1981.

Rusk, Lauren. *The Life Writing of Otherness: Woolf, Baldwin, Kingston, and Winterson*. New York and London: Routledge, 2002.

Sapir, Edward. 'The Status of Linguistics as a Science', *Language* 5 (1929): 207–14. Reprinted in D. G. Mandelbaum (ed.), *The Selected Writings of Edward Sapir in Language, Culture and Personality*. Berkeley: University of California Press, 1949, pp. 160–6.

Seaboyer, Judith. 'Second Death in Venice: Romanticism and the Compulsion to Repeat in Jeanette Winterson's *The Passion*', *Contemporary Literature* 38.3 (Fall 1997): 483–509.

Sexton, David. 'A Serious Case of Solipsism. Review of *Gut Symmetries*', *Spectator* (4 January 1997): 27–30.

Sharman-Burke, Juliet and Liz Greene. *El tarot mítico: Una nueva aproximación a las cartas del tarot*, trans. Felicitas di Fidio. Madrid: Editorial EDAF, 1988 (1986).

Sheehan, Aurelie Jane. 'Review of *Written on the Body*, by Jeanette Winterson', *Review of Contemporary Fiction* 13 (Fall 1993): 208–9.

Shelley, Percy Bysshe, 'A Defence of Poetry' (1821), in Harold Bloom and Lionel Trilling (eds), *The Oxford Anthology of English Literature IV. Romantic Poetry and Prose*. Oxford: Oxford University Press, 1973 (1840).

Shiach, Morag. *Hélène Cixous: A Politics of Writing*. London and New York: Routledge, 1991.

Showalter, Elaine. 'Eternal Triangles', *Guardian* (2 September 2000): 9.

Sinkinson, David Lloyd, '"Shadows, signs, wonders": Paracelsus, Synchronicity and the New Age of *Gut Symmetries*', in Helena Bengston, Marianne Borch and Cincide Maagaard (eds), *Sponsored by Demons: The Art of Jeanette Winterson*. Odense: Scholars' Press, 1999, pp. 81–92.

Siropoulos, Vagelis. 'The Dionysian (Gay) Abject: Corporeal Representation in *The Birth of Tragedy* and *Death in Venice*', in Parkin-Gounelas (ed.), *The Other Within*, pp. 93–103.

Smith, Evans Lansing. *Rape and Revelation: The Descent to the Underworld in Modernism*. Lanham, NY and London: University Presses of America, 1990.

Stevenson, Robert Louis. *Treasure Island*. Cambridge: Cambridge University Press, 1995 (1883).

Stowers, Cath. '"No legitimate place, no land, no fatherland": Communities of Women in the Fiction of Roberts and Winterson', *Critical Survey* 8.1 (1996): 69–79.

—— 'The Erupting Lesbian Body: Reading *Written on the Body* as a Lesbian Text', in Grice and Woods (eds), *'I'm telling you stories,'* pp. 89–101.

Stuart, Andrea. '"Terms of Endearment": Review of *Written on the Body*, by Jeanette Winterson', *New Statesman and Society* (18 September 1992): 37–8.

Sutherland, John. '"On the Saliery Express". Review of *Written on the Body*, by Jeanette Winterson', *London Review of Books* (24 September 1992): 18–20.

Swift, Jonathan. *Gulliver's Travels*. Peter Dixon and John Chalker (eds), Introduction by Michael Foot. Harmondsworth: Penguin, 1967 (1726).

Taylor, D. J. 'The Solace of Solitude: *Lighthousekeeping*', *Literary Review* (May 2004): 49.

Traherne, Thomas. 'The First Century', in *Centuries of Meditations*, 2004 (1908). www.ccel.org/t/traherne/centuries/. Consulted on 7 August 2004.

Troberg, Anna. The Jeanette Winterson Reader's Site, 2000 (1997). http://web.telia.com/~u18114424/. Consulted on 14 January 2002.

Turner, Jenny. 'A Tulip and Two Bulbs', *London Review of Books* 22.17 (7 September 2000): 10.

Unsworth, Tania. '*Art & Lies*: Contempt and Condescension', 1999. www.geocities.com/WestHollywood/Heights/3202/ARTANDLIES.HTML. Consulted on 14 January 2002.

Vaux, Anna. 'Jeanette Winterson: *Written on the Body*', *Times Literary Supplement* (4 September 1992), 20.

Veeser, H. Aram (ed.). *The New Historicism*. New York and London: Routledge, 1989.

Wachel, Eleanor. 'Eleanor Wachel with Jeanette Winterson: An Interview', *Malahat Review* 111 (1997): 61–73.

Wang, Zhen. 'The Time's Arrow within the Uncertainty Quantum', 2004 (1998). http://arxiv.org/abs/quant-ph/9806071. Consulted on 27 July 2004.

Waugh, Evelyn. *Decline and Fall*. London: Penguin, 1940 (1928).

Waugh, Patricia. *Practising Postmodernism: Reading Modernism*. London: Edward Arnold, 1992.

—— 'Harvest of the Sixties': English Literature and its Background 1960 to 1990. Oxford and New York: Oxford University Press, 1995.

White, Hayden. Metahistory: The Historical Imagination in Nineteenth-Century Europe. Baltimore and London: Johns Hopkins University Press, 1985 (1973).

Whorf, Benjamin Lee. 'Science and Linguistics', Technology Review 42 (1940): 227–31, 247–8.

Wildman, Eugene. 'Sexing the Cherry, by Jeanette Winterson', Chicago Tribune (5 June 1990): Section 5, 3.

Williams-Wanquet, Eileen. 'Jeanette Winterson's Boating for Beginners: Both New Baroque and Ethics', Études britanniques contemporaines 23 (2002): 99–117.

Wilson, Scott. 'Passion at the End of History', in Grice and Woods (eds), 'I'm telling you stories,' 61–74.

Wingfield, Rachel. 'Lesbian Writers in the Mainstream: Sara Maitland, Jeanette Winterson and Emma Donoghue', in Hutton (ed.), Beyond Sex and Romance?, pp. 60–80.

Wittig, Monique. Le Corps lesbien. Paris: Éditions du Minuit, 1973.

Wood, Graham. 'Truth or Dare', Times Magazine (4 January 1997): 9–10, 13.

Wood, James. 'England', in John Sturrock (ed.), The Oxford Guide to Contemporary Writing. Oxford: Oxford University Press, 1996, pp. 113–41.

Woolf, Virginia. The Waves. London: Vintage, 1992 (1931).

—— To the Lighthouse. London: Vintage, 2000 (1927).

—— Orlando. A Biography. London: Vintage, 2000 (1928).

—— 'A Room of One's Own' and 'Three Guineas'. London: Vintage, 2001 (1929).

Yates, Frances A. Giordano Bruno and the Hermetic Tradition. London: Routledge and Kegan Paul; Chicago: The University of Chicago Press, 1977 (1964).

Yeats, W. B. A Vision. New York: Collier Books, 1965 (1937).

—— Poems of W. B. Yeats. Introduction and Notes by A. Norman Jeffares. Basingstoke and London: Macmillan Education, 1985 (1962).

Index